Buying and Selling the Poor

PUBLIC AND SOCIAL POLICY SERIES

Gaby Ramia, Series Editor

The Public and Social Policy series publishes books that pose challenging questions about policy from national, comparative and international perspectives. The series explores policy design, implementation and evaluation; the politics of policy making; and analyses of particular areas of public and social policy.

Australian social attitudes IV: the age of insecurity
Ed. Shaun Wilson and Markus Hadler

Buying and selling the poor: inside Australia's privatised welfare-to-work market
Siobhan O'Sullivan, Michael McGann and Mark Considine

Globalisation, the state and regional Australia
Amanda Walsh

Markets, rights and power in Australian social policy
Ed. Gabrielle Meagher and Susan Goodwin

One planet, one health
Ed. Merrilyn Walton

Risking together: how finance is dominating everyday life in Australia
Dick Bryan and Mike Rafferty

Wind turbine syndrome: a communicated disease
Simon Chapman and Fiona Crichton

Buying and Selling the Poor

Inside Australia's Privatised
Welfare-to-Work Market

Siobhan O'Sullivan, Michael McGann
and Mark Considine

SYDNEY UNIVERSITY PRESS

Contents

Acknowledgements

This book was made possible by an Australian Research Council (ARC) Linkage grant (LP150100277). We wish to thank the ARC for their support, as well as extend a heartfelt thank you to our industry partners: the National Employment Services Association (NESA), Westgate Community Initiatives Group (WCIG) and Jobs Australia (JA). We are grateful for the insights our industry partners afford us. Our partners have an amazing wealth of knowledge and continually support our efforts to understand and critically evaluate Australia's welfare-to-work system. In particular we acknowledge the support we have received from Ron Miers, Sally Sinclair, and David Thompson, who sadly passed away while this book was being written.

We must also thank Jenny M. Lewis (University of Melbourne) and Phuc Nguyen (La Trobe University), who are both centrally important members of our larger research team. While they did not come with us on this book journey, they helped conceptualise the project and worked with us on complementary aspects of our research.

Gabrielle Meagher (Macquarie University) very graciously read an early version of the manuscript and offered us both insights and encouragement. It was a pleasure to work with Gaby Ramia (University of Sydney), whose passion for, and knowledge of, the welfare-to-work sector made the editorial process wonderfully smooth and intellectually stimulating. We are also grateful to Susan Murray and Agata

Mrva-Montoya from Sydney University Press and Nikki Lusk who worked with us closely, and to Evelyn Brodkin (University of Chicago) for her enthusiasm for the book and for contributing such a thought-provoking foreword.

We are indebted to the Department of Education, Skills and Employment (DESE). The department staff have shown a welcome interest in this research and, in particular, they facilitated this project by allowing us access to data on high-performing offices. Our research design would have been less reliable were it not for the department's support.

Of course, we must thank all the agency managers, case managers, receptionists and support staff who allowed us to watch them at work and to talk through the complex issues they face. It took a lot of trust to allow us into your worlds so completely, and we sincerely appreciate your help. We have much admiration for the work you do.

Finally, we must, of course, say a very big thank you to all the jobseekers who allowed us to observe them obtaining employment services – including at times when they were feeling vulnerable, stressed, unsure or frustrated. The system exists to support you, so being able to include your stories in this book is incredibly important to us. In particular, it is our sincere hope that our use of language in describing the work of First Nations people engaged with Australia's welfare-to-work system is respectful and reflects the way in which they wish to be identified.

Foreword: On history, poverty, and the continuous quest for reform

Evelyn Z. Brodkin

Welfare and labour market policies are boundary-setters; straddling the line between two, large structuring institutions: state and market. From this perspective, one can understand why policies that shift the balance between welfare and work, even if relatively modest, may assume outsized political significance. One can also appreciate why these boundary-setting policies might be perpetually unsettled, as they are regularly subject to adjustment pressures created by changes in society, the polity, and the economy.

Tension at the boundaries is evident in the history of Western democracies, reflected, in part, in shifting strategies for grappling with poverty and unemployment. At times, states have provided food, cash, or employment supports that help enable individuals to make it in a market economy. At other times, states have deployed regulatory strategies that discipline the labour force (e.g., the workhouse and workfare), intensifying pressures to participate in the paid labour force by withholding aid or making it conditional. The distinctions between these approaches (one *enabling*, the other *regulatory*) are not clear cut, and often they are coupled to one another.[1] Since the 20th century, it has become common to combine strategies, offering cash benefits

---

1   For a fuller discussion of the boundaries between work and welfare as well as enabling and regulatory approaches, see Brodkin 2013a.

to sustain individuals during periods of poverty and unemployment, providing services (e.g., education, training, job matching) to move them into the paid labour market, and, at the same time, asserting discipline by making benefits conditional on service participation or work-for-the-dole.

These combined strategies may appear sensible on their face, particularly if one assumes that services largely perform an enabling function, helping the unemployed to make it in the market, eventually making benefits unnecessary. This assumption has contributed to the popularity of service strategies despite their mixed record (as detailed in depth in this book). After years of studies and evaluations, it seems reasonable to expect that *if* employment services are well designed, well funded, and well run, they *may* build human capital, provide access to job networks, and, best of all, link individuals to good jobs. But those 'ifs' are too infrequently realised.

Yet services strategies remain popular, a standard part of the toolbox policymakers reach for to address poverty and unemployment. Thus, it is important to understand these strategies and consider, not only what functions they claim to perform, but also *what else* they do. Beyond their manifest function in facilitating the inclusion of the unemployed in the labour market, services also perform latent, regulatory functions. This occurs when participation in service programs is not voluntary, but a condition for receiving income support. Under these conditions, employment programs function as a modern-day work test that supposedly sorts the willing from the unwilling-to-work and, most critically, disciplines the latter by excluding them from income support. They accomplish this regulatory function irrespective of how well they meet their manifest purposes, even when service participants remain workless or continue to struggle with recurring unemployment and low wages, common experiences for those relegated to precarious sectors of the labour market.

To be fair, as this book's richly described case studies show, workers in the employment services industry may try their hardest and against tough odds to support program participants. Some of their efforts are nothing short of extraordinary. Yet, it is clear that the challenges of service work have only increased under the constraints of contracting and new public management strictures. That said, even at their best, it is important to recognise that employment programs cannot affect the structure of the economy, nor the labour market or social conditions that shape the possibilities for surviving, much less thriving, in a market system. Although services can be useful, they are fundamentally limited to the extent that they offer largely behavioural solutions to structural problems. In effect, they aim to 'fix' the unemployed by making them 'market ready' but leave unchanged the labour market structures that create unemployment and economic precarity.

Given these limitations, there is a certain illogic to policies that treat employment services as if they provided a realistic alternative to the provision of income support, rather than a complement to it. Yet welfare-to-work, activation, and workfare policies tend to do precisely that. They make cash benefits conditional on either finding a job (virtually any job) or participating in employment services of uncertain value. Moreover, as carefully detailed in this book's case studies of Australian employment services agencies, there are distinctly regulatory dimensions to these programs. Those who run afoul of program rules or requirements (whether reasonably administered or not) are subject to penalties: financial sanctions, work-for-the-dole, or, simply, the discipline of the market.

Under these circumstances, it should not be surprising that, like previous boundary-straddling policies, present day welfare-to-work and activation strategies have been subject to continuous revision. This reflects both the practical difficulties of administering these strategies and the enduring political difficulties of setting the balance between welfare and work. Over centuries, such difficulties have produced repeated cycles of reform, disillusionment, and promises of new reform.

The contemporary Australian experience vividly recounted in this book is the latest example in a continuing process. Although, as the aphorism has it, history repeats itself but never in precisely the same way. Australia's Jobactive program, the main publicly funded employment support services program for people on jobseeker payments, may be more closely connected to its historical ancestors than one might expect.[2] Even aspects of the new public management strategies

---

2   An interesting approach to 'archaic anthropology' as a way to 'historicize the present' of labour market politics can be found in Boland and Griffin (2021).

advanced as part of the Australian reformist agenda are, in a sense, pre-figured in administrative strategies deployed centuries earlier.

Before looking ahead to the contemporary Australian experience, a brief glance backward into history provides insights into the centuries-long journey that has led to 'buying and selling the poor'. If history is any guide, one might expect that the *new* reforms so aptly described in this book will be followed by *new new reforms* as the journey continues.

Setting boundaries: the legacy of the British Poor Laws

Writing in 1927, Sidney and Beatrice Webb offered this observation upon reviewing some 600 years of British Poor Law experience:

> For a period of 600 years, the continuously shifting and perpetually developing legal relations between the rich and the poor, between the 'haves' and the 'Have-nots', [have been] embodied in a multitude of statutes and administrative devices ... [Yet] the story ends as it begins with the (as yet unsolved) problem presented by the Unemployed, whom our grandfathers called the Able-bodied.[3]

In their epic two-volume history, Webb and Webb trace the British response to poverty, beginning in the 16th century with the establishment of the workhouse as an alternative to 'outdoor relief'. The workhouse provided a strategy for regulating the activities of the unemployed, in part, by making support (e.g., rations of bread) contingent on unpaid work. A more conspicuously disciplinary dimension to this strategy made workhouse conditions sufficiently onerous to discourage all but the most desperate from seeking aid. As Webb and Webb describe it, the workhouse required gruelling work in return for meagre rations. Yet, in its day, the workhouse represented reform, a reaction against the severity of the prior Henrician Poor Laws, which provided for the enslavement and harsh physical punishment

---

3   Webb and Webb 1963, v.

of unemployed 'vagrants'.[4] The workhouse reform, by linking food and shelter to unpaid work, suggested a rough prototype for workfare strategies that would arrive centuries later.

However, the Poor Laws failed to produce a stable resolution to setting the balance between welfare and work. Unemployment persisted, driven by economic and social changes that regularly generated new sectors of unemployment, first as medieval tenants were dispossessed of their land, and later as jobs shifted from rural to mercantile and eventually to manufacturing. Apparently, neither the miseries of the workhouse nor the conditionality it imposed were sufficient to stop the so-called 'able-bodied' poor from seeking aid.

The failure of the workhouse to fully deter the poor was a disappointment to public officials. An inspector responsible for overseeing the poor expressed surprise that, although workhouse conditions were clearly 'demoralising,' 'the test of work failed, in many cases, to deter able-bodied applicants from coming for relief'.[5] (Note that sorting the 'able-bodied' – now labelled 'ready-to-work' – from those deemed unable to work has long been a central concern of welfare administration.) It seems that public officials then, as now, are all too ready to believe that the poor prefer welfare over work. But they also recognise that mass unemployment and deprivation posed dangers to social and economic stability. How to set the balance between welfare and work?

Pressures for reforming the workhouse grew over the 18th century and came to include, not only policy but also administration. A series of financial and other scandals led reformers to seek new ways for the state to locally operate workhouses and hold them accountable for their use of public funds. Taking the first, incipient steps on a path to bureaucratic formalism in welfare administration, reformers deployed inspectors, instituted new reporting requirements, and threatened legal action against local officials for abuses of administrative discretion.

While reformers pursued accountability through these measures, their interests were narrowly drawn. Presaging later strategies that obscured accountability while ostensibly promoting it, 18th-century

---

4   See Kunze 1971.
5   Webb and Webb 1963, 374.

reformers directed administrative oversight towards containing expenditures for the workhouse and the dole. But they were decidedly disinterested in documenting the hardships and ill-health besetting those relegated to the workhouse. Reformers celebrated 'a drastic reduction in the number of applicants for Poor Relief, and in the expenditure from the Poor Rate' but made no inquiry into the rate of illness, mortality, or infant death.[6] Apparently, administrative systems that skew accountability towards cost containment and caseload reduction, while disregarding evidence relevant to the wellbeing of the poor and unemployed, are not an entirely modern invention.

In the mid-1800s, reformed Poor Law Boards changed the way they provided information to Parliament, ending the practice of providing reports that included narrative descriptions of local workhouse conditions and replacing them with selected statistical accounts. The new reports were:

> devoid of description of incidents; omitting the Inspectors' reports; confined in the main, to statistical records ... hardly ever illuminated by a pregnant phrase; and, in consequence, almost unspeakably dull.[7]

Webb and Webb suggest that loading ministers and members of Parliament with 'dreary detail' was purposefully intended to discourage political oversight by creating an atmosphere of 'business-like dullness'. Whether or not this was, in fact, a purposeful strategy, it was surely strategic. The power to conceal under the guise of administrative statistics and business-like efficiency resonates to this day.

Resetting boundaries in the modern era: the 'activation turn'

Fast forward to the first part of the 20th century and the rise of the modern welfare state, a development that brought a major shift in the boundaries between state and market. The advent of the welfare state,

---

6   Webb and Webb 1963, 462.
7   Webb and Webb 1963, 190.

the various forms it took in different nations, and its development over time have been the subject of extensive academic discussion and debate far too varied and complex to be neatly summarised here. For purposes of this brief introduction, suffice it to say that the welfare state ultimately did not fully resolve fundamental tensions between welfare and work; but it did reshape the playing field upon which struggles to determine the balance would continue.

As social and economic conditions changed over the course of the century, familiar tensions between providing relief and regulating labour animated new policy strategies and created new political dilemmas. In the latter part of the 20th century, these tensions led to a pushback of sorts against the welfare side of the work-welfare equation, most notably (but not only) in those countries Esping-Andersen refers to as 'liberal' regimes,[8] notable among them the USA and Australia.

This pushback was exemplified by the introduction of a national workfare scheme in the USA, a forerunner of a broader *activation turn* which eventually circled the globe. Touted by the Clinton administration as 'welfare reform', the 1996 welfare law increased federal expenditures supporting employment services for low-income families. However, it tied this increase to imposition of a new work test, conditioning cash benefits on participation either in paid work or in designated 'work activities', including welfare-to-work programs.

The law was accompanied by management reforms establishing national performance metrics to determine federal welfare payments to state agencies. The metrics rewarded states for placing cash beneficiaries in 'work activities', paid work, or simply removing them from the benefits rolls. In effect, states were rewarded equally for helping adults find good jobs, pushing them off the benefits rolls, or placing them in service programs of uncertain value. The law also created incentives for privatising employment services, leading to an increase in contracting to for-profit and non-profit providers (although initially with a fairly modest for-profit footprint in most states).[9]

---

8   Esping-Anderson 1990. On the shifting balance between work and welfare in this period, see Brodkin and Larsen 2013.
9   For a more detailed discussion, see Brodkin 2013a.

When work increased and welfare rolls declined, the Clinton Administration was quick to claim success. However, the role of a booming economy and increased job creation in achieving these results was largely overlooked as was troubling evidence that poverty was rising despite greater work participation. How to explain the apparent discontinuity between the success narrative supported by selective performance metrics and the fact of increasing poverty, measured by the census and other surveys?

It is here that street-level research, which is at the centre of this book, comes into the picture. Street-level studies of welfare agencies began to look beyond the 'business-like dullness' of performance metrics to investigate what took place under the rubric of law in everyday practice and to interrogate how those metrics were achieved. Studies revealed that staples of new public management, contracting, and especially the relentless pressures of performance management, eventually reached down to shape the discretionary practices of frontline practitioners. Under these administrative pressures (described in detail elsewhere[10]), the discretion to help was substantially constrained and discretion to discipline effectively encouraged. In this context, the regulatory features of the American workfare scheme came to substantially eclipse its enabling features. By the year 2000, in a prequel to what would later unfold in Australia, in the states in the USA were paying a larger share of their program funds to service providers than to the poor themselves. All the while, poverty and unemployed persisted and then worsened as the boom economy went bust.

Turning to Australia, in the decades since the *activation turn*, labour market reforms have moved through multiple cycles of reform and disillusionment, bringing yet new promises of reform as decribed in this volume. The most recent of these, Jobactive, is carefully detailed, unpacked, and interrogated in this important book. It suggests that, beyond continuing along the path of the late 20th-century activation turn, Australia has been at the forefront of a parallel *privatisation turn*. This turn may be understood as part of the continuing process of

---

10   See, for example, Brodkin 2013a; Brodkin 2017b; Dias and Maynard-Moody 2006; Soss et al. 2013.

resetting the balance between welfare and work, and more broadly, the boundaries between state and market. Over the past 20 years, Australia has pressed forward with a program of privatisation, performance management, and profit maximisation that goes further than its European or Northern American counterparts have to date.

Yet, even as Australia has advanced its commercialised policy model, it has carried with it the legacy of the British Poor Laws, along with their complicated contradictions and dilemmas. As one proceeds through this book, one encounters familiar patterns and practices Without attempting to cover ground that is presented comprehensively and deftly in the chapters to come, it may be useful to point out some notable historical artefacts unearthed in this contemporary excavation.

Among the historical legacies that appear throughout this book's account of Australia's Jobactive practices, several are particularly striking. First, the most obvious is the deployment of conditionality as a modern-day work test. As noted earlier, the requirement that individuals seeking income support participate in employment services has resonance to previous efforts to sort 'willing' from 'unwilling' workers. Second, replacing the crude 16th- and 17th-century practices that sorted the *able-bodied* from *unworthy vagrants*, Jobactive uses the patina of science to identify characteristics that distinguish among the *job ready* and the *unready*, the latter of whom are channelled into *Stream C*, where they are subject to increased intervention and oversight. Third, in place of the reviled workhouse, with its harsh surveillance and working conditions, Jobactive disciplines individuals it finds in violation of its work rules by requiring them to keep *dole diaries* and imposing *demerit points* that can send individuals to the *penalty box* where cash benefits are reduced or withdrawn.

Fourth, there are historical resonances in administrative arrangements, as well. It seems that the development of administrative reporting strategies purported to assure accountability have been substantially refined from earlier eras, with performance metrics providing a sophisticated penumbra of accountability. Yet, with a nod to the 'dreary' 19th-century reports that focused almost exclusively on controlling costs and caseloads, Jobactive's administrative reporting also focuses on costs and caseloads, as well as employment program participation. It also monitors aspects of work-enforcement and services production. Much like its historical ancestors, Australia's reporting system is largely indifferent to the health, wellbeing, or even the medium-to-long-term labour market outcomes for those it channels through its programs.[11] But unlike its historical ancestors, Jobactive's reporting system packs a punch. Its metrics are used to publicly rank providers and offices, a system nominally designed to advance accountability and make low-ranking agencies uncompetitive. In an ironic twist, the algorithms used to rate performance are confidential.

Contested boundaries and the path ahead

This historical review, while necessarily too brief, suggests that certain boundary-setting features have become embedded in the contemporary architecture of welfare and labour market policies. As discussed, enabling features from cash welfare to supportive services, as well as regulatory features from the workhouse to workfare have been instrumental in adjusting the boundaries between welfare and work and, more broadly, state and market. Certain types of features appear to diminish in importance, perhaps even disappear for a time, only to re-emerge, in updated form, in later periods.

Although a common architecture of boundary-setting devices seems to persist over time and national contexts, there is substantial variation in how elements of this architecture are used, refashioned, and deployed. These variations matter as both the policies and the street-level practices that implement them are instrumental in readjusting the boundaries.

The role of street-level organisations (SLOs) in the processes of reform may be under-appreciated in the policy debates that capture the attention of legislators and the public. Yet, the periodic advancement of administrative reforms that target SLOs suggests their relevance has not entirely escaped notice. From the local workhouse operators of the

---

11 Jobactive does measure short-term job placement; but that obscures job precarity, a common feature of the contingent labour market which makes economic wellbeing and stability difficult to achieve.

Elizabethan era to the public welfare and employment agencies of the 20th century, to the contracted firms and non-profit service providers of the current period, SLOs (like the policies they implement) straddle the boundaries between welfare and work.

This book reveals how Australia's policy and administrative reforms are reshaping these boundaries. It shows how policy reforms have ramped up regulation of the unemployed by imposing work as a condition for receiving welfare, part of an activation turn that has now been in progress for several decades. The authors also direct attention to the privatisation of employment services as a distinct type of boundary-setting strategy. In the grand tradition of street-level research, they probe beyond the policy rhetoric and political claims about privatisation to directly examine how privatisation works in everyday organisational life, tracing its indirect consequences for how formal policies are realised on the ground and illuminating its direct consequences for the experiences of unemployed citizens.

For decades, critics of policies that condition welfare on work requirements have argued that these provisions commodify the poor and unemployed, in effect, recognising their value as workers, but not as citizens. These policies, now prevalent around the world, have to varying degrees pushed back the boundaries of the welfare state, eroding its promise that citizens would have the means necessary to become full participants in society and the polity.[12]

However, this book identifies a significant development in the long-running reform saga, demonstrating how the marketisation of employment services in Australia has led to double-commodification of the poor. Double-commodification represents a unique development in boundary-setting. As this book traces the evolution of Australia's fully privatised employment services program, it reveals ways in which it commodifies the unemployed, effectively transforming them into profit units in the production of employment services. The authors argue that the value of these citizens now derives, not only from their value to the labour market, but also from their value to service providers, for whom they are both necessary inputs and outputs of production.

---

12 On the welfare state, social rights, and the global workfare project, see: Esping-Andersen 1990; Marshall 1950; Brodkin and Marston 2013.

This admittedly crude language (mine, not the authors') is intended to highlight the political importance of what appears to be a modest administrative reform manifestly aimed at increasing competition and efficiency, but apparently achieving neither.

As in previous periods, it seems that the seeds of dissatisfaction may have already been sown, and pressures for a new round of reform are germinating. In Australia, the authors note reform proposals advocating digitisation of service work and more intensively targeted conditionality that would further advance the activation turn. However, there also is evidence of counterstrategies emerging in Australia and elsewhere that would enlarge welfare entitlements through a universal basic income or, at the street-level, implement models of service delivery that expand the space for practices directed more towards enabling than regulating the unemployed.[13]

Nonetheless, some readers may find the Jobactive experience described in this book to be disheartening, a troubling turn on the long road to reform. But that is not the entire story. This book also recognises the dilemmas of service workers, who find their efforts to provide meaningful assistance increasingly constrained, yet find spaces for acts of resistance, pushback, even subversion, offering a glimpse of possible struggles yet to come. Importantly, the authors also bring to light the experiences of low-income and unemployed individuals who turn to the state for help. By telling their stories it gives them voice and elevates them to their rightful place in this saga, as citizens and human beings, not simply as units of services production or labour market commodities. When considered along with previously mentioned attempts to advance welfare-broadening reforms in other countries, it should be clear that the struggle is not over.

History suggests that the boundaries between welfare and work, state and market are likely to remain unsettled and subject to further adjustment. Undoubtedly, the next phase in the ongoing struggles at the boundary will be informed by this important book.

---

13   See Caswell and Larsen 2020; Standing 2017.

Introduction

This book has its origins in the mid-1990s, when part of Australia's case management services, previously delivered by the Commonwealth Employment Service (CES), were first contracted out to for-profit and not-for-profit organisations. As the Keating Labor government began what would become Australia's long march towards privatising countless public services, Mark Considine saw an opportunity to investigate and explain what was taking place. In the late 2000s, an expanded research team, including Jenny M. Lewis and Siobhan O'Sullivan, revisited that early research to document conditions within Australia's now fully privatised Job Network system. This was after the Howard government moved to full competitive tendering in 1998. Whereas, under Keating, the CES had been assured of delivering the bulk of services, now it was in direct competition with private agencies in an open bid for government contracts. Unemployed people are among the poorest in the country and what the new private system achieved was to make the services they receive a profitable commodity. Entrepreneurs could now bid for different groups of unemployed people in various parts of the country, hoping to make money from the services provided to them. This new world of services being bought and sold had many supporters and not a few critics. Our task has been to peel back the layers and explain how it works.

As the team surveyed frontline employment services staff about their work lives, their relationships with jobseekers, management and policymakers, we found a system that had already deviated markedly from the promises of enhanced flexibility and tailoring made by prime ministers from both the left and the right of Australian politics. The team continued to track the evolution of Australia's system through Job Services Australia, which was introduced by the Rudd Labor government in 2009, and its replacement, Jobactive, which was an Abbott Coalition government initiative in 2015, all the while comparing the Australian experience to that of the UK, the Netherlands and beyond. The differences between these successive iterations of Australia's employment services market are described in detail in chapter one. Policy makers have tended to focus their reform agenda around the payment model and the performance framework that governs how employment services are contracted out. What has remained constant, until now, is the Australian government's belief in the benefits of marketisation and competitive procurement even if, over time, the number of private service agencies delivering the program(s) has shrunk from over 300 providers in the late 1990s to just 44 agencies by the time of Jobactive.

In 2016, once our team – which had expanded to include Phuc Nguyen and Michael McGann – had a bird's eye view of the Australian system, we decided to focus more closely on its 'Achilles heel': the under-explained failing of the Australian system to help more disadvantaged jobseekers into ongoing employment.[1] If a welfare-to-work system can be judged on any single measure, surely the assistance it affords the most vulnerable among us should be that marker.

Our research to that point had told us that the Australian system is a lean, administratively driven apparatus with key performance indicators (KPIs) that put considerable pressure on frontline staff to work quickly, simultaneously assisting large numbers of jobseekers. Yet we also knew from government data that some offices, within particular agencies, had managed to distinguish themselves in helping the most

---

1   This expression was first used to describe the failings of Australia's employment services system by Peter Davidson, the Australian Council of Social Service's (ACOSS) principal policy advisor. See Davidson 2014.

disadvantaged jobseekers. Why were some offices able to achieve more than others within the context of a largely standardised system? Our sizable, longitudinal dataset was unlikely to offer us the answers. Instead, we decided that to comprehensively capture the secrets to success we would have to work locally in those high-performing, or as we now prefer to describe them for reasons that will become apparent in chapter two, 'best-performing' offices. With the help of the Department of Education, Skills and Employment (DESE) we selected four sites from their larger list, with two of us observing every office interaction over multiple days, including the staff's interactions with jobseekers, office meetings and phone calls made to employers. Once we finished watching and listening to frontline staff carry out the business of welfare-to-work, we followed the stories of more than 100 highly disadvantaged jobseekers as they moved between offices, jobs and institutional settings. Some of these jobseekers we were following disappeared from the welfare-to-work system and, sadly, we have no way of knowing what happened to them.

This book is the result of that work, taking readers behind the scenes of Australia's multibillion-dollar welfare-to-work system, the largest area of government procurement activity in Australia outside of defence.[2] While some readers may have worked in the sector, and others may have been a jobseeker at some point, the perspective we bring is, we believe, unique and revealing. As we moved between offices, we quickly saw similarities and differences in how case managers did their jobs. Some of what we saw was confronting. Much of it was mundane. But combined, it paints a picture of critically important social services, which many people are aware of, but few properly understand.

In chapter one we place Australia's welfare-to-work system within a broader socio-political framework. We outline the political arguments behind the policy design and the volatile, often hostile environment in which Australia's long-term unemployed must survive.

In chapter two we introduce the study methodology and research approach, situating the book within the developing field of street-level

---

2   When the initial Jobactive contracts were signed in 2016, they were worth a combined $7.6 billion over five years. Figure from Henriques-Gomes 2019.

bureaucracy research and understanding welfare-to-work from the frontline point of delivery.

We then dedicate a chapter to each of the offices we studied. Chapter three is set in the suburbs, where welfare offices nuzzle up against the flashy consumerism of aspirational shopping centres. The most highly disadvantaged jobseekers there are recent immigrants, struggling with English and trying to build a new life in a foreign land. In chapter four we venture out to the city limits, finding cheaper real estate and more open spaces. But we also discover a genteel despair. The ritzy shopping centre of chapter three has been replaced by a tired mall featuring discount shops and no public transport. The highly disadvantaged jobseekers here are mostly white, with limited education and opportunities. In chapter five we find ourselves near the centre of one of Australia's largest cities. The suburb is in transition, with a mix of upwardly mobile hipsters, recent immigrants and people battling a range of demons, including serious drug addiction. In chapter five we discover that one way to 'assist' the long-term unemployed is to transfer them to another provider or service. In a world full of 'carrots and sticks', we quickly become acquainted with the stick. Then in chapter six we settle back and relax a little in a regional office, where the sun is always shining and the surf is always up. But with that enviable lifestyle comes a lack of jobs and the trauma of job losses as industries shut down and are not replaced.

Our original aim was to find something singular to unite these four best-performing offices, which we could then describe to others and which policymakers could perhaps use to make the system better overall. We found more diversity than we had expected. But, as we shall see, once you zoom out slightly, these offices start to become similar within the larger social security picture. None of the people whose story we tell here are fully autonomous. Each is bound by a constrained and relentlessly demanding system. The people who design the system, the people who bring the system to life in practice and the people who depend on the system to get by, all have some modicum of power. But that power is often tenuous and is not shared equally – far from it.

As we tell the story of these offices, the case managers and their jobseeker clients, we contextualise our discussion within a broader understanding of welfare-to-work in Australia. We recount how the profile of frontline staff has changed over the years. We explain how Work for the Dole is managed, joining the dots between decisions made by public servants in Canberra and the lived experience of the Australian citizens who have to perform a series of very precise actions to continue receiving welfare payments while also trying to deal with complex, long-term disadvantage.

We end the book with a brief look into the future. Welfare-to-work is nothing if not dynamic. As we write this book, public servants around Australia are busy finalising the design of Australia's next welfare-to-work system. So far we know very little. But we do have some clues. It is likely to be much less personalised than the rhetoric of Job Network/Jobactive, or indeed the reality. The narrative has always been that the dismantling of the CES, and the introduction of privatised service delivery, makes services more responsive and individualised. That narrative has seemingly been abandoned. In its place is a focus on efficiency and ease. If policy designers can get the technology to work, Australia's next system, post-2022, will be predominantly computer driven. For all but those with the most complex needs and challenging employment barriers, Australia's welfare-to-work system, long touted as a world leading example, will become defined by an app on a phone.

The road from human- to robot-driven social services is likely to be rocky, especially for the people whose stories we tell here. As you will read in the coming pages, Australian welfare-to-work agencies hand out new mobile phones to many of their clients. What we did not see, and what is difficult to imagine, is how the highly vulnerable people we met in Jobactive offices around Australia, will be able to maintain their new devices in good working order. While 'employment services by app' may be more convenient for some, will it be effective for all? To date the government has not clearly articulated what will happen to those who simply cannot work out how to engage digitally. Some form of 'enhanced' face-to-face support is proposed to be available to the 'hardest-to-help' cohort of jobseekers featured in this book. But it is not yet clear what shape this support will take or how jobseekers' needs for face-to-face rather than digital services will be reliably determined. As will soon become evident in the pages of this book, the current assessment practices for determining jobseekers' employment support needs are beset with difficulties and are frequently disputed by both jobseekers and providers. Moreover, the government has not – to the best of our knowledge – articulated a plan to retain frontline staff. For those who work with jobseekers because they derive satisfaction from getting to know the individual and eventually seeing them succeed, will this new system hold any appeal? Or will these skills be lost? But that is a problem for another day. For now, our aim is to tell the story of very disadvantaged people traversing our current in-person system, so readers gain an appreciation of what life is like for those who work with a system of contracts and incentives and where enormous pressure is brought to bear both on jobseekers and frontline staff, with surprising results.

1
The politics of managing the poor

The title of this book, *Buying and selling the poor*, refers to the transformation of Australia's public employment services system into a market for welfare-to-work services. It captures how people on welfare payments have been organised into purchasing lots, for which private agents bid to win a share of the services to support them, discipline them and make money from them. People receiving these welfare payments are among the poorest in the country, with many of them waiting more than five years for a chance to get back to work. Successful bidders win the right to try and improve jobseekers' employability and sell them to employers, in the very real sense that they earn a direct payment for each successful placement and lose money for those who are not selected for work. Marketising Australian's public employment services treats unemployed people as objects 'of calculation and exchange' that can be bought and sold 'just like any other commodity' in a free market.[1]

Labor Prime Minister Paul Keating was the first advocate for a more competitive approach to providing this service. His scheme involved case management for those deemed long-term unemployed, together with training and other support. He broke the mould of public service by putting part of the case management program out to tender.

---

[1]   See Adkins 2017, 300. Also Grover 2009, 501.

He wanted to energise the Commonwealth Employment Service (CES) by making part of its service contestable. There was also a widely held view in his government that senior management had lost control of the CES to an activist union and that greater market pressure might reset that balance.

Several privatising iterations later, we find Australia organising this service through a program called Jobactive, the welfare-to-work program introduced by the Coalition Abbott government in July 2015. It became the latest version of this welfare-to-work market – more accurately called a *quasi-market*, because purchasing power is centralised in a single Australian government agency.[2] Sellers, in this case employment services providers, must transact with and compete for business from the Department of Employment.[3] The service users (jobseekers) are not actually the purchasers or customers in this market; the Australian government is. You will see this in the language that the frontline staff repeatedly use to talk about Jobactive participants. They are always 'clients' or 'jobseekers', never 'consumers' or 'customers', of the services these providers have been contracted to deliver. This 'monopsony' purchasing power gives the Australian government much leverage over providers, and the requirements of the department feature heavily in the minds of frontline employment services staff.

Australia's welfare-to-work system is also considered a quasi-market because some of the participating providers are not ostensibly in the business of making profit. In contrast to conventional

---

2   The differences between quasi-markets and conventional markets are discussed in detail by Julian Le Grand and Will Bartlett in their introduction to the edited collection *Quasi-markets and social policy.* They point to three main differences: purchasing power is concentrated in state agencies (often a single agency), the sellers/providers of services include not-for-profit and publicly owned organisations that are not driven to maximise profits, and consumer purchasing power is not expressed in monetary terms but through vouchers that permit them to buy services specified by the government. See Le Grand and Bartlett 1993.

3   During our research period, the department underwent numerous name changes, but for consistency's sake, we refer to it throughout this book as the Department of Employment.

marketplaces, not all employment services providers are privately owned or driven to maximise profits. A significant proportion are not-for-profit and, in principle, mission-driven organisations. This is becoming rarer as more and more profit-driven corporations enter the market. There are even examples of for-profit and not-for-profit organisations combining to compete for contracts, such as Mission Providence. This Jobactive provider was a joint venture between Christian charity Mission Australia and Providence Service Corporation, a US-based multinational human services delivery business that is listed on the stock exchange. The short history of Mission Providence is emblematic of how welfare and employment services have become commodified, not only in Australia but globally as well. It is not only the unemployed jobseekers who are traded in this marketised system, but also the government contracts to deliver employment services. In 2017, Mission Providence was sold to Konekt, one of Australia's largest private sector providers of organisational health and return-to-work solutions, for a reported US$22 million.[4] In December 2019, Konekt was in turn acquired by Advanced Personnel Management (APM), a multinational employability and human services organisation headquartered in Perth.[5] By this stage, APM had coincidentally already acquired Ingeus – a company established by Thérèse Rein, the wife of former Australian prime minister Kevin Rudd – from Providence Service Corporation in 2018, meaning that it now held government contracts to deliver employment services in not only Australia but also the USA, the UK, Canada, Switzerland, South Korea, Germany, Singapore and Spain.[6]

Despite the enduring presence of not-for-profit organisations in Australia's employment services landscape, the differences between the for-profit and not-for-profit sectors of the market are becoming less and less clear. As we have argued before, the extent to which the not-for-profit organisations that remain in the market can be characterised as *mission*-driven is open to doubt.[7] This has been a longstanding concern since the very early days of privatised

---

4   GlobeNewswire 2017.
5   APM 2019.
6   MergerLinks 2018.

employment services, with social policy researchers such as UNSW's Tony Eardley cautioning about the 'serious conflict' facing mission-driven agencies delivering government contracts: between their traditional impulse towards knowledge sharing and mutual collaboration to address poverty and social exclusion, on the one hand, and, as providers in a quasi-market, 'the need to jealously guard market knowledge and power', on the other.[8] Another concern was that contracting to deliver services for the government could drastically narrow agencies' critical distance from policymakers and limit their capacity to independently advocate for the needs of the most marginalised members of the community. For the not-for-profit providers that have endured through repeated contracting rounds and new iterations of the system, surviving in Australia's competitive welfare market may have proven to be something of a poisoned chalice. They have managed to keep, and in some cases grow, their contracts, but at the cost of perhaps losing their purpose. We certainly do not claim that this is true of *all* the not-for-profit organisations delivering employment services. But our research, dating back more than 20 years, on frontline employment services staff and the agencies delivering welfare-to-work, certainly supports the view that 'the surviving for-profit and not-for-profit providers [are now] much more alike' than 20, or even 10, years ago.[9] This is a proposition we return to throughout this book.

---

7   See, for example: Considine, O'Sullivan and Nguyen 2014a; Considine, O'Sullivan and Nguyen 2015. We also discuss this issue in two related papers: Considine, Lewis and O'Sullivan 2011; Considine, O'Sullivan, McGann and Nguyen 2020. The tension between delivering marketised employment services and the mission orientation of faith-based and other charitable organisations has also been discussed by numerous other scholars and commentators on the Australian quasi-market in employment services. See, for example, Rogers 2009; Ramia and Carney 2003.

8   Eardley 2002, 311.

9   Considine, O'Sullivan, McGann and Nguyen 2020, 866. The loss of diversity between for-profit and not-for-profit providers was also previously addressed in a much earlier paper tracking changes at the frontline of service delivery under Job Network. See Considine, Lewis and O'Sullivan 2011.

Marketisation: 'the reform that never ends'

The contracting-out, or marketisation, of employment services in Australia has a long and ever evolving history, one that Mark Considine had already dubbed 'the reform that never ends' back in 2005.[10] This description of Australian welfare-to-work reform still tells an essential truth. The privatised system has never settled the big questions it raises about the nature of public services for very vulnerable people: can the conflicting interests of the parties be reconciled in a truly public service?

As we write this book, the Australian government is trialling designs for yet another major iteration of the country's welfare-to-work market, what it is provisionally calling the New Employment Services Model. The impetus for the reform is the recognition that the current system, while supporting many Australians to return to work, can and must 'do better for the long-term unemployed'.[11] Prior to the Covid-related surge in unemployment, about one in five jobseekers were registered with employment services for more than five years. Among more disadvantaged client cohorts, this duration of registration with employment services was the norm.

The future is digital, with the Australian government planning to deliver the bulk of employment services online through chat bots and machine-learning platforms that will assist jobseekers in self-managing their own return from welfare-to-work. Only when this online system fails to produce a result will jobseekers be directed to call centres. Those call centres will probably be staffed by a small number of people, who will likely have little experience working directly with highly vulnerable people. Their employer will in all likelihood be a private, contracted multinational. The face-to-face services that are contracted out under the new system will be reserved for those jobseekers who are considered harder-to-help: mainly those jobseekers who are currently in what is termed Stream C of the current Jobactive system.[12]

---

10 Considine 2005.
11 Department of Jobs and Small Business 2018a, 4.
12 The blueprint for this new system, which is being trialled in two employment regions before national rollout in mid-2022, is set out in the final report of

This Stream C contains the highly vulnerable jobseekers who are the focus of our study and of this book. We are going to address the question: what works in helping the people who are hardest to help? While answering this question, we will also show the character of the commercial system for welfare delivery and the challenges associated with it. We will do this from the bottom up and by weaving together detailed descriptions of the local organisations, employment offices, frontline service staff and jobseekers that we followed closely in doing the research for this book. But it was this question, what works with those who are hardest to help, that set us along this journey in the first place.

When politicians and experts debate the success or failure of welfare markets like this one, they generally focus on summary data – such as the number of jobseekers who successfully found jobs, or the speed with which the average jobseeker moved into work. But the people in our study are not average jobseekers. An average jobseeker is someone who finds themselves temporarily out of work, often because of layoffs or economic downturn in their industry. With the right opportunity, this group will return to work quickly. But at the other end of the spectrum, where this book shines a light, are hundreds of thousands of Australians who have been left outside the mainstream labour market. The reasons can be many, but they include lack of training, health challenges and negative perceptions from employers caused by being out of work for a long period.

Working nation

As we have noted, contracting-out this public service goes back 25 years to the Keating government's Working Nation reforms. Some scholars go back further than this, pointing out that local non-government organisations (NGOs) were already being contracted by government agencies to deliver training programs to the unemployed in the 1970s and 1980s.[13] However, it wasn't until the mid-1990s that end-to-end

the government's Expert Advisory Panel on Employment Services. See Department of Jobs and Small Business 2018a.

case management of jobseekers began to be transferred from public to private organisations. Up until this point, public employment service delivery was within the purview of the Commonwealth Employment Service (CES), a public labour exchange service established in the aftermath of World War II. It was institutionally structured as a labour market support rather than a welfare delivery agency, although throughout the late 1970s and 1980s it became increasingly involved in 'work or activity testing' people on benefits.

'Work testing' requires unemployed people to prove that they have genuine reasons for claiming benefits by demanding that they look for work and undertake other activities designed to demonstrate that they are involuntarily unemployed. Normatively, it is associated with an influential theory of social justice known as 'luck egalitarianism'. According to this view of equality, which underpins contemporary understandings of equality of opportunity, justice demands compensating people for inequalities or disadvantages that result from luck or misfortune.[14] Consequently this approach argues that we are under no obligation to alleviate inequities that flow from people's poor decisions or lifestyle choices. So, people who are unemployed through their 'own fault' have no legitimate claims to social assistance. Activity testing tries to ensure that the right to claim benefits stems from circumstances beyond an individual's control, not from 'unresisted dependency'.[15] It thereby legitimates their claims for social assistance 'as those of the "deserving poor".[16] However, the flipside of this activity testing is that it can lead to a wider stigmatisation of people on welfare as lacking in motivation to work. For demanding that claimants *prove* they are involuntarily unemployed, through the performance of mandatory job searching and other activity requirements, rests on a deeper suspicion about the trustworthiness of welfare recipients and their commitment to work. To this extent, as Greg Marston has argued, the politics of welfare-to-work are heavily guided by the belief that the sources of poverty and economic disadvantage are attributable 'to

---

13   See Struyven 2014.
14   See Cohen 1989.
15   Attas and De-Shalit 2004, 310.
16   White 2004, 280.

the behavioural problems and moral shortcomings' of the long-term unemployed rather than structural economic factors.[17] Unemployed people live with the effects of these policy narratives in the form of stigmatisation and shame.[18]

The CES's delivery of a comprehensive public employment service was challenged by the Working Nation reforms. The Keating government argued for the introduction of 'healthy competition', and a shift 'away from processing large numbers of jobseekers through relatively rigid national programs'.[19] This would be achieved by harnessing the entrepreneurialism of the private sector and the community spirit of the not-for-profit sector to produce a more flexible and better tailored employment services system. While Labor did not want the CES dismantled, it felt that private for-profit and not-for-profit agencies could 'augment established services' to provide enhanced training and work experience opportunities. Moreover, introducing competition into the public service delivery supply chain also afforded a way for the government to 'activate public servants working for the CES'.[20] Thus, a new dual system was created, in which approximately one-third of case management services were contracted out to around 300 privately owned for-profit and community organisations. A publicly owned case management provider, Employment Assistance Australia, was also created to compete with the private and not-for-profit case management providers. Jobseekers who were required to participate in case management services could choose which agency they wanted to work with, and whether this was a public, private or not-for-profit provider. The contracted agencies, in turn, received fees for each client they worked with, comprising an initial upfront attachment sum, and placement and outcome payments when clients obtained and completed 13 weeks of either work or training.[21] The central plank of the new Working Nation model was the 'Jobs Compact'. This was a guarantee by the government that those on

17   Marston 2008, 359.
18   Peterie et al. 2019b, 1047.
19   Keating 1994, 127.
20   Considine, Lewis, O'Sullivan and Sol 2015, 34.
21   Considine 1999, 189.

benefits would be provided with subsidised employment or training, or both, after 18 months in the program. This might have been a compelling approach had it lasted but it did not.

Shortly after coming to power in 1996, the Coalition Howard government cut the training programs and the job creation elements of the Working Nation reforms. Philosophically, it favoured reorienting Australia's active labour market programs further towards intensified job search activities and a policy emphasis on enforcing what was termed *mutual obligation*. Under this approach, the onus was on clients to 'prove their worth' and '*earn*' their welfare benefits' through behavioural compliance demonstrating their attachment to the labour market.[22] This was in keeping with the emerging activation agenda promoted by the Organisation for Economic Co-operation and Development (OECD) in the late 1990s, which sought to redirect countries' investment in active labour market policies away from vocational training and subsidised public-sector employment programs towards less costly job search assistance programs, and a policy emphasis on 'work first'. However, the Howard government was also attracted to the market competition logic that the Keating government had layered onto Australia's public employment services system. During the late 1990s, competition for clients and contracts would quickly become the system's 'major driving force'.[23]

The Job Network era

In 1998, the Howard government opened up the entire public employment service system to full competition with its Job Network reform. The remaining public service was corporatised into Employment National, a government-owned provider. But its place in the system was no longer guaranteed, as Australia became the first country to submit its employment services to full competitive tendering. Over 1000 agencies bid for contracts to deliver a combination of job matching, job search training and intensive

22   Carney and Ramia 2002, 279.
23   Ramia and Carney 2001, 66.

assistance services to jobseekers referred into the welfare-to-work system by the recently created benefits administration agency, Centrelink. Centrelink categorised jobseekers into one of three service streams: Flex One (most 'job ready'), Flex Two or Flex Three ('hardest-to-help'). This assessment was made through a statistical profiling tool, the Job Seeker Classification Instrument (JSCI), which scored the unemployed on various indicators of vulnerability and labour market disadvantage. Providers received better payments and profits depending on which stream jobseekers were in, ranging from $245 per placement for Flex One participants to up to $9,200 in payments for Flex Three participants. Payments to providers were a mixture of upfront service fees, interim outcome payments and final outcome payments (as remains the case to this day). The long-term goal 'was to have providers earning more than 50 per cent of their income based on outcome payments',[24] a milestone that was eventually achieved under the Jobactive contract almost 20 years later.

Job Network was seen at the time as an 'internationally important social policy experiment'.[25] It remains so to this day, being a significant turning point in the development of welfare-to-work markets, not only in Australia but internationally. As O'Flynn observes, it went 'much further' than the Working Nation reforms 'not only in the range of services contracted out, but also in its greater emphasis on paying providers for employment *outcomes*'.[26] The OECD considered it 'without parallel' internationally, and Job Network quickly became the exemplar for its active labour market policy reform agenda.[27] In a report on population ageing and the role of active labour market policy reforms, the OECD celebrated Job Network's active participation model as, 'perhaps, the most innovative [employment services] model, given its heavy reliance on the private sector'.[28]

Under the first Job Network contract (1998–2000), two-thirds of public employment services delivery was shifted outside the public

---

24 O'Flynn 2007a, 5.
25 Ramia and Carney 2001, 60.
26 O'Flynn 2007a, 1.
27 Quoted in Finn 2011, 5.
28 Organisation for Economic Cooperation and Development 2006, 128.

sector as a total of 306 private, not-for-profit and publicly owned providers successfully bid for contracts. The Howard government signalled to the new Job Network providers its intent to take its hands off the wheel by not specifying what form of assistance should be provided to the long-term unemployed, hoping instead 'that fees tied to employment outcomes would encourage providers to invest efficiently in assistance tailored to individual needs'.[29]

This became known as a 'black box' approach to service contracting, whereby the purchaser set the program targets and policy direction but let contracted agencies determine how to get there. This 'separation of policy from service delivery'[30] was a revolution in the role of government – from a public service provider that designed programs for jobseekers to predominantly a purchaser of employment outcomes from market providers. As one public administrator put it in an early study of Job Network: 'We give the provider a client with a set of characteristics, they get the outcomes and then we pay for it.'[31]

This administrative reorientation epitomised a broader governance shift that had been gaining traction internationally since the early 1990s; namely, from public administration and public service to New Public Management (NPM), or enterprise. The thrust of this governance shift was to replace so-called direct command-and-control forms of accountability with arms-length managerial forms of accountability such as performance monitoring and financial incentives. Evelyn Brodkin summarises this shift as it applies to public service delivery:

Referencing the familiar trope of 'steering not rowing', NPM positions higher level officials to create incentives and set the destination, while leaving it to lower-level organisations to figure out how to get there. The underlying assumptions are that if performance indicators provide the equivalent of a bottom line and incentives (or penalties) are attached to them, then one can

---

29 Davidson 2011, 62.
30 Ramia and Carney 2010, 266.
31 Quoted in O'Flynn 2007a, 9).

leave it to street-level organisations to determine how best to do policy work.[32]

Put differently, government ministries would now be 'more likely to purchase services than to deliver them, more concerned with regulating contracts than managing public services ... [and] increasingly concerned with managing an economy of incentives ... than with traditional forms of bureaucratic organisation.'[33]

In short, the delivery of public services and use of public resources was to be increasingly governed by 'commercial as opposed to public accountabilities'.[34] The creation of Job Network was arguably the world's most radical NPM experiment in the social services field. But it was not a static experiment, and Job Network would evolve dramatically over the next 10 years.

In 1999, the new service market was put out to tender again for contracts that would run from 2000 until 2003. This time, the government-owned provider was left with just eight per cent of the market as the total number of providers was slashed to 205 agencies. It promptly went out of business. Under the second tendering round, agencies could bid on price as well as quality for intensive assistance, plus job matching and job search training contracts. But by the third Job Network contracting round in 2003, the government had decided to abandon price competition altogether. The price bids that providers were submitting were almost at floor price, 'and at a level that was insufficient to ensure proper employment assistance for the most disadvantaged jobseekers'.[35] There was also mounting empirical evidence that providers had gamed the earlier Job Network contracts by 'churning' jobseekers through short-term placements and even 'creating phantom jobs' to collect payments.[36] Plainly the interests of for-profit companies were not so easily aligned with those of a public service for vulnerable people.

---

32 Brodkin 2011, i254.
33 Considine and O'Sullivan 2015, 2.
34 Ramia and Carney 2010, 267.
35 Thomas 2007, 8.
36 O'Flynn 2007a, 4.

Providers had responded to the new performance environment by 'targeting their most job ready clients' for assistance and giving clients 'with more problematic profiles, including a lack of skills or health issues ... only very cursory attention'.[37] These practices of what are now commonly referred to as 'creaming' and 'parking' became such a problem during the early Job Network era that the Howard government referred the matter to the Productivity Commission. These practices arose directly from one of the key control mechanisms that the Australian government relied on to drive policy outcomes in the new welfare-to-work market: the payment structures embedded in the Job Network contract. These payment structures were backloaded towards payment-by-results. The fear was that frontloading payments towards start-up fees would encourage agencies to take large numbers of clients onto their books to earn the attachment payments but not necessarily to place them in work.

However, as the early Job Network proved, an unintended consequence of backloading the payment structure was that it motivated providers to cream their caseloads by focusing their resources on clients they thought were likely to find a job with little effort by them. Creaming and parking, while a rational response to the business environment established by the government purchaser, worked to further marginalise the most disadvantaged citizens. At first the government hotly denied that creaming and parking were taking place. In one of our first studies of the problem delivered to a seminar at the Australian National University, the Secretary of the Department of Employment rejected the survey data we presented and countered with the claim that there was no creaming or parking in the system and that, if any parking was going on, this was due to jobseekers 'self-parking'. This blaming of the problem on jobseekers illustrates the wider stigmatisation and distrust of claimants' motivation to work that we highlighted earlier as animating the politics of welfare-to-work.

The government started to default from 'black box' commissioning under the second Job Network contract, introducing a code of conduct for providers. However, it had few means of monitoring what services were delivered or enforcing this code of conduct. This changed from

---

37   Considine, Lewis, O'Sullivan and Sol 2015, 36–7.

the third Job Network contract onwards, when the Howard government reacted to the problems of creaming, parking and other frauds by trying to regain control through more traditional bureaucratic means. It 're-regulated' the system, introducing detailed contractual specification or service standards and applying performance monitoring and auditing frameworks more intensively and more regularly.[38] One key development was the introduction of a mandatory computerised case management system for providers' frontline staff to document various workflow processes and expenses. Significantly, the information in this system could be viewed by agency managers and by government officials, and the latter had the power to take back payments to providers if caseload audits or client files revealed evidence of gaming. As a result, the administrative discretion of frontline service staff became substantially curtailed. This not only made it more difficult for providers to game contract payment models through strategies of creaming and parking; as Greg Marston argues, the new computer system also made it harder for frontline staff 'not to apply harsh new financial sanctions and penalties to the unemployed'.[39] More detailed (and prescriptive) minimum servicing requirements were written into contracts. The department also started to produce more regular guidance documentation about the processes and requirements for frontline employment services staff.

The third Job Network contract signified an important development in Australia's welfare-to-work market for two additional reasons: the intensification of Australia's famous star rating system and the full advent of privatisation. This denoted an end to the government's direct involvement in the day-to-day delivery of employment services to out-of-work citizens in Australia. From this point forward, all street-level bureaucrats working within Australia's welfare-to-work system would be employed on short-term contracts by a private for-profit or not-for-profit agency.

Unlike previous contracting rounds, not all providers were required to bid for their new contracts in 2003. Indeed, 60 per cent of contracts were rolled over on the basis that these existing agencies were

---

38   Bredgaard and Larsen 2007.
39   Marston 2005, 91.

deemed to be 'high-performing' providers and could therefore avoid competition. This assessment was based on their individual star rating. The star rating system monitors and ranks the performance of the private agencies and each of their local employment offices. It was introduced in 2001 as a kind of 'Michelin Guide' for signalling providers' relative performance to jobseekers.[40] This followed evidence that jobseeker choice, the primary goal identified by Keating, 'was playing a minimal role' in the selection of providers, because they had no reliable information to make a choice about which provider to go with.[41] So, the star rating system was created to measure each local office's performance in the hope that this would 'drive competition between providers for clients'.[42]

The system uses a confidential regression analysis of performance to control for differences in client characteristics, local labour market conditions and other relevant variables. This allows agencies in similar parts of the market to be compared on job placements, which drives their rating. Providers that exceed the national performance average for their sector by more than a given percentage are awarded five stars, whereas those who underperform against the national average by a given threshold are awarded one star. Providers on the cusp of the national performance average are rated three stars, and so on.

Star ratings, which were originally issued biannually, are now published quarterly for every single service site in Australia. Employment outcomes are the KPI used to calculate a site's star rating, although the type and weighting of indicators that feed into agencies' star ratings have changed over time. One of the most controversial changes to star ratings was under the Jobactive contract (2015–22), when the Work for the Dole program became a key part of the performance measurement framework. As a result, 20 per cent of agencies' star ratings now have nothing to do with their track record of securing job placements or employment outcomes. Instead, they relate to the proportion of clients they place in the Work for the Dole program and the speed at which their clients start Work for the Dole activities

40   Considine, Lewis, O'Sullivan and Sol 2013, 30.
41   O'Flynn 2007b, 5.
42   Jarvie and Mercer 2018, 286.

during their annual activity phase.[43] This is one of the reasons we did not use star ratings to select 'best-performing' Jobactive offices to study for this book.

Agency star ratings were influential in determining which providers were awarded Job Network contracts in 2003, and again in 2006, when less than 10 per cent of contracts were competitively tendered.[44] In between contracting rounds, every 18 months or so, the government also uses star ratings to reduce the caseload of the poorly rated agencies, giving those clients to more highly rated providers. The process is designed to progressively eliminate low-performing agencies from the market by making employment services a survival-of-the-fittest contest. And because star ratings are a *relative* measure of agencies' performance, there will always be winners, losers and bloodletting. Needless to say, the reallocation process causes high anxiety among the agencies and often disrupts any sense of local affiliation, since an office may be lost in one part of the country and another gained in subsequent rounds.

Market models after Howard

It is now well over a decade since the end of Howard's Job Network. The program was decommissioned by the Labor Rudd government in 2009 and replaced by the Job Services Australia (JSA) model. That model was in turn decommissioned by the Coalition Abbott government and replaced with Jobactive in 2015. Essentially, Australia's employment services system has been overhauled with every change of government over the past 20 years. The one constant throughout this turbulent pattern of change is the apparent political consensus 'that welfare-to-work is best delivered by private agencies operating under short-term government contracts'.[45]

These two versions of the system have each maintained the core design of the third Job Network, with some adjustments to the payment

---

43   See Australian National Audit Office 2017.
44   Finn 2011.
45   Considine, O'Sullivan and Nguyen 2014b, 470.

model, size and duration of the contracts. For example, under JSA, the payment model increased the incentives for providers to focus on securing sustained employment outcomes for their more disadvantaged clients. A fourth stream was also added for Centrelink to use to refer jobseekers to contracted providers.

This increase in the number of service streams reflected an important change in the profile of clients that providers would have to work with. JSA rolled the old Job Network and six other employment assistance programs into a single contracted out program, increasing the challenge and complexity of the clients on providers' caseloads. This change eliminated many smaller, specialist employment services providers from the Australian welfare-to-work market, as they did not have the resources to offer an entire suite of services across bigger territorial areas. Hence, although the total number of employment services agencies increased under the JSA contract from around 100 to 141, the number of smaller agencies 'was much reduced and now tended to be confined to remote locations and Indigenous specialists'.[46]

The pressures on smaller agencies intensified even further when Jobactive replaced JSA in July 2015 and further increased the contracted territorial areas. The Australian government's purchasing agency, the Department of Employment, wanted to reduce the number of contracts it had to manage. It divided the country into 51 'employment regions' rather than the 110 'employment service areas' that had been used to apportion JSA contracts. The duration of agencies' initial contracts also increased from three to five (since extended to seven) years, to give providers greater certainty and to encourage longer-term and more strategic investments in employment support. However, this added contractual certainty was offset by changes to provider funding that made Jobactive a predominantly payment-by-results system. More than 50 per cent of the total payments available to providers now depended on their securing employment outcomes with clients. This had not been the case under JSA, where fixed administration and service fees had comprised the bulk of provider payments. The implications of this change are discussed in greater detail in chapter four, but suffice it to say here that it was detrimental to smaller community organisations,

---

46   Considine, Lewis, O'Sullivan and Sol 2015, 45.

which did not have the capital reserves or access to borrowing needed to take on the financial risks of managing a payment-by-results contract. Big international businesses gained influence because of the Jobactive contract which had the effect of concentrating the market, with just 44 agencies winning contracts to deliver the program. Compared with JSA, a greater proportion of contracts were now held by for-profit providers. And by shifting the model to favour these big profit-taking firms, the government also made itself more dependent on them and more open to political pressure to support their sustained role in the market.

Multiple motives drove the replacement of JSA with Jobactive. The more conservative Abbott government wanted a welfare-to-work system that would be stronger on its mutual obligation demands on jobseekers. The Labor government's JSA reforms had been seen as softening the emphasis on jobseeker compliance compared with the Howard government's Job Network. Gaby Ramia and Terry Carney suggest that the JSA system saw a partial return to 'more traditional concepts of "social citizenship"' and access to services as a matter of right rather than subject to mutual obligations and sanctions.[47] However, this interpretation is contested by Simone Casey, who observes how consolidating pre-employment assistance programs for cohorts such as lone parents and people with disabilities with mainstream employment services under JSA had the effect of widely extending mutual obligation requirements and subjecting more and more recipients 'to behavioural supervision'.[48] The Abbott government also criticised JSA as heavily 'constrained by administrative requirements' that offered 'limited scope for provider-initiated service design';[49] an accusation that the Rudd government had previously levelled against Job Network when making the case for JSA. As the then Minister for Employment, Julia Gillard, had argued at the time, JSA was to replace Job Network's '"one size fits all" approach ... with greater flexibility for employment services providers to tailor services'.[50]

---

47   Ramia and Carney 2010, 270.
48   Casey 2019, 1019.
49   Department of Employment 2015, 9.
50   Gillard 2008.

However, by the end of the first JSA contract in 2012, providers' scope to tailor services was heavily constrained by the more than 3,000 pages of procedural guidelines that the department had issued to providers about various administration requirements.[51] A key objective of the Jobactive reform was therefore to reduce the level of 'service prescription' by the purchasing department and of the associated regulatory and administrative burden for providers.[52] During the tendering process, providers were encouraged to propose their own service models, in the hope that this would free them 'to deliver flexible solutions tailored to an individual jobseeker's circumstances'.[53] Even so, by the end of the first year of the Jobactive contract, there were still over 30 different (and sometimes contradictory) guideline documents covering frontline employment service delivery, with some of these documents up to 45 pages in length.[54]

The activation turn in social policy

The market delivery of public employment services is not unique to Australia, but Australia has gone further down this path than any other OECD country. The contracting-out of social services is, however, only one half of the major institutional transformations that have occurred to Australia's welfare state since the early 1990s. A series of 'activation turns' in social security policy have unfolded alongside this trajectory of service marketisation. The term 'activation turn' is an umbrella concept used to describe the reconfiguration of labour market policies away from demand-side, job creation measures towards 'supply-side employability interventions' focused on rapidly moving social security claimants into work.[55] Within the now vast literature on activation, a common distinction is drawn between enabling and demanding activation measures.[56] The former incorporate support services such as

---

51   Australian National Audit Office 2014.
52   Department of Employment 2015, 1.
53   Australian National Audit Office 2017, 54.
54   Australian National Audit Office 2017.
55   Whitworth and Carter 2020, 845.

training and work experience programs designed to develop jobseekers' skills and improve their competitiveness in the labour market. Demanding activation, by contrast, places the accent on more behavioural policy tools for motivating employment and penalising welfare dependence such as job searching and other conditionality requirements, tightening eligibility criteria for benefits, reducing payments, and imposing sanctions for non-compliance with mandatory activation measures. It is the spread of this more demanding approach, which is also often referred to as 'workfare',[57] over recent decades that has dominated much of the debate about welfare reform and shaped the activation turn in social security policy. According to Adam Whitworth and Eleanor Carter, demanding activation or 'workfare' has now 'become the standard welfare orthodoxy at the heart of international welfare systems', motivated by governments' pursuit of fiscal austerity and 'growing desire to responsibilise individuals for their own welfare provision'.[58]

These changes to the rights and obligations of citizens receiving welfare payments have been a core part of the transition towards a new welfare state model, one that purports to 'end welfare as we know it'.[59] As the then Australian Treasurer, Joe Hockey, pronounced in a much-publicised speech to the Institute of Economic Affairs in London, 'The age of entitlement is over.' Hockey's speech lauded the frugality of Hong Kong's social security system over the 'enormous entitlement systems' spanning Western democracies, arguing that the notion of entitlement 'corrodes the very heart of the process of free enterprise that drives our economies'. While he did not say so, his speech took up ideas that conservative politicians across the globe had been championing since the early 1980s. This conservative critique of the welfare state was captured in the title of Lawrence Mead's influential book *Beyond Entitlement*, published in the mid-1980s.

While Mead was not the first neo-conservative to challenge thinking about welfare entitlement, his book set out a spirited case for a

---

56   See, for example, Dingeldey 2007.
57   See Bonoli 2010.
58   Whitworth and Carter 2020, 845.
59   Considine 2000, 274.

form of 'Big Government' conservatism that would later become known as the 'the *new paternalism*'.[60] Rather than calling for dramatic cuts to monetary benefits, as many of his conservative peers such as Charles Murray were arguing for, Mead argued for making benefits increasingly conditional on the performance of various behavioural obligations: specifically, a requirement to undertake work-like activities that would instil work motivation in unemployed people. Social assistance payments, Mead argued, fostered a culture of welfare dependence because the long-term unemployed had 'too many other sources of income ... to work reliably unless programs require them to do so'.[61] His solution to the rising welfare caseloads of the era was to couple rights to social security 'with serious work and other obligations' and to impose a regime of sanctions on those who breached these behavioural requirements.[62] The welfare state would be re-purposed as a vehicle for shaping conduct and culture, converting 'passive' benefit recipients into active citizens capable of self-sufficiency through employment.

Mead defended this supervisory approach as a form of justifiable state paternalism, and as being in poor people's own interests. In contrast to previous generations, Mead argued that the capacity of poor people to look after themselves could 'no longer be taken for granted'.[63] They needed to be helped to help themselves, which government programs would do by subjecting them to much tougher requirements to seek and take work of any kind. Any job was better than no job in what would become widely adopted internationally as a 'work-first' model of activation. No longer was the welfare system to be treated as a social safety net or judged by the level of social assistance it provided. Instead, as US President Reagan announced in a radio address on welfare reform, it would be judged by how many citizens 'it makes independent of welfare'.[64]

It was not long before these arguments crossed the Pacific and started to take root within Australian social policy. Unlike in the USA

---

60   See Mead 1997; Soss et al. 2011a, 25.
61   Mead 1986.
62   Mead 1986, 3–4.
63   Mead 2014 [1991], 89.
64   Reagan 1986.

where conservative criticism focused on single mothers as 'welfare queens', however, the primary targets of activation in Australia were the long-term unemployed.[65] Also, as with marketisation, it was the progressive rather than conservative side of politics that took the first steps towards activation in Australia.

The genesis of the compliance regime that currently underpins jobseeker activation in Australia was the Social Security Review, chaired by Bettina Cass on behalf of the Labor Hawke government in the late 1980s. The Hawke government came to power on the promise that it would restructure Australia's social security system. Long-term unemployment was rising rapidly in Australia, accompanied by 'a record high ratio of jobseekers to job vacancies'.[66] The Cass Review argued for the introduction of a more rigorous activity test that required people on out-of-work payments to attend mandatory workforce participation activities like job search assistance clubs, job creation and training programs.[67] While an obligation to look for and accept 'suitable' work had been a condition of receiving unemployment benefits since their introduction, these conditions were not strongly enforced until the late 1980s, when the CES became obligated to officially report jobseekers who no longer attended appointments with them, which would result in the Department of Social Security stopping their payments.

The rules concerning what types of work those receiving benefits could reasonably refuse were also narrowed and, in 1991, unemployment benefits were renamed the Job Search Allowance for those under 18 or who had been unemployed for less than 12 months, and Newstart Allowance for those over 18 who were long-term (12 months or more) unemployed. The names of the new payments were meant to be significant. No longer were people entitled to *benefits*. Those who were out of work now merited a short-term *allowance* that would come with significant strings attached. Recipients of out-of-work payments would also now be designated as 'jobseekers' rather than 'unemployed' people, a term that, Greg Marston observes, 'places the

65 McDonald and Chenoweth 2006, 113.
66 Bennett et al 2018, 13.
67 For discussions of these reforms see: Bennett et al. 2018; Deeming 2016.

problem firmly within the mode of the individual'.[68] Newstart recipients could be compelled to attend CES appointments when requested or face payment suspensions. Breaches of the activity-test requirements were punishable by a two-week loss of payments in the first instance, a six-week loss of payments in the second, and a further six-week loss of payments for subsequent breaches.[69]

As Gaby Ramia and Terry Carney observe, this shift towards a more active and conditional welfare system denoted a fundamental transformation in 'the social division of welfare' and basis of entitlement. No longer were welfare payments considered benefits payable to citizens on the basis of their socio-economic circumstances and need, like the age pension and other payments. They were reserved for good jobseekers who 'prov[ed] their worth, and in the process earn[ed] their benefits and services'.[70] This emphasis on behavioural activation was soon followed by the introduction of a new case management model under the Keating government's Working Nation reforms. This case management model required jobseekers to not only search for jobs but also to accept any suitable offer of employment. Caseworkers could recommend payment suspensions if clients failed to attend interviews, training courses or 'other activities deemed to be helpful'.[71] Penalties for non-compliance with activity-test requirements were toughened to increase the loss of payment period for initial compliance breaches to four weeks for the long-term unemployed, and to six weeks for those unemployed for 18 months or more. In exchange, the government committed to a reciprocal obligation to provide paid work opportunities for those who had been unemployed for 18 months or more.

However, reciprocal obligation quickly became 'mutual obligation' under the Howard government. Jobseeker Diaries, referred to by many as 'dole diaries', were introduced in 1996, requiring welfare recipients to list more detailed employer contact information and to keep a diary of the activities they had undertaken, and number of jobs applied for

---

68   Marston 2005, 86.
69   Ziguras et al. 2003.
70   Ramia and Carney 2001, 63.
71   Considine 1999, 189.

over a certain period. A year later, the Howard government introduced compulsory Work for the Dole for those aged 18 to 24 years. Younger jobseekers were required to perform unpaid community work for six months out of every year they were on benefits. A new sanctioning regime was also put in place that extended the maximum total loss of payments period, following a third breach of compliance requirements, from six to eight weeks. Over the late 1990s and early 2000s, as the policy emphasis on mutual obligation deepened, Work for the Dole was progressively extended, first to those aged between 18 and 34 years of age and then to all jobseekers under 50.[72] Now it was simply the fact of receiving income support – not the additional investments in training and support services as under Keating's reciprocal obligation – that generated 'the obligation to "give something back" to the community' in various forms, including Work for the Dole.[73]

The circumstances under which payments to recipients could be suspended also dramatically increased to include 56 different possible reasons for stopping jobseekers' payments.[74] Not surprisingly, sanctioning jobseekers for compliance breaches became far more widespread. A study by Terry Carney and Gaby Ramia showed that the number of breach penalties applied to jobseekers increased by some 260 per cent during the first four years of the Howard government, from 10,060 breaches per month in 1997/98 to 25,208 breaches per month in 1999/2000.[75] By 2001, 18 per cent of Newstart Allowance recipients and 26 per cent of young unemployed people were breached for non-compliance, resulting in losses of up to a quarter of their payments for up to 26 weeks.[76] Welfare agencies reported consequent increases in homelessness and related distress.[77]

Some years later, in 2003, the Howard government moved to a so-called active participation model for all jobseekers, not just those who were long-term unemployed. This significantly expanded the reach of

---

72   Deeming 2016.
73   Ziguras et al. 2003, 9.
74   Bennett et al. 2018, 17.
75   Carney and Ramia 2002, 281.
76   Davidson 2011.
77   Australian Council of Social Services 2001.

behavioural conditionality requirements, which were further extended in 2006, under the Howard government's Welfare-to-Work reforms. These reforms increased 'the range and number of people required to look for and accept work', with principal carers, parents, people with disabilities and mature-age jobseekers all being targeted for activation.[78]

After it came to power in 2007, the Labor Rudd government attempted to soften the punitive compliance framework that had emerged especially during the Job Network era. Changes to the *Social Security Act* introduced alongside the JSA reforms narrowed the number of circumstances under which jobseekers' payments could be suspended. The compliance framework was adjusted to motivate 'connection and co-operation' via temporary payment suspensions rather than non-payment periods. Jobseekers who failed to attend activities such as job interviews, training or employment service appointments without a valid reason would have their fortnightly payments reduced by 10 per cent for each day they committed a 'connection failure' rather than losing their payments for a period of weeks.[79]

The Rudd government also moved away from a sole focus on Work for the Dole, giving people more options to meet their mutual obligation requirements through training or volunteer work. It removed specific funding for Work for the Dole programs, meaning that providers had to use Employment Fund credits or their own resources to finance Work for the Dole placements. This funding change motivated greater use of training programs by providers during clients' annual activity phase.[80] However, this softening of jobseeker compliance was short lived.

When the Abbott government came to power in late 2013, it toughened the jobseeker compliance framework, subjecting Australian jobseekers to some of the strictest conditionality requirements in the OECD.[81] In July 2014, it gave private providers the power to directly suspend jobseekers' payment for non-attendance by submitting a Non-Attendance Report (NAR). These new sanctions were not

---

78   Thomas and Daniels 2010, 1.
79   Ramia and Carney 2010, 268.
80   Davidson 2014.
81   Senate Education and Employment References Committee 2019, 102.

scrutinised by the Department of Human Services other than to verify that jobseekers had mutual obligation requirements on the day a NAR was submitted. Initially, payments were suspended only until jobseekers agreed to attend a re-engagement appointment. But this was quickly changed to a 'suspend till attend' policy. From July 2015, providers could also recommend a payment penalty be applied, usually 10 per cent of jobseekers' fortnightly payments for each day of non-attendance, if they believed clients did not have a valid reason for non-attendance. The maximum no-payment period for voluntarily leaving a job or being dismissed for misconduct was also extended to 12 weeks for jobseekers who had received relocation assistance to find a job.

The Jobactive reforms also saw a return to Work for the Dole as the default annual activity requirement for all jobseekers under 50 years of age. This was in line with the emphasis on a stronger approach to activation. As Minister for Employment under the Howard government, Tony Abbott had been a key architect of the original Work for the Dole program, introduced in the late 1990s, advocating mandatory Work for the Dole on precisely the sort of new paternalist grounds that Mead had used to defend workfare; namely, that Work for the Dole was trying to 'change a culture of welfare to a culture of work'. 'We're trying to replace an ethic of entitlement with an ethic of responsibility,' he argued at the time, and 'for Newstart beneficiaries the era of unconditional welfare is over.'[82] So, it was no surprise that Abbott's ascendancy to Prime Minister marked a return to the workfare policies of the late 1990s and early 2000s.

Once people had participated in Jobactive for 12 months, they would be required to complete 50 hours of activities each fortnight for six months, on top of their usual job search and appointment attendance requirements. By any international standard this was a punitive regime that was bound to result in problems. Those aged between 50 and 59 were required to complete 30 hours of activities per fortnight, and those aged 60 years or over had an annual activity requirement of 10 hours per fortnight. Whereas under the JSA system jobseekers had been encouraged to meet their annual activity requirements through investments in education and training, the

---

82   Quoted in Fowkes 2011, 6.

Abbott government narrowed the range of activities that jobseekers could undertake. Specialist Work for the Dole coordinators were contracted to manage this aspect of the jobseeker compliance regime in each of the 51 Jobactive employment regions.

These Work for the Dole coordination contracts were separate to the contracts signed with providers to deliver employment services, although some Jobactive providers won both. Work for the Dole coordinators acted as intermediaries between employment services providers and host organisations such as charity shops and other social enterprises, taking responsibility for identifying potential host organisations, securing Work for the Dole places for jobseekers and connecting Work for the Dole host organisations with providers.[83] Moreover, Jobactive providers' overall performance rating was now partly determined by their clients' level of participation in Work for the Dole. However, in July 2018, the separate Work for the Dole coordination contracts were ended, and these functions were transferred directly to Jobactive providers.

The elevation of Work for the Dole was one of the most divisive aspects of the Jobactive reforms. While some providers saw its value as a work experience program, many others questioned its contribution to improving jobseekers' employability, viewing it instead as having a predominantly punitive function.[84] It was also argued that the jobseeker's search activity was constrained while they were occupied on this program, delaying their efforts to find work. Several safety concerns were also raised about the program, after one young jobseeker died from a head injury sustained on a Work for the Dole placement in April 2016. While every Work for the Dole activity is required to have a work health and safety assessment, and adequate supervision of jobseekers must be provided by all Work for the Dole host organisations, a report by auditing firm EY found that more than a third of Work for the Dole activities 'did not fully meet the average safety benchmarks'.[85]

---

83 National Employment Services Association 2019.
84 For a discussion of the mixed evidence on the effectiveness of Work for the Dole, see Senate Education and Employment References Committee 2019.
85 Senate Education and Employment References Committee 2019, 124.

A series of other controversial activation reforms have been introduced in recent years. These include Parents Next, a pre-employment program rolled out nationally in 2018 that extended activation requirements to parents with children as young as six months old. The jobseeker compliance framework was also overhauled, moving to a new 'demerit points' system known as the Targeted Compliance Framework (TCF) in July 2018, under which jobseekers accumulate demerit points for every mutual obligation or activity failure they commit over a six-month period. Once they accumulate five demerit points, they enter the penalty zone. In this penalty zone, where jobseekers remain until they have met all their activity requirements for three consecutive months, any subsequent compliance failure results in a 50 per cent loss of a fortnightly payment. A penalty of this magnitude obviously has catastrophic impacts on jobseekers' housing, food and health.

A second compliance failure in the penalty zone incurs a 100 per cent loss of payment, and a third or subsequent failure results in total cessation of payments for four weeks. One of the most notable aspects of the TCF is its automated approach to compliance. In addition to accumulating demerit points that move them closer to the penalty zone, jobseekers' payments are also automatically suspended if they do not 'self-report' attendance at an activity listed in their Job Plan. This self-reporting can be done online or via a smartphone app, but it shifts the burden onto jobseekers to demonstrate their compliance, whereas previously the onus had been on providers to demonstrate jobseekers' non-compliance. Scope for exercising discretion in administering sanctions is consequently much narrower. It also makes the system more difficult to traverse for those with low levels of digital literacy or people who are trying to manage chaotic lives for one reason or another.

'Double' activation

What we can see from the above discussion is that welfare-to-work reform in Australia has followed a 'twin track'. The radical administrative and governance reforms of the institutions that deliver policy (i.e. private agencies and profit motives) have gone hand in glove with major social security policy reforms tightening the eligibility conditions for receiving payments and intensifying obligations. This combination of a social policy turn towards activation and the creation and expansion of quasi-markets in employment services is far from unique to Australia. It has occurred in numerous other countries, including the USA and the UK, along with a wave of European countries, including the Netherlands, Denmark, Germany and, in more recent years, Ireland and Sweden. It is fair to say, however, that Australia has travelled further along these reform tracks than most countries and, in the case of marketisation in particular, is widely considered to be a pioneer and at the vanguard of employment services delivery reform.

As Evelyn Brodkin observes in relation to what she terms the unfolding global workfare project, managerial reforms such as marketisation and workfare-oriented social policy reorientations 'have become closely intertwined'.[86] Joe Soss, Richard Fording and Sanford Schram argue that we need to understand these twin reform tracks as 'two sides of a single political project' involving the societal embedding of a neoliberal market rationality.[87] Just as welfare payments have been increasingly reconfigured to promote and compel participation in the labour market, so too have states increasingly looked to organise the delivery of social services via the market. For some public policy and social policy scholars, this is no mere accident. There is a view, especially among European scholars, that outsourcing employment services delivery to non-public agencies is a deliberate political strategy to smooth the way for implementing contested workfare policy practices; that changes in the structure of employment services are designed to support policy shifts in the direction of 'work-first'. For example, policy designers might assume that a work-first activation model 'can more easily be implemented through a non-public implementation structure than by traditional public employment officers' such as those employed in the CES.[88] Or policy designers might suspect that unionised public-sector workers will try to resist redefining their job roles to require them to enforce mutual obligations

---

86   Brodkin 2013b, 11.
87   Soss et al. 2013, 139.
88   Bredgaard and Larsen 2007, 294.

or impose payment penalties on jobseekers for compliance breaches. Conversely, as Thomas Bredgaard and Flemming Larsen argue, private sector workers and agencies motivated by economic incentives might be expected to be tougher in their 'use of sanctions, demands, and other motivational initiatives'.[89] In short, quasi-market reforms can change the substance of welfare and activation policy on the ground.

Viewed from this perspective, the turn towards a more regulatory welfare state over the past 30 years reflects not only the legislative project of conditioning income support on particular behaviours but also strategies of public management reform aimed at disciplining workers involved in policy delivery. Elsewhere, we have described this as *double activation*, meaning that marketisation and related public service delivery reforms have exposed the agencies and frontline workers responsible for delivering policy to the same behaviour-change instruments (activity monitoring and financial incentives) relied on to activate the unemployed.[90] People on benefits have been reconfigured by policy 'as individual units of (paid) labour which need to be financially incentivised to sell their labour' while service providers have been simultaneously repositioned by governance reforms as 'market agents who need to be financially incentivised to place people in paid work'.[91] Put differently, the governance instruments that are applied to monitor and steer the behaviours of case managers and service providers 'are cut from the same neoliberal cloth as the systems designed for their clients'.[92]

Julian Le Grand, a leading quasi-markets theorist and former senior policy adviser to UK Prime Minister Tony Blair, characterises this change as a shift away from viewing public service delivery agents as altruistic 'knights' towards governing them as 'knaves' motivated only by self-interest. It is an administrative orientation animated by public choice theory in economics, which sought to explain the growth in public expenditure and public employment in many countries over the 1960s and 1970s as partly the product of rent-seeking behaviours by

---

89   Bredgaard and Larsen 2007, 294.
90   Considine, Lewis, O'Sullivan and Sol 2015.
91   Shutes and Taylor 2014.
92   Soss et al. 2013, 138.

bureaucrats concerned with maximising their own salaries, patronage and prestige rather than pursuing the public interest.[93]

As Owen Hughes observes, public choice theory gave neoliberal critics of the welfare state 'a plausible weapon' to support their criticisms that government had become 'too big and inefficient'.[94] Repositioning bureaucrats and public service workers as driven by self-interest fostered distrust in bureaucracy and provided the conceptual ammunition to justify outsourcing and privatisation. Public choice theorists argue that policy reforms fail not because they mistake the nature of the problem they are trying to address, but because they often do 'not serve the self-interest of the people delivering that policy'.[95] Quasi-markets try to remedy this agency problem by using outcomes-based contracting and payment-by-results to harness the self-interest of policy producers towards the public good. In this way, they embody the alleged invisible hand of the market 'whereby, simply through pursuing their own advantage, suppliers are led to contribute to socially desirable ends'.[96] A core tenet of employment services marketisation is that competition between providers for clients and contracts should motivate agencies to innovate, achieving services that deliver greater employment outcomes which are more responsive to users' needs. Likewise, outcomes-based contracting should reduce the overall cost of program delivery through price competition and ensuring that purchasers only pay for successful interventions.

The 'double activation' story is a reform agenda that various members of our research team, led by Mark Considine, have been following since the mid-1990s. This began with Mark's comparative interview and survey research of frontline staff working in the three different sectors (public, private and not-for-profit) of what was then a mixed welfare market.[97] That survey research was followed up a decade later (with Jenny M. Lewis and Siobhan O'Sullivan) to examine how frontline employment service delivery had changed as a result of

---

93   See, for example, Schwartz 1994.
94   Hughes 2003, 10.
95   Le Grand 2010, 60.
96   Le Grand 1997, 159.
97   See Considine 1999; Considine 2000; Considine 2001.

privatisation.[98] We have tracked the sector ever since, with Phuc Nguyen joining the larger research team in 2012 and Michael McGann coming on board in 2016.

The Howard government consistently maintained that Job Network was more efficient than its predecessors, delivering a higher proportion of employment outcomes at lower average cost. Results from the department's own quarterly post-program monitoring survey showed a steady increase in the proportion of jobseekers who entered employment three months after participating in welfare-to-work: from around 30 per cent of participants in the late 1990s to over 45 per cent by 2004, but plateauing thereafter. The average cost paid by the government per employment outcome also declined considerably, from approximately $6,500 per outcome during the first Job Network contract to approximately $3,500 per outcome by 2005.[99] However, observers questioned the extent to which these higher outcome rates had to do with the success of Job Network rather than external economic factors, particularly a stronger labour market.[100] There was also concern that the cost savings may have been achieved 'at the price of weakened service quality' and 'at the expense of difficult-to-place jobseekers'.[101]

By the time of the economic downturn in 2009, the number of long-term recipients of dole payments stood at more than 300,000 people. This, as Peter Davidson notes, was 'well above the number two decades earlier, despite robust employment growth and an unemployment rate that plummeted to 30-year lows'.[102] Indeed, by the end of Job Network, the proportion of unemployment payment recipients classified as *very long-term unemployed* (unemployed for two years or more) had risen to 43 per cent, compared to 16 per cent in 1990. In short, the profile of participants was now more disadvantaged, 'with a higher incidence of Indigenous peoples, people of mature age, people with disabilities and people with social barriers to work such as homelessness, addictions, or mental illness'.[103]

---

98 See Considine and Lewis 2010; Considine, Lewis and O'Sullivan 2011.
99 Finn 2011, 12.
100 Finn 2011, 12.
101 See Finn 2011, 12; Thomas 2007.
102 Davidson 2011, 83.

Privatisation may have produced a system that was economically more efficient when averaged across the entire cohort of payment recipients. However, contrary to the expectations of reformers that marketisation would also deliver greater flexibility in service delivery for the benefit of jobseekers, our comparative research published in 2011 showed that employment services became *less flexible* over time.[104] The level of service standardisation or 'one size fits all' was more pronounced as Job Network matured. But more than this, there was also little left to distinguish between the approaches of agencies located in different sectors.

Both Keating and Howard strongly favoured a mixed market that included both for-profit and not-for-profit providers. The presumption was that each would bring different characteristics to the system, enhancing the flexibility of employment services overall. But research showed that over time, providers responded to commercial imperatives in much the same way, regardless of whether they were a small faith-based or secular charity or a large multinational human services corporation. The findings of our research team cohered with the analyses of several other scholars. In a report commissioned by the UK Department for Work and Pensions, the UK social policy scholar Dan Finn concluded that privatisation had given rise to an 'inflexible' pattern of outsourced services in which 'up to half of the available service hours were being consumed in meeting administrative and compliance requirements'.[105] One of the most detailed independent studies of Job Network, from the point of view of clients, is Greg Marston and Catherine McDonald's longitudinal study of jobseekers' experiences of activation. In their study, which involved three waves of in-depth interviews with 75 long-term unemployed jobseekers, they likewise reached the conclusion that people, in general, 'are churned through what is experienced as an indifferent system, with " personalised service" being the exception, rather than the norm'.[106] Imposing greater administrative and compliance demands over

---

103 Davidson 2011, 83.
104 Considine, Lewis and O'Sulllvan 2011.
105 Finn 2011, 13.
106 Marston and McDonald 2008, 265.

successive contracting rounds, allied to a fall in the value of service fees and outcome payments, had driven agencies 'to focus on the most "job ready" and avoid more expensive interventions that were needed for the harder to place'.[107] Contracting-out social services, we concluded, did 'not produce a new industry of service innovators ... but a "herd" of profit maximisers who are highly responsive to threats to their viability and who embrace standardisation of services as a way to minimise risks'.[108] Added to this standardisation of frontline delivery was a loss of professionalism among case managers that was driven, in part, by low wages, a lack of job security and the increasingly administrative nature of frontline work.[109]

Our research team has since repeated this survey research in 2012 and again in 2016, finding consistent results. There has been no reversal in the pattern of routinised service delivery despite repeated reform attempts to reintroduce flexibility and personalisation into the system. If anything, our most recent survey findings suggest that the level of service standardisation has deepened further and that there is even less to distinguish the for-profit and not-for-profit elements of the system than there was under Job Network.[110] Recent sociological studies of jobseekers' experiences of Jobactive, and the quality of support delivered to clients by providers, reinforce this observation. Participants in the study by Michelle Peterie and her colleagues of social networking patterns among 80 unemployed Australians described experiencing a dehumanising and 'impersonal system' where participation in employment services was characterised by the performance of 'bureaucratic requirements' rather than progression towards paid work.[111]

In this book we will not restate those findings or earlier evaluations we have made of the trajectory that welfare-to-work reform has taken in Australia. Where appropriate, we will draw on the larger body of

---

107 Finn 2011, 12.
108 Considine, Lewis and O'Sullivan 2011, 18.
109 The de-professionalisation of Australia's frontline employment services workforce following marketisation is discussed in detail in Considine and Lewis 2010.
110 See Considine, O'Sullivan, McGann and Nguyen 2020.
111 Peterie et al. 2019b, 1051. See also O'Halloran et al. 2019.

research to provide context and supporting data for the observations and arguments developed in this book. However, our aim in this book is to offer a more local, ethnographic account of Australian's welfare-to-work system; one that is told from the *street level*. In the next chapter, we will explain what such an ethnographic perspective brings to the study of welfare-to-work markets. But first it is necessary to touch on what drew us to undertake this kind of research in the first place – the particular predicament of the most disadvantaged.

(Not) working with the 'hardest-to-help'

A recurring theme throughout the research that our team has undertaken over the last 20 years is the low rates of success that welfare-to-work markets have had in supporting the more disadvantaged jobseekers into work. While Australia's system of privatised employment services has had success in achieving outcomes with jobseekers who are comparatively close to the labour market, employment programs to date have been plagued by 'their lack of impact on outcomes for the most highly disadvantaged jobseekers'; namely, those long-term unemployed jobseekers, who in addition to a lack of employment, experience a range of personal issues that increase the difficulty of finding work such as mental health problems, substance dependency, domestic violence, homelessness and/or criminal records.[112]

This is not only an Australian problem. Studies from colleagues in other countries show that it reflects the international experience of welfare-to-work markets.[113] We have already considered this issue in relation to Job Network. The two systems that replaced it, JSA and Jobactive, have fared little better. Long-term unemployment, as Peter Davidson argues, has become the 'Achilles' heel' of the Australian welfare-to-work market. Whereas just under 47 per cent of Newstart recipients were considered very long-term unemployed towards the

---

112 Borland et al. 2016, 3.
113 See, for example, Fuertes and Lindsay 2016; Greer et al. 2017; van Berkel 2014.

end of Job Network (June 2008), in June 2019 this was true of 63 per cent of Newstart recipients.[114] As the caseload has become more disadvantaged, the success of providers in placing people into jobs has tailed off, despite millions of dollars flowing to the profits of these companies every year. When we drill down deeper and examine the incidence of very long-term unemployment among those who are classified as requiring the most intensive assistance, the picture becomes even more bleak.

As noted earlier, when people claim activity-tested payments they are assessed by Centrelink to determine their 'distance' from employment. Under the current system they are organised into one of three service streams: A, B or C. Stream C, the most disadvantaged cohort, accounts for around 16 per cent of the Jobactive caseload. Among the Stream C members, who are the focus of this book, more than 44 per cent have been clients of employment services for over five years and nearly 90 per cent are classified as long-term unemployed.[115] Official data reported for the period from 1 July 2015 to 31 May 2018 shows that only 29,310 Stream C clients in total were supported by providers into six months or more of employment during almost the first three years of the Jobactive contract. To put this figure into perspective, during the first year of the Jobactive contract, providers worked with almost 130,000 Stream C clients.[116] So, over the first three years of the contract, they would have worked with a considerably greater number of Stream C clients than this.

Only about one in five Stream C jobseekers that are placed into employment by a Jobactive provider sustains that job placement for 26 weeks or more. The positive results in the Australian system come from the least disadvantaged. This has led to the criticism that Australian governments have essentially been paying providers 'to administer rules relating to "activation" rather than provide real employment

---

114 For June 2008, data on the proportion of Newstart recipients on income support for two years or more is taken from Department of Families, Housing, Community Services, and Indigenous Affairs 2010, 43. Data for June 2019 is taken from Department of Social Services 2019.
115 Department of Jobs and Small Business 2018b.
116 Department of Employment, Skills, Small and Family Business 2020, 91.

assistance'.[117] More than this, some critics have suggested that the Australian quasi-market may even be causing direct psychological harm to long-term unemployed jobseekers by exposing them 'to services focused on making them "active" with no improvement to employability or income'.[118] Over time, this exposure may corrode jobseekers' sense of self-efficacy and esteem, leading to longer-term unemployment scarring. In short, large parts of Australia's welfare-to-work market do a very poor job of supporting highly disadvantaged unemployed people back into work. But we wanted to know more about the agencies and sites that were doing well with this group. What was their secret and how could it be explained and perhaps extrapolated to the broader system? To answer that we had to dig deep and watch closely, as we will see in the chapters that follow.

117 Casey and Lewis 2020, 10.
118 Casey and Lewis 2020, 11.

2
Thinking inside the box

In popular understanding the 'black box' is an Australian invention installed in aircraft to record key data that might be needed in case of misadventure or system failure.[1] Black box recorders, of course, are famously not black. They are fluorescent orange. But the reason they are described as 'black box' recorders is not a misnomer. It stems from their function to record and document the conversations, exchanges and decisions that are made inside aeroplane cabins – a domain otherwise hidden from the view of passengers, aviation authorities and often even other airline crew.

A more formal definition of the black box exists in organisation theory and philosophy. This more apparently resembles the intentions of those who design and advocate for quasi-markets in public policy. In this form of black box, the policy system is a behavioural device that has only two important points of observation – what goes in and what comes out, with no information about its working.[2]

We use the notion of a black box deliberately for its double meaning. On the one hand, the image of a black box stands for a certain domain of action, or in this case policy delivery, which is completely

---

1 It was invented by David Warren at the Aeronautical Research Laboratories in Melbourne in 1953.
2 Ashby 1956, chapter 6: The black box.

obscured from view and may therefore remain unknown or poorly understood. This is how the term is often used in relation to quasi-markets in employment services, where 'black box contracting' denotes a specific form of output, or results-based contracting; one where the government purchaser allows the service provider to determine the workings, including staffing, style of interaction with clients, and the frequency and nature of the services provided. Service providers are predominately paid on the basis of the outcomes they produce, not the internal services actually provided, which may remain invisible to policy designers. It is in this sense that Department of Employment officials have described the frontline of employment services delivery to us as a 'black box'; namely, that the detail of the frontline of jobseeker-client interactions remains obscured from view despite all the data on frontline interactions being collected via provider audits, and accumulated in computerised case management systems. This takes us to the second meaning of black box, as a way of showing why some providers' offices work better than others by looking inside and seeking to reconstruct the paths taken by staff and clients. This assumes that what happens inside is most important, as we describe below.[3]

A street-level perspective on assisting the long-term unemployed

In this book, we narrate the internal workings of the program for very disadvantaged jobseekers from a frontline service perspective. Each local office, with its manager and client consultants, forms its own micro-system. Management directions from the government and head office, and the skills of the staff are all inputs to this frontline drama. Demands for meeting targets and making profits are the understood outputs. In the research literature this is also known as street-level bureaucracy, where the interactions between frontline employment services staff and their clients, and the background organisational

---

3   The counter hypothesis would be to argue that the black box is largely irrelevant and that it is simply the assets of the jobseeker and the level of demand in the labour market that determines outcomes.

routines and work practices shaping these encounters make a big difference to the way a program runs. This frontline perspective has situated our team's approach to studying welfare and employment services reform for the past 20 years. This focus on the frontline recognises the key role case managers and other 'street-level bureaucrats' play as not only program administrators or service providers but policy producers. While a program template will describe its main intentions, it will be always and everywhere subject to adjustment and interpretation, because clients come with a great diversity of experiences and needs. Some of these local adaptations will be trivial but others will express the requirement to manage ambiguity in rules, management's excessive optimism about simple solutions and differences in the skills of frontline staff. To this extent, 'the process of policy making continues *while policies are delivered* at the frontline'.[4] This is perhaps the central insight of, and key motivation behind, the discipline of street-level bureaucracy research that has arisen since Michael Lipsky published his seminal study on the topic 40 years ago.

Lipsky challenged how political scientists and public policy scholars conventionally understood the process of policymaking. In the preceding decades, positive models of policymaking had characterised policymaking as a largely instrumental and rational process involving clear demarcations between the phases of policy design, option comparison, choice of instruments and implementation, and finally policy evaluation. However, Lipsky's work broke from this tradition by characterising the frontline officials responsible for implementing policies – such as police officers, teachers and welfare agency case managers – as policymakers shaping programs to fit both design intentions from above and real-life circumstances from below. While policy elites and political officials set the major dimensions of policy such as eligibility rules and the level of benefits, Lipsky argued that lower-level frontline workers still held considerable discretion in determining the nature and quality of the services, benefits and, perhaps more importantly, the use of any sanctions required by their agencies.[5] Students of street-level bureaucracy who have taken up this

---

4   Caswell et al. 2017, 2.
5   Lipsky 2010, 13.

research orientation treat discretion as an inherent feature of frontline activity that can never be fully constrained by rules and regulations. This is not least because such rules and regulations are never, as Bernardo Zacka argues, 'as tight as it may appear to outsiders'.[6] Frontline work in delivering welfare and other public services, as Stephen Maynard-Moody and Michael Musheno put it, may be 'rule-saturated' but it is not 'not rule-bound'.[7]

Policy delivery or implementation, in short, is more like an interpretive skill than the 'relentlessly routinised' administrative process it is so often caricatured as being.[8] Frontline staff must navigate between a plurality of demands, ambiguous and even conflicting policy directions, and the specificities of complex individual cases. This is certainly true of welfare-to-work policy implementation, which Dorte Caswell and her colleagues describe as 'a type of policies *par excellence* where the role of frontline workers as mediators of politics becomes tangible'.[9] A key tension for frontline employment services staff lies in their dual roles as enforcers of disciplinary rules imposed on clients and as advocates for these same clients in motivating them to find work. Reconciling the punitive instruments (sanctions and benefit withdrawal) and the facilitative elements (training, job brokerage) contained within the policy parameters of welfare-to-work is an ongoing and challenging task confronting frontline staff. Choosing when to be harsh and when to be supportive involves complex professional and moral dilemmas, which the rules can never fully resolve. Formal welfare-to-work policies are thus indeterminate, and the work of policy implementation remains 'suffused by moments of policymaking', as Bernardo Zacka puts it.[10] This is what street-level bureaucracy theorists mean when they describe frontline workers of the type featured in this book as 'de facto policymakers.'[11]

---

6   Zacka 2017, 4.
7   Maynard-Moody and Musheno 2000, 334.
8   Brodkin 2012, 941.
9   Caswell et al. 2017, 4.
10   Zacka 2017, 247.
11   See van Berkel 2013, 88; Brodkin 2013a, 23; Gofen 2014, 477.

When Michael Lipsky published his study at the start of 1980s, almost all street-level bureaucrats were public-sector workers or government employees. In fact, he defined street-level bureaucrats as: 'Public service workers who interact directly with citizens in the course of their jobs, and who have substantial discretion in the execution of their work.'[12] This is no longer the case today, with a great many of the public services Lipsky described as street-level bureaucracies now contracted out to private and not-for-profit organisations. This is one reason why Evelyn Brodkin uses the terms street-level workers rather than bureaucrats, and street-level organisations rather than bureaucracies: to account for the 'varieties of *street-level organisations* – the public, private, and hybrid agencies – now engaged in policy delivery around the world and increasingly operating under the influence of new governance and managerial regimes'.[13]

Of particular interest to contemporary street-level bureaucracy theorists such as Brodkin are the governance and managerial forces shaping how street-level organisations and frontline staff deploy their policy discretion 'in patterned ways'.[14] She points out that frontline workers do not make decisions as isolated individuals but rather as people who are firmly embedded in particular organisational cultures, in structured workplaces and social contexts that inform the decisions and choices they make. Dorte Caswell and her colleagues note that these contextual factors shape frontline workers' 'room for discretionary decision-making' by 'framing and limiting their options'.[15] Indeed, Brodkin argues that governance instruments associated with what we have described as double activation constitute an explicit effort by governments to affect what she terms the 'calculus of street-level choice'.[16] Government purchasers direct the choices of street-level bureaucrats 'at a distance' by applying performance incentives and sanctions, and monitoring these frontline providers and agents. Here, Brodkin is listing the kinds of elements that would be seen

---

12 Lipsky 2010, 3.
13 Brodkin 2013b, 4.
14 Brodkin 2012, 943.
15 Caswell et al. 2017, 2.
16 See Brodkin 2011.

as inputs to a black box model by those who advocate that idea, as her metaphor of distance suggests. Joe Soss, Richard Fording and Sanford Schram take a more determinist view in arguing that frontline workers are not at liberty to treat clients as they would like. They 'make their choices as actors who know they are being observed and evaluated'.[17] So the question of who is doing the observing is obviously important. Plainly, performance measurement tools and forms of monitoring and incentivising are not neutral technical devices for tracking what people do. They also affect what frontline employment services staff and other street-level bureaucrats do, and the choices they make when implementing policy.

Recognising the informal policymaking role of delivery agencies and frontline staff has important implications for the study of welfare and activation policy reform. As Brodkin argues in her introduction to a series of studies on street-level organisations and the welfare state, we cannot assume 'a simple correspondence between what policies say and what they do'.[18] Or, put differently, we need to be cautious about reading 'official policies as proxies for policy practices' as Rik van Berkel argues in a recent commentary on welfare conditionality from a street-level perspective.[19] Much more is carried out *in the name of policy* than is written, and much of policy-as-written never finds its way inside the box at the street level. Not all of these differences between formal intentions and actual policy practice suggest a breakdown in what governments seek to do, however. Indeed, the literature on discretion is full of examples of successful innovation and adaptation that honour the spirit of policy by pushing beyond its formal limits. Part of the challenge in research is to separate the more pathological discretions from real learning and improvement.

What we find inside the black box is not always more flexible and adaptive than what is written on the lid. Consider the example of Employment Pathway Plans, commonly known as Job Plans. These contractual agreements between employment services providers and clients stipulate what activities jobseekers need to undertake to satisfy

---

17   Soss et al. 2011b, i225–i226.
18   Brodkin 2013b, 11.
19   van Berkel 2020, 200.

their mutual obligations. Formally, according to the Australian government's Social Security Guide (sec 3.11.2), Employment Pathway Plans must be tailored to 'take into account the job seeker's individual circumstances' and 'job seekers should be encouraged to consult with their employment services providers to identify appropriate activities they are interested in, or may prefer to undertake, to meet their mutual obligation requirements'. The stated intention is for plans to be personalised, carefully tailored and jointly negotiated between providers and clients. However, studies drawing on in-depth interviews with jobseekers who have entered into Job Plans suggest that the process of agreeing to a Job Plan can often be experienced as little more than 'going through the motions', where the plans are pre-filled in advance from generic templates and jobseekers have little agency to negotiate or dispute the contents of the agreement.[20]

In short, what happens between frontline workers and jobseekers can often be different from what is envisaged in official policy guidelines, legislation and contract deeds. However, all too frequently this issue of how policy is brought 'into being' and changed during implementation is missed in official evaluations and policy studies. As a result, much remains to be understood about *how* policies produce the outcomes that they do. Evaluation studies that measure changes in exit rates from welfare caseloads or employment outcomes among program participants tell us about the aggregate outputs that policies produce. But they rarely give insights into the mechanisms by which policies achieve those outcomes, and nor do they reveal policies' unintended consequences. Brodkin describes this as 'the *missing middle*' in policy analysis: the practices constituting welfare-to-work on the ground 'may be noticed and casually remarked upon' but they are rarely 'systematically examined'.[21]

Besides the importance of 'separating policy fact from policy fiction',[22] studying welfare-to-work from a frontline perspective is also important because it is at the street-level that the welfare state 'comes

---

20 See, for example: O'Halloran et al. 2019; Peterie et al. 2019a; Marston and McDonald 2008.
21 Brodkin 2013b, 8.
22 Brodkin 2008, 325.

alive' for individual citizens.[23] What service providers and frontline staff do, how they treat clients, and how they distribute benefits and services to concrete individuals all fundamentally matters 'for the relationship between citizens and the state'.[24] As Deborah Rice puts it, 'the welfare state as an institution does not live in abstract regulations and legal texts but rather in the day-to-day interactions between caseworkers and clients in local welfare offices'.[25] Indeed, Michael Lipsky extends this to the institutions of government and the state more generally. If citizens encounter government, it is mostly not through letters to political representatives or attendance at political-party or school-board meetings but, as Lipsky remarks, 'through their teachers and their children's teachers and through the policeman on the corner or in the patrol car'.[26] For those citizens unfortunate enough to be without work, this extends to the consultants they interact with at their employment services provider and the case managers in their local Centrelink office. Nadine Raaphorst and Steven Van de Walle further reason that the quality of citizens' experience of a public or bureaucratic encounter is 'a crucial aspect in fostering trust, commitment, and collaboration between public officials and citizens, which in turn could help to democratise and legitimate the state'.[27] Bernardo Zacka echoes this view, arguing that the demeanour of frontline workers during citizen-encounters can go a long way towards 'shaping what citizens think of their state, and of their own standing in it'.[28]

Opening the black box

To deepen our understanding of the marketisation of employment services and the turn towards a more behaviourally oriented approach to welfare provision, we need to 'open up the black box of

---

23   Bovens and Zouridis 2002, 175.
24   Brodkin 2012, 942.
25   Rice 2013, 1055.
26   Lipsky 2010, 3.
27   Raaphorst and Van de Walle 2018, 1368.
28   Zacka 2017, 240.

[welfare-to-work] policy implementation, as Caswell and her colleagues describe it.[29]

Several Australian researchers have studied how welfare-to-work unfolds at the street level, using a multiplicity of methodological and disciplinary perspectives. Our own previous work – with our colleagues Jenny M. Lewis and Phuc Nguyen – has largely applied survey methods to comparatively study the changes in the frontline delivery of welfare-to-work over time and between countries (Australia, the UK, the Netherlands and New Zealand). This has been supplemented, on occasion, by more in-depth interviews with frontline employment services staff and agency managers, which have afforded us deeper insights into, and explanations of, the changing patterns of frontline decision-making observable in our large-scale survey data.[30] Through this intertemporal collection of data, we have been able to trace the progressive standardisation of employment services delivery over the Job Network era, and subsequent iterations of the system, as well as the changing demography of frontline workers following privatisation. More recently, we have also shown how frontline workers' attitudes towards jobseekers – along with those of the more general population – have hardened over time, and that frontline staff have become increasingly inclined to report jobseekers for sanctioning over various compliance breaches. Catherine McDonald and Greg Marston have also surveyed the attitudes of frontline workers towards their clients, and compared differences between the perceptions and understandings of unemployment held by Job Network staff and Centrelink social workers.[31]

Generally, however, it is uncommon for social policy researchers to directly interview frontline employment services staff. There are some notable exceptions, including the work of Tony Eardley studying the tensions experienced by not-for-profit employment service providers enacting mutual obligation during the first years of Job Network.[32] More recently, in their respective work on the activation of lone parents,

---

29   Caswell et al. 2017, 2.
30   See, in particular, Considine, Lewis and O'Sullivan 2011.
31   See McDonald and Marston 2008.
32   Eardley 2002.

Simone Casey and Michelle Brady each interviewed frontline employment services staff during the transition from Job Network to Job Services Australia.[33]

Notwithstanding these exceptions, the vast bulk of Australian research on welfare-to-work at the street level has focused on *jobseekers'* experiences of activation. This is important work that gives voice and visibility to a hard-to-reach, much stigmatised and highly disadvantaged group of citizens who are frequently acted *upon* rather than engaged *with* by policy officials. Greg Marston's work with Catherine McDonald, studying participants' changing experiences of employment services over the course of the Job Network era,[34] and then more recently with Gaby Ramia, Roger Patulny and Michelle Peterie, examining jobseekers' social networks and experiences of activation under Jobactive,[35] deserves mention. This body of qualitative work, which is remarkable for its sample sizes (75–80 jobseekers per study), has shed important light on the stigma, shame and feelings of worthlessness induced in many jobseekers by their interactions with what many perceive as either a punitive or indifferent, but rarely helpful, system of welfare-to-work services. As Marston and McDonald put it, in relation to their study of participants' experiences of Job Network:

> While the rhetoric of the market model of employment services espouses individual service, for the most part it is experienced as a model that 'radiates indifference' ... towards the plight of the long-term unemployed ... In general, people are churned through what is experienced as an indifferent system, with 'personalised service' being the exception, rather than the norm.[36]

Our study reported here departs from both our own earlier survey work and the interview-based work of our aforementioned colleagues

---

33 See Brady 2018; Casey 2019.
34 See, for example: Marston and McDonald 2008; McDonald and Marston 2005. See also: Murphy et al. 2011.
35 See, for example: Peterie et al. 2019a; Peterie et al. 2019b; Ramia et al. 2020.
36 Marston and McDonald 2008, 265.

in at least one especially important way. It is heavily, although not exclusively, observational in its approach. We physically sat in on appointments between frontline staff and jobseekers and spent multiple days at each of the four different Jobactive offices: taking notes, interacting with staff and carefully observing what was going on *inside the black box* of service delivery. Some researchers, such as Michelle Brady, have spoken of bringing an 'ethnographic imaginary' to their work through practising 'engaged listening' when interviewing frontline staff.[37] Ethnography often refers to immersive research approaches in anthropology and sociology that study other cultures or sub-cultures in depth. While this can involve observational research, some ethnographies are based solely on in-depth interviewing without any direct observation of the cultures under study.[38] This is not the case with our study. To the best of our knowledge, it is one of the very few Australian studies that actually reports on direct observational research of employment services offices.[39]

The 'ethnographic turn' in policy studies

In recent years, more and more researchers studying the 'missing middle' of policy analysis have turned to ethnographic methods such as observational fieldwork as 'a way of seeing big by looking small'.[40] An early example is Evelyn Brodkin's study of a welfare-to-work program in Chicago, the Job Opportunities and Basic Skills (JOBS) program, which showed the unintended consequences of benchmarking welfare offices' performance by client participation rates in job search activities.[41] One response from case managers to participation quotas was to register more clients and churn them through basic job search classes 'to make up the numbers'. The study also showed how internal

---

37 Brady 2018, 836.
38 For a helpful discussion of the distinction between ethnography and observational research see Wright 2003, 84–86.
39 One other example is Michelle Brady's study of personalised planning programs targeted at Australian single parents. See Brady 2011.
40 Brodkin 2013a, 18.
41 Brodkin 1997.

budget cuts gave rise to underinvestment in administrative resources, creating mounting paperwork for caseworkers, who frequently misplaced important documentation. These costs, however, were shifted onto clients by frontline workers who required clients 'to resubmit missing records' that the workers themselves had lost.[42]

Brodkin's study is just one example of the numerous American ethnographies of welfare-to-work at the street level, alongside the many examples of ethnographic studies of welfare delivery in European countries, such as the observational studies of UK Work Programme providers by Ian Greer, Lisa Schulte, David Jordan and others;[43] Sharon Wright's ethnography of a Jobcentre in Scotland;[44] or the ethnographies of French welfare offices written by Vincent Dubois.[45]

In the US context, many welfare ethnographies have highlighted systematic patterns of racism and discrimination in how welfare-to-work programs and benefit-conditionality policies are delivered and applied by caseworkers at the street level. One prominent example is the work of Joe Soss, Richard Fording and Sanford Schram, which combined observational research with experimental survey method to highlight systemic racial bias in the delivery of welfare-to-work programs in Florida, and to examine the role played by performance management systems in driving caseworkers to sanction their clients.[46] Their observational studies of case managers sanctioning clients led them to conclude that caseworkers employed sanctions because performance measurement systems pressured them to achieve results with clients while resource constraints and budgetary cuts left them with few tools or resources to do so. Faced with clients that 'put their performance at risk', caseworkers turned to sanctions out of frustration rather than any belief that sanctions were effective instruments for promoting work attachment.[47] Significantly, their study also suggested that clients from non-white backgrounds (i.e., Black or

---

42   Brodkin 2011, i263.
43   Greer et al. 2018; Jordan 2018.
44   Wright 2003.
45   See, for example, Dubois 2009, 2016.
46   See Soss et al. 2011a.
47   Soss et al. 2011b, i227.

Hispanic) were more likely to be sanctioned by case managers than white jobseekers, even when their behaviours were almost identical. They later tested and verified this insight from their ethnographic work through experimental survey research to develop the Racial Classification Model (RCM) of policy choice.[48]

The RCM explains racial disparities in policy outcomes as the result of unconscious biases replicated by policy narratives and cultural discourses concerning the target populations of interventions. Rather than viewing these racial disparities as the product of white administrators' overt prejudice and discrimination, the RCM interprets them as the product of racially coded policy discourses and negative stereotypes of non-white groups implicit within the program logics of social policy interventions. These social scripts of problem populations – whether it be intergenerational welfare dependence, so-called welfare queens or at-risk youth – 'give rise to mental structures that work in implicit ways to racialise policy choices and, thus, to produce racially biased policy outcomes'.[49] Black participants in welfare-to-work programs are sanctioned at a higher rate than white participants not because of any actual behavioural differences between black and white clients, but because policy discourses have implicitly made caseworkers more sensitive to behavioural deviance when dealing with black jobseekers than when working with white clients.

The number of ethnographically oriented welfare studies has grown over recent years. Among the most prominent recent contributions to the field is Bernardo Zacka's *When the state meets the street*, in which Zacka takes up Michael Lipsky's call from 40 years ago to theorise street-level bureaucracy as an enterprise replete with moral agency and personal dilemmas. Zacka sets out to understand frontline service staff as necessarily moral and political agents, who must remain sensitive to plural considerations of efficiency, fairness, respect and responsiveness when making discretionary decisions. Zacka argues there is a fundamental 'predicament' at the heart of street-level policy work: the delivery of public services depends 'on the moral agency' of frontline workers; yet the organisational environments and policy

---

48   See Schram et al. 2009.
49   See Soss et al. 2011, 80.

contexts in which they work frequently give rise to 'working conditions that tend to undermine that very agency'.[50] Zacka reached this conclusion after six months of intensive fieldwork as a participant observer: volunteering as a receptionist in a not-for-profit agency contracted to deliver several local welfare programs in a major US city. This approach of participant observation, while the preferred mode of ethnography in fields such as anthropology – and even considered by some as the only legitimate form of ethnography – is rare among scholars pursuing street-level research or *policy* ethnography. For the most part, ethnographies of the street-level delivery of welfare-to-work rely instead on a combination of in-depth interviews and direct observation of the institutions and people under study by researchers who remain outsiders to the organisations they are researching.

One reason for the 'ethnographic turn' in street-level bureaucracy research, and particularly the use of observational methods, stems from a methodological limit associated with the more widely used social scientific methods, survey research and participant interviews; namely, that there can be a gap between what people say they do and what they actually do. What they do in practice may be habitual and local or 'workarounds' for things that the systems struggle to manage. Observational methods can help address this issue by bringing researchers closer to the people and organisations they are studying, and by affording them a window into actual service encounters as they happen in real time. This is especially important for street-level bureaucracy studies, which are animated by the understanding that there is typically a disjuncture between policy-as-written and policy-as-produced on the ground. Ethnographic methods help to bridge this disjuncture by 'draw[ing] attention to how social institutions actually function, rather than how they are supposed to function'.[51] In so doing, they help to surface the 'practical logics' propelling the enforcement of welfare-to-work,[52] and by which 'institutional norms are reproduced'.[53] Direct observation, as Evelyn

---

50   Zacka 2017, 241.
51   Zacka 2017, 257.
52   Dubois 2009, 236.
53   Weeden 2010, 262.

Brodkin argues, can also 'giv[e] visibility' to the sources of ambiguity in policy implementation that are less likely to be revealed by other methods.[54] This in turn, argue Matthew Longo and Bernardo Zacka, can destabilise official categories of understanding to expose 'new avenues of moral concern'.[55]

To take an example, in earlier work published from the study reported here, we have shown that Centrelink's categorisation of jobseekers into different streams (currently streams A, B and C) is actively contested by Jobactive providers.[56] Providers rarely take these official categorisations at face value, instead working to change them through practices of up-streaming and re-categorisation. Moreover, contractual performance incentives such as Jobactive's differentiated payment model – by which providers earn higher payments for outcomes achieved with clients in Stream C rather than B or A – feed into these 'category manoeuvres'.

This kind of research orientation, which Vincent Dubois terms 'critical policy ethnography', depends on researchers becoming immersed in the experience of the people and institutions under study.[57] This makes for a demanding and time-consuming field methodology, but the payoff can be rich. As Evelyn Brodkin argues, because observation 'does not depend on the recall of interviewees or their reconstruction of events', it can be especially fruitful 'as a strategy for distinguishing between what caseworkers *do* versus what they *say* or may *think* they do'.[58] Immersive fieldwork of this kind can enable researchers to look beyond the presented face of policy implementation in interviews to see what happens when welfare-to-work reforms 'meet the worlds, subjects and processes they aim to transform'.[59] This in turn, as Lisa Herzog and Bernardo Zacka suggest, can promote a more nuanced and detailed understanding of the policy issues 'than one ... from afar'.[60]

54　Brodkin 2017a, 132.
55　Longo and Zacka 2019, 1066.
56　See O'Sullivan, McGann and Considine 2019.
57　Dubois 2009.
58　Brodkin 2011, i261.
59　Brady 2011, 267.
60　Herzog and Zacka 2017, 768.

However, the success of this approach depends on going beyond just describing what is observed and being 'interested not just in what people *do*, but also in why they do it'. As Zacka argues in developing this point, this means engaging in description and interpretation 'at once': observing people's responses to specific situations 'and trying to make sense of what these situations look like to them' and the political implications of, and rationalities behind, their actions.[61] Put differently, the observational field data 'become the point-of-departure for analyses of broader macro-level political phenomena'.[62] Here, what policy ethnography does, in a way that few other social scientific methods attempt, is try to understand political institutions from the inside out. As we hope the remainder of this book shows, this approach can be particularly fruitful when studying organisations such as contracted welfare-to-work providers, which have political as well as commercial reasons for screening aspects of their institutional behaviour when presenting these 'to the outside world'.[63]

Study method in detail

The study behind this book is based on more than 18 months of intensive fieldwork and data collection at four of the best-performing Jobactive offices in the states of Victoria and New South Wales. These offices were chosen based on their success rate in achieving employment outcomes with their Stream C, or most disadvantaged, clients. As we discussed in chapter one, supporting these 'hardest-to-help' clients into sustained employment has been the major challenge for Australia's privatised employment services market for more than 20 years.

While the overall success rate of providers with their Stream C clients is very low, a number of agencies consistently outperform the rest in assisting this group into employment. Providers who outperform the national average by 30 per cent or more are awarded a five-star

---

61   Zacka 2017, 255.
62   Brodkin 2013a, 18.
63   Longo and Zacka 2019, 1068.

rating, and less than a quarter of Jobactive sites typically receive such a rating.[64] To maintain this rating over a sustained period is an impressive and difficult achievement. That said, being consistently ranked among the best-performing Jobactive agencies does not necessarily mean that those agencies are achieving a particularly high rate of employment outcomes with their Stream C clients, as we will see.

When we commenced our study, we described the four agencies featured in this book as 'high-performing' sites, but we now prefer the term 'best-performing' Jobactive sites. This change in terminology reflects the low threshold for reaching the upper performance echelons of the Jobactive system – at least for Stream C outcomes. Being a 'best-performing' Jobactive site is one thing. Being an employment service office that achieves outcome rates that would impress people outside the industry is something altogether different.

This discrepancy became apparent when we were selecting the four Jobactive offices for our study. Given the reservations we expressed in chapter one about the criteria that feed into Jobactive sites' star ratings, we asked the department for a list of the best-performing sites in Victoria and New South Wales based on those sites' 26-week outcome rate among their Stream C clients, which means that the agency has placed Stream C clients into work, and they have stayed employed for at least 26 weeks. This is the longest duration of client employment outcomes that is measured in the Australian system. So if there is one indicator of success, this is it. The department was supportive of our study's aims and agreed to our request on the proviso that they would only identify individual sites to us with those organisations' consent. Shortly after the first performance ratings for Jobactive sites were published in August 2016, we received a list of 29 of the highest performing Jobactive sites in Victoria and New South Wales. We were also given the raw data, in de-identified form, on sites' employment outcomes by stream, for all Jobactive sites in Victoria and New South Wales, so we could verify that these 29 sites were indeed among the best-performing Jobactive sites in those states.

---

64   The criteria for calculating Jobactive sites' star ratings are discussed in detail in Australian National Audit Office 2017.

Two things immediately struck us about this list. First, the majority were offices with relatively small Stream C caseloads – often no more than 50 clients in this category. Second, and most significantly, the benchmark for reaching the department's high-performance rating was low.

The department frequently publishes Employment Services Outcomes reports on the overall performance of Jobactive. These reports suggest about a quarter of the Stream C caseload are placed into employment. For example, between 1 October 2018 and 30 September 2019, nationally across Jobactive, 26.7 per cent of Stream C clients achieved some form of employment placement while, across all streams, 42.8 per cent of people placed into work remained employed for at least 26 weeks.[65] One might reasonably assume that about 11.4 per cent of Stream C clients achieved at least 26 weeks of employment (i.e., 42.8 per cent of 26.7 per cent). However, Stream C jobseekers placed into work are much more likely than jobseekers in other streams to fall out of employment before reaching 26, or even 12, weeks. So, the actual 26-week outcome rate among Stream C jobseekers is much lower.

The threshold for making it onto the list of 'best-performing' Jobactive sites provided to us was managing to place just 4.1 per cent of Stream C clients into 26 weeks or more of employment. The best-performing site on the list had a Stream C 26-week outcome rate of just under 16 per cent, which it had achieved by placing seven out of 44 clients into jobs lasting six months or more. However, the vast majority of the 29 sites on our list had a Stream C 26-week outcome rate of under eight per cent. Five sites had made it onto the list of best-performing sites by placing just three clients into sustained jobs over a 12-month period. This tells us that measured performance in relation to those who are 'hardest to help' is a matter of marginal gains: where the difference between being rated a high or average performer could come down to just one or two outcomes across a site's caseload over a year.

After discussing the choice of sites and eliminating those that had placed fewer than five clients into sustained employment, we

---

65   Department of Education, Skills and Employment 2019.

approached five different providers about participating in the research. Two were for-profit providers and the other three were not-for-profits. One of the for-profit agencies was unresponsive to our requests, but the other four agencies were enthusiastic about the research. We eventually included four sites operated by different contracted providers in different employment regions. We deliberately chose a wide variation between the four sites, seeking to identify and explore common elements of success among the best-performing sites, which could be embedded and reproduced in different organisational contexts and locations. We also selected sites with at least 60 Stream C clients on their caseloads to avoid the risk that their 'high' performance levels had been skewed by small caseloads. While small caseload sizes are conducive to more personalised approaches to working with clients, they can also artificially drive up performance levels because each outcome potentially has more impact on those sites' performance ratings than the equivalent additional outcomes realised by sites with larger caseloads. Each of our four 'best-performing' Jobactive sites are described in detail in the chapters that follow.

Over the 18 months of field research that we conducted, we collected various types of data at each site. First, two of the authors together visited each office for two to three days to conduct observations and interviews with all frontline staff. This included sitting in on appointments with clients (with their permission) and watching the interactions between the site staff, management and a range of other key actors, such as employers and training organisations. Having two of us present allowed us to record more of what was going on at each office than if one of us had visited alone. Frequently, for example, one team member sat in on an employment consultant's client appointment while the other observed the rest of the office – as other staff chatted about problem clients, raised the latest administrative issue of the day or sought pieces of critical documentation that had gone missing. We then swapped positions, enabling us to compare notes and ensure that we were both seeing 'the same thing'. If a limitation of survey and interview-based research is that what people say they do can sometimes be different from what they actually do, an issue that observational studies sometimes run into is 'the potential for observer bias'.[66] This is where the researcher 'sees what she wants to see' rather than what is happening. Having two researchers observing at the four sites under study helped mitigate this risk, as did the debriefings with the research team back at the university, where observations and interpretations were systematically assessed, and counter-explanations tested.

We repeated the observational research approximately a year later to test some of our early findings and to gather additional fieldwork data on the progress being made with the client group we had identified. Each office visit generated around 30 pages of typed field notes, from each of the researchers, providing a documented basis for checking themes and insights, for reviewing exemplary interactions and for assessing our level of confidence in our observations. The observations were supplemented by interviews with client-facing staff at each site, including interviews with new staff who commenced partway through the study. Twenty-one staff were interviewed in total from across the four sites, including: six site managers (the manager at one site changed three times during the study), ten employment consultants, two reverse marketers (who work to connect with employers) and three other specialist staff. To protect the privacy of the individual organisations and staff that participated in this research, we have changed the names of all four employment services providers and staff members referred to in this book. We have also anonymised the research locations and used pseudonyms for any employers, training organisations, labour hire agencies or other complementary service providers.

Another major component of the research involved tracking the progress of the four sites with a selection of Stream C jobseekers. We chose approximately ten clients to follow per full-time case manager at each site, interviewing those case managers every eight to ten weeks about each jobseeker's progress. These interviews were a mixture of face-to-face and phone interviews, and tracked changes in clients' circumstances, forms of support that staff had recommended, and any issues of non-compliance that had emerged and how consultants had responded. We used pseudonyms for clients, to protect their privacy, and we also designed the tracking sample to include a diverse range of jobseekers by age, gender and duration on benefits. Initially, we followed the cases of 74 jobseekers across the four sites. However, we

---

66   Brodkin 2008, 330.

began following a further 32 jobseekers midway through the research to compensate for those who were indefinitely suspended, transferred to another Jobactive site, or who were automatically exited from the system by Centrelink (without being placed into employment). This brought the total number of tracked jobseekers across the four sites to 106, although some of these jobseekers were tracked only very briefly. This issue of caseload churn proved to be an important challenge for us and for the agencies. At least a quarter of the original sample of jobseekers that we started following *at each of the four offices* dropped off site caseloads *without finding employment*. So, we had to adapt our approach to capture sufficient information about how the offices and staff were working with jobseekers.

In short, our study method blended direct observational research with more structured interviewing of frontline staff and, importantly, with qualitative longitudinal research tracking of progress with a sample of their clients. This incorporation of qualitative longitudinal research marks a further innovation of our study for Australian research on the street-level delivery of welfare-to-work. Although longitudinal studies have been widely used to understand *jobseekers'* experiences of employment services,[67] the perspective of frontline workers – and their attitudes towards their jobseeker clients – has rarely been examined in such an ongoing way. Mostly, studies of the frontline delivery of welfare-to-work have followed a cross-sectional design, gathering data about practices *at specific moments* through surveys or interviews rather than tracking the evolution of caseworkers' approaches over a sustained period. Adopting this longitudinal approach enabled us to consider how client servicing strategies evolved over time, and as clients moved through distinct phases of activation. Re-interviewing the same frontline workers six or seven times in a period of well over a year also helped us to build up trust with the participants, facilitating deeper revelations than we could have achieved in a single wave of interviews.

This high level of access to welfare-to-work providers is very rare in research of this kind, particularly for such a sustained period. Street level scholars and others who have tried to study the frontline

---

67   See, for example, Marston and McDonald 2008; Wright and Patrick 2019.

delivery of welfare-to-work have often been frustrated by the refusal of employment services providers to allow their staff to take part in research. For example, when a team of researchers led by Peter Dwyer and Sharon Wright approached UK employment services providers about taking part in a major longitudinal study of activation and welfare conditionality funded by the UK's Economic and Social Research Council, the UK government's Department for Work and Pensions prevented Jobcentre Plus and Work Programme staff participating.[68] Thankfully, that was not our experience. We spent well over a year studying the four offices documented in this book and encountered almost no resistance to our research from either Jobactive providers or the Australian government's Department of Employment. Other researchers certainly have interviewed frontline employment services staff several times before. But it is rare, even internationally, that they have been allowed to observe client interactions first-hand, or to repeatedly discuss individual cases with case managers. One reason for this is that the employment services field is, after all, a competitive market. Providers are understandably cautious about disclosing business practices that may give them a commercial advantage. While employment services may be publicly funded, the contracts between the government and individual providers are shrouded by commercial-in-confidence restrictions.

We acknowledge that even under these positive conditions there are limits to what can be achieved. Looking inside the box is not the same as working there. And while we secured a high level of access and good will, we have no doubt that some issues remain undisclosed. Frontline staff managing ambiguous demands and difficult clients must often work hard to hold a coherent sense of purpose and value in their work. This is especially the case when the formal results of their efforts register only a low level of official success. So we argue that this method is not a complete picture but, rather, highlights local patterns of conduct and forms of adaptation that are important and capable of being generalised – at least in answering our two major questions: How do the best-performing agencies work with the most disadvantaged

---

68   Welfare Conditionality Project 2018.

jobseekers to get results? And what does this tell us about the welfare-to-work system itself?

3
Wilmore, the heart of Australian suburbia

It's a Tuesday in late November. We are on the outskirts of Melbourne, in Wilmore, one of the city's more established satellite suburbs. It's about 40 minutes by train from the CBD – a little shorter by freeway if you can stand the traffic – and home to around 17,000 people. It's the first day of our fieldwork, so we are both excited and a little apprehensive about what to expect.

Things do not get off to the best start. We arrive at the Wilmore office of Pegasus Employment at midday, prepped and ready to go, only to be told by Gill, a bubbly receptionist in her mid-20s, that it is lunchtime and none of the staff are available for us to meet. We should have guessed this from the vacant reception area, an entrance foyer no larger than 10 square metres with a row of seven empty seats for people to wait for their allotted appointment. Although, as we will soon learn, the appointment process is highly elastic.

Employment offices are not spaces that always remain on schedule. Appointments are routinely missed, run late or can happen randomly when 'walk-ins' arrive. Waiting is therefore a characteristic experience of the system – for frontline staff as much as for their clients. But unlike the spaces where consumer-citizens wait to buy services, here there are no television broadcasts or lifestyle magazines to entertain those waiting.[1]

In his book *When the state meets the street*, Bernado Zacka argues that the interior architecture of welfare spaces tells us a lot about their normative worlds.[2] The physical design helps to control interactions between caseworkers and clients, through shielding or exposing workers to direct contact with clients. Colour palettes and material textures aesthetically signal the purpose of the encounter and the power relations at play between frontline professionals and their clients. Think of the tonal differences between the waiting areas of medical practices and travel agents, or the 'brutalist architecture' of social security offices in the past, monochrome concrete buildings that, as Tom Boland and Ray Griffin observe, 'have little enchantment' and project an atmosphere 'of seriousness and heft.'[3]

The Pegasus reception area is muted and restrained, with a faded burgundy counter guarding a small corridor of rooms where the company's employment consultants meet with jobseekers. To the right-hand side is a small room filled with computer terminals for clients to use to search for jobs online, or to work on their résumés and applications. An A4 poster above one of the terminals passive-aggressively asks, 'Are you doing enough to get a job?' But nobody is watching.

The office walls are hued mostly in magnolia, although the wall adjacent to the reception desk is a soft shade of lilac. Two cork noticeboards advertise the company's service standards, procedures for lodging customer complaints or compliments and a selection of jobs notices sourced from the local paper. There's the usual array of Australian government-issued guidelines about jobseekers' mutual obligation and Work for the Dole requirements, although these are pushed as far towards the door as physically possible – perhaps symbolically distancing Pegasus from the government's activation policy, given that the guidelines are hidden by the front door whenever

---

1   As Tom Boland and Ray Griffin observe in their ethnography of Irish social welfare offices, 'Such distractions might seem like a luxury or an admission that the process itself is an imposition to be alleviated by entertainment.' Boland and Griffin 2017.

2   Zacka 2017.

3   Boland and Griffin 2017, 15.

someone enters. With Christmas a few weeks away, the only bright decorations in sight are a rack of brochures next to the reception counter. These advertise a variety of short courses offered by private training organisations to jobseekers seeking accreditation to enter various occupations.

With a warm politeness, Gill suggests that it would be better if we returned in an hour. We head across to the large shopping centre over the road. For, unlike the unemployed clients we will meet later that afternoon and over the coming days, time is ours to waste rather than to fill with 'job-seeking' or owe in mutual obligation.[4]

The business of unemployment

It's not quite the 'fashion capital', but Wilmore's shopping centre certainly aspires to be. There's a Myer, a Country Road, one of those trendy Japanese clothing stores and an expensive pseudo-French patisserie where shoppers can quaff coffee and croissants. Spotting a Sunglass Hut, Siobhan wonders about buying a pair. After all, we're heading towards summer and it's blistering outside. This is certainly no scene from *Struggle Street* but scratch the surface and the area's veneer of affluence soon fades.

We know from the official statistics that Wilmore is an area of above average unemployment. At the time of our visit, it had an unemployment rate of 7.2 per cent, not as high as some other parts of Victoria but still well above the state's seasonally adjusted unemployment rate, which was then 5.7 per cent.[5] Beyond the official statistics, further evidence of the area's underlying disadvantage comes from the strip of social and public services juxtaposed to the temple of consumerism: a Centrelink office, a Magistrate's Court, a legal aid office, and at least five different employment services providers occupy a distance of about 200 metres. Pegasus Employment is one of these providers, nestled between two of its competitors on the ground floor of a suite of corporate offices stepped just off the street. On this street,

---

4   Marston and McDonald 2008.
5   Data derived from Department of Employment, 2016b.

there's a bustling trade, it seems, in finding employment and administering other services to those on welfare.

According to National Employment Services Association (NESA), one of the two peak bodies that represents employment services providers, the agencies currently contracted to deliver Jobactive collectively employ 14,713 people across Australia.[6] However, it's a volatile workforce that expands and contracts with the ebbs and flows of contracting rounds and business reallocations. Across the industry, the annual turnover of staff is estimated by NESA to be well over 30 per cent, and as high as 42 per cent in years when contracts are re-tendered. This is approximately three times the average annual turnover of staff in the Australian economy.[7] Our own previous survey research shows that fewer than half of all client-facing staff have been working in the industry for more than five years, and only one in four case managers have a university degree. Only half of frontline employment services staff are satisfied with their present working conditions, such as pay, hours, and opportunities for promotion.[8] Rates of unionisation, around three per cent, are especially low for a social services sector workforce. This reflects what others argue is a trend towards the 'disorganisation of employment relations' in market-based welfare systems – characterised by declining union coverage, more individualised employment contracts and an increase in hiring via non-standard employment contracts.[9]

Among those in managerial roles, the situation isn't much better. Indeed, NESA's survey findings suggest that almost half of managers in employment services have no formal qualifications, neither completing secondary school nor undertaking further education. Job churn is also high among site managers, who, on average, have been with their employers only a year longer than the caseworkers they manage.[10]

In this deskilled and largely low-paid employment context, the biographies of frontline workers and the welfare recipients whose cases

---

6   Maguire 2017.
7   Senate Education and Employment References Committee 2019, 93.
8   Lewis et al. 2016.
9   Greer et al. 2017.
10   Maguire 2017.

they manage often intersect. This observation – that frontline workers today 'share defining elements of personal history and social identity with their clients' – is a point much reflected on by Joe Soss, Richard Fording and Sanford Schram in their book *Disciplining the poor*, a detailed ethnography of welfare-to-work offices in Florida, in which they observe:

The contracted providers who hire case managers today are not required to consider markers of skill … And with much of casework focused on documentation and data entry, they have few incentives to forgo low-wage workers in favour of hiring professionals. As a result, the legitimacy and credibility of the case manager (beyond his or her formal policy authority) has become disconnected from any credential or claim to diagnostic and prescriptive expertise. Life experience is the trait that fills this vacuum … a kind of wisdom that, for many, is more profound than professional expertise and more deserving of client attention.[11]

The Australian employment services system is a different context to the welfare bureaucracies described in *Disciplining the poor*. But parallels exist in relation to the frontline working conditions and the backgrounds of those employed in the sector.

We learn from Jessica, the manager of Pegasus' Wilmore office, that she herself was a jobseeker once and, indeed, a client of the very agency she now works for:

The employment consultant that I had … She said, 'We've got a receptionist role going here, perfect opportunity.' And do you know what my response was? 'They're not going to hire me, I'm a jobseeker.' Because that was my perception. I thought, 'There's some stigma attached to this industry, like they must think I'm a jobseeker, I'm probably not capable of this.' Then they ended up setting me up an interview a couple of days later, I went in for an interview and then ended up getting a job.

---

11   Soss et al. 2011a, 242.

Now in her early 30s, she reflects on the journey she has taken from being on Youth Allowance to becoming a site manager just over 12 months ago, after working her way up from the reception desk:

It wasn't as though I planned to get into this industry. However, I always had a passion, or I guess a want and need, to help people. But at that point in time when I started in this industry, I didn't realise how massive it was ... I wouldn't change it for the world.

Jessica is only the first of three site managers that we encounter over the course of our time at the Wilmore office, as she begins parental leave shortly after our first visit. It's a pattern that repeats at other sites, with only one of the four offices retaining its manager for the study's 18-month duration.

Jessica's journey from being a client to managing the office says something about how Pegasus, as a wider organisation, perceives and values the potential of both its clients and employees. Jessica's own formative experience as a jobseeker, of being encouraged by her consultant to go for the receptionist role, inflects her view of the case management relationship and the qualities she encourages in staff. Her goal, she says, 'is to not have any jobseeker leave our office without being helped', by which she means making sure that jobseekers 'never leave the office without a referral to an employment opportunity'. She says, in a matter-of-fact way, 'Because technically we're an employment service, we're not here to manage the barriers.'

The other main industries in the Wilmore area are health care and social assistance, construction and manufacturing which together account for a third of all employment in the area. Responsibility for sourcing employment opportunities (or vacancies) for the Wilmore office's clients lies with Troy, the business development consultant (BDC) also known in the sector as a reverse marketer. He prefers to work with smaller manufacturing businesses 'where the manager that I'm speaking with also does the recruiting rather than going through the whole HR department and whatnot'. His job, as he sees it, hinges on building personal relationships with employers who are prepared to employ people based on their attitude as much as their ability. He has little time for larger employers with 'their own recruitment processes' and policies to stick to 'rather than come to us'.

As a Jobactive agency, Pegasus is in the minority in resourcing most of its offices with a reverse marketer dedicated to that site. It's a model not replicated at any of the other offices we study. We quickly discover that for many agencies, reverse marketer roles are shared across multiple sites or an entire region. This means that branch offices within an organisation compete with each other to place their clients into whatever vacancies are 'gathered' by the agencies' reverse marketers – whose customers are the employers, not the jobseekers their colleagues are working with. The advantage of being a site-focused BDC, explains Troy, is that 'you get to know the clients more' because 'you're seeing them on a more regular basis' than if you were moving from site to site. We witness this 'hands-on' approach ourselves over the coming days, with Troy regularly joining consultants' appointments to talk about work opportunities that the jobseekers they are seeing might be interested in or at least suitable for.

Troy has a commanding familiarity of the site's caseload. Like the Wilmore office's employment consultants, he knows most of the jobseekers by name. He is a popular staff member and is highly praised by Jessica, his manager, for being 'very jobseeker-focused' and having a 'brilliant rapport' with clients. It's one of the main reasons, she thinks, behind the site's Stream C success, along with his collaborative way of working with his employment-consultant colleagues.

Troy, who dresses professionally in black trousers and a business shirt and looks to be in his early 30s, has been working in the industry for three years – although he's only been with Pegasus for two of these years. Before that, he was a reverse marketer with one of the largest for-profit agencies in the sector and he sees a palpable difference in the work culture at Pegasus, a not-for-profit: 'I think there's not so much discussion about money as there was previously. It's still important … But I think at Pegasus there's more of an understanding of people's barriers and also finding the right jobs for people.' For Troy, this means making sure that people 'are getting referred to work that they want, that's for them'. As much as his colleagues might want him to refer their clients to whatever jobs he has on his books, he's very clear in his mind that he's not about 'to start forcing people to do a job that they don't want, because it's just not going to last'.

Systems compliance

Troy's stance is at odds with the Australian government's mutual obligation policy, which requires people on activity-tested payments 'to be actively seeking and willing to accept any offer of suitable paid work in a variety of fields'.[12] What 'suitable' means in this context is open to interpretation, but the fact that jobseekers may not like, or want a job to which they are being referred, is not a valid reason for refusal under the *Social Security Act*. Jobseekers who do so risk incurring significant payment penalties and suspension. At the Wilmore office, however, frontline staff appear to favour softer sanctions in the form of verbal warnings rather than submitting official participation reports (PRs) that could result in clients losing their payments for several weeks.

Indeed, only three out of a total of 27 jobseekers we tracked at the Wilmore office were PRed. On the days that we visit the site, it seems to us that they are an agency that uses more 'carrots' than 'sticks'. The staff emphasise building understanding and trust with clients, critical commodities that can soon perish if case managers heavily police their clients' behaviour. 'I've seen a lot of people change in here', Troy tells us about some of the Wilmore office's clients who have come from other providers 'where they've been pushing them too hard and they've lost trust in the whole industry'. They come in 'a bit sour', he says, 'and from the employment consultant building that relationship, they become a lot more trusting in us'. We quickly wonder whether this is at least part of the secret to the Wilmore office's success.

We witness this softer approach later with Oli, a recently released prisoner and newly commenced Stream C jobseeker that we track for a period of months. During a follow-up interview, his consultant, Sharmaine, accuses him of sabotaging a vacancy that she referred him to by 'telling Troy that he wasn't really interested because he wanted to start his own business'. Being the only reverse marketer for a site

---

12   Australian Government 2021, section 3.11.1.20.

of around 600 clients, Troy has little time for clients he suspects do not want to work, so he goes cold on Oli for the remainder of the study. While he says he's prepared to give everyone a couple of chances, 'because there's so many people I sort of focus on the ones that … not so much want to work, but that want our assistance'.

Sharmaine, in her 30s with bleached blonde hair and piercing eyes, is the main consultant managing the Wilmore office's stream B and C clients. She's taken over the caseload from Amelia, the Wilmore office's long-term consultant of more than seven years, who went on parental leave in the middle of the year. Sharmaine's body language is comfortable and at ease, and she often sits cross-legged in meetings with an elbow on her knee and her chin perched on one hand. Her demeanour is disarming and belies the fact that she has been working as a consultant for only seven months, previously working as a hairdresser, bistro manager and flight attendant. We later learn from Laura, who is seconded from another site to manage the Wilmore office soon after our first visit, that Pegasus has employed 'quite a few hairdressers' and that they've generally taken to being employment consultants 'like a duck to water': 'Whether it's their rapport building, their troubleshooting, they're talking to people all day when they are doing that other skill set – it's just amazing.'

Sharmaine has between 120 and 140 jobseekers on her caseload at a time, although she says that she does not 'really look at what stream they are' but treats 'them all like individuals with individual barriers'. Partly, this is because she has little confidence in how jobseekers are classified and streamed. This is an issue that, it quickly becomes apparent, is systemic across the Australian sector. These assessments, which dictate the level of resources available to providers to assist clients and the intensity of jobseekers' mutual obligations, are done by staff at Centrelink. In the view of some frontline staff, these decisions about how to categorise jobseekers relate not only to what the jobseeker is willing to disclose, but also to the amount of money the government wishes to make available for employment assistance. Stream C jobseekers are more expensive than Stream A jobseekers, from the Australian government's perspective. Centrelink's assessments are frequently carried out by phone in the first instance. But Sharmaine tells us that 'they are often fairly out of whack' and that she prefers to wait for jobseekers to tell her 'in their words', because significant barriers – such as the fact that people have been in prison or have a serious mental illness – are often missed by the faceless, bureaucratic assessment process. We witness this for ourselves with Kendrick, a jobseeker we track via the Wilmore office, who is categorised by Centrelink as a Stream A jobseeker, despite being a twice-released prisoner and presenting to Sharmaine as homeless and on heroin.

Given that Sharmaine prides herself on building 'a rapport' and gaining clients' 'trust', when she suspects Oli has sabotaged a vacancy, she sees this as a significant betrayal of their relationship. But rather than submitting a PR, as she is entitled to do, Sharmaine chooses to phone Oli to personally convey 'that it's not acceptable' and that he needs 'to be accepting work'. She does not formally note the discussion, so it does not show up in the 'compliance history' tab of Oli's file record on ESS Web, the computerised case management system that frontline staff are required to use to document workflow processes, the vacancies they have referred clients to, and the activities clients are undertaking to meet their Job Plan requirements. If clients miss appointments or other activities, frontline staff are supposed to make a record that is visible to the Department of Employment and Centrelink. In this way, the computerised system is a tool used to circumvent case manager discretion, and therefore ensure a work-first approach at all times. However, as our previous survey research demonstrates, case managers retain some discretion in sanctioning jobseekers. For example, when asked under what circumstances they would typically report clients for sanctioning, almost 80 per cent of frontline staff that we surveyed in 2016 reported that they would do so if 'a jobseeker refuses to apply for a suitable job'. However, 94 per cent said that they would report clients for sanctioning if they did this for a second time.[13] Clearly, this indicates that a proportion of frontline staff would typically not report clients for their first infringement, contrary to Australian government guidelines.

Much of an employment consultant's job involves interfacing with ESS Web. For the department, it 'underpins the operation of employment services':[14] managing access to jobseeker information,

13   Lewis et al. 2016.
14   Department of Employment 2016a, 3.

storing the digital information for processing payment claims and serving as a virtual panopticon for the department to monitor provider activity. Misuses of administrative discretion by case managers and providers show up as 'red flags' in the computerised system, which allows agency managers and departmental contract managers to continuously audit the decision-making powers they have delegated to frontline staff. This puts pressure on frontline staff to follow procedural guidelines, such as minimum job-search conditionality requirements, to the letter. The challenge for frontline staff such as Sharmaine is to find the space in between the bureaucratic rules that allows them to treat their clients with a degree of empathy and compassion:

> I would like to remove that [job search] requirement for some jobseekers, but no I can't. Because it will flag. It will show up in an audit … But if you can use discretion, and you're 100 per cent sure as you can be … then you use as much discretion as you can.

Since it was first introduced in 2003, ESS Web has become more and more intensively used to guide, monitor, and discipline frontline–client interactions. No less than other public services, welfare and employment services have become what Mark Bovens and Stavros Zouridis term 'screen-level bureaucracies'. While frontline workers may still have face-to-face contact with citizens, 'these contacts always run through or in the presence of a computer screen'.[15] Indeed, almost 80 per of the case managers that we surveyed in 2016 reported that they were *always* accessing a computer during their appointments with jobseekers. A further 13 per cent said that this was the case *most of the time*.[16] In other words, when meeting with clients, 93 per cent of frontline staff are also working on their computers most, if not all, of the time. This is up marginally from the end of the Job Network era, when just under 74 per cent of frontline staff reported being always logged on to their computers, and a further 17 per cent said they were accessing their computers most of the time in client meetings.[17]

---

15 Bovens and Zouridis 2002.
16 The full survey results are summarised in the report: Lewis et al. 2016.
17 Considine, Lewis and O'Sullivan 2009.

In nearly every appointment that we observed at every office that we studied, consultants met with their clients in the company of their computer screen – ticking boxes and entering data on a jobseeker's digital profile as they moved through the appointment. As they did this, the client invariably sat quietly and waited. Computers underline the transactional nature of the meetings. Jobseekers under Australia's privatised system seem accustomed to being given less attention than the computer screen. When case managers are not physically taking appointments with clients, they spend much of their time completing file notes, digitising documentation to enter on the system or looking at data on their screens. These computers partially dictate the tempo of appointments, as internet connections slowed, files failed to upload properly and login details were misplaced. This problem is one faced by almost everyone in Australia. The Australian government aspires to be a world leader in digital public management, but Australia's internet infrastructure is some of the poorest quality in the world.[18] And Wilmore is in the 'big smoke'; how do case managers do their jobs, and jobseekers find the patience to wait, in more remote parts of Australia?

'This computer is so slow', Sharmaine says aloud in an appointment that we are invited to observe. It's 2.17 pm and we are sitting in one of the three small interview rooms that look out onto the corridor guarded by the reception desk. Sharmaine is meeting with Karl for one of his regular three-weekly appointments. The meeting was supposed to be almost an hour earlier, but when Karl arrived late, Sharmaine pushed back her 2.30 appointment with Tang, a newly commenced Tibetan-born client she has not met before, to take the appointment with Karl. Tang waits patiently in the reception area.

Karl is Australian born and in his late teens. Unlike many jobseekers who visit the Wilmore office, Karl's English language is first rate, but he speaks with a mild speech impediment. He's one of Sharmaine's Stream B clients, but Sharmaine tells us before the meeting that she thinks he should be in Stream C. The meeting starts out as a conversation about Karl's ideal job, which he says is 'working outside'. But Karl does not have a mobile phone, so he is uncontactable for jobs. 'We can't get you a job if we can't get in contact with you', Sharmaine

---

reiterates to Karl as she calls in Gill from reception, who goes across to the shopping centre to buy Karl a new mobile phone. We quickly learn that Gill has no need for the gym as she spends a large portion of her day beating a path from the office to the shopping centre. Staff members at all the sites we visited would do the same.

While Australia has had a decade-long debate about whether the Newstart rate should be increased from just below $278 per week, what is clear is that there is money in the system to make purchases for jobseekers, which benefits any shop located near an employment services office. Mobile phones are the items we saw purchased most often at Wilmore. At the Cove, our fourth site, seemingly every jobseeker who walked through the door left with new boots or office wear.

Sharmaine and Karl's conversation quickly turns to Work for the Dole, which is showing up as a red flag on Karl's profile in the case management system. 'What I want is to get you into work. But I now have to place you into Work for the Dole', Sharmaine tells Karl as she tries to open the Work for the Dole activity referral tab on her computer system. The screen freezes, opening a brief window for some small talk about Karl's family before the system finishes loading and the appointment continues:

> Sharmaine: We need to refer you to an activity for Work for the Dole. Don't feel like it's a punishment. It will be good for your CV.
> Karl: What's an activity?
> Sharmaine: You have to do something for 25 hours per week. Previously your training covered that. The department wants you to be doing something; they don't want you just sitting at home on the lounge. They don't want you getting gaps on your CV, sitting at home doing nothing.

Sharmaine does little to hide the implication that Karl, as an unemployed person, is doing nothing productive with his time. But she also employs a subtle verbal tactic of distancing herself from what is being asked of Karl, conveying that it's the government system – and not her – that is insisting Karl does Work for the Dole or faces a payment penalty. She tells us in a later interview that it's a tactic she uses because 'you don't want to be the bad cop', so you blame Centrelink and the department instead.

Sharmaine returns to filling in the online forms – 'This computer is so slow!' – before warning Karl that if he does not do Work for the Dole, his payments will be cut. 'It's not me, it's the department,' she tells him.

Karl: When do I start this?
Sharmaine: Tomorrow.
Karl: That's bullshit.
Sharmaine: But I am buying [you] a phone.
Karl: Will you phone me tomorrow?
Sharmaine: I will phone and hassle you. You will wish you didn't have a phone!
Karl: I can't believe I have to start tomorrow.

Sharmaine (pointing to her computer screen): See this red flag, it has been against your name since you finished [the TAFE course]. If I had a number for you, you would have been in this earlier.

'Don't go slow today, please', Sharmaine mutters to her screen as she proceeds to work her way through the referral interface. While she does this, Karl asks to go outside for a cigarette. But Sharmaine tells him that he needs to stay in the room 'to sign stuff'. Altogether, the appointment runs for nearly 50 minutes. It's one of the longest that we sit in on at the Wilmore office, dictated by the slow pace of the computer.

However, as the earlier example of Sharmaine's phone conversation with Oli illustrates, much of what happens between frontline staff and their clients goes officially unrecorded. Rationalising her decision not to report Oli for refusing a vacancy referral, Sharmaine argues:

I just don't know that it's going to be beneficial to me in order to get compliance out of him by slapping him with an eight-week non-payment period. If I want to get a placement from him that is not the way to go about it … If I got him offside and he did get a job he would never ever give me the details.

Her concern about getting Oli 'offside' alludes to one of the more controversial outcome payments that agencies can receive: cases where clients have 'found own employment' and the fact, as mentioned in a Senate inquiry into Jobactive, 'providers receive their outcome payments regardless of the degree to which they contributed to the participant securing work'.[19] Provided that they lodge the details of clients' employment on ESS Web and those clients either drop off payments for the required 26 weeks or report their earnings to Centrelink of their own volition, Jobactive agencies can earn thousands of dollars in outcome payments even if they did not facilitate that employment.

From the providers' perspective, it is administratively much simpler to claim outcome payments automatically in this way – via jobseekers dropping off benefits entirely for the necessary period or, if in part-time employment, 'declaring' their earnings voluntarily every fortnight to Centrelink. As Claire, who processes the outcome payments for the Wilmore office, explains, this removes the need to provide payslip evidence that clients are working. More importantly, it reduces the risk of opening jobseekers up to a departmental audit:

> This contract is all about how they [jobseekers] declare their income … If you're doing the payslip evidence there's more options for scrutiny by the department. So, if they've declared and it's showing it's 100 per cent, great, there's no scrutiny. If we have to put documentary evidence in, there's that option that that might come up as a desktop audit. If there's one line that you've missed or done wrong, that may cause them to open up for everything else.

Claire is in her late 40s and has been with Pegasus for three years. Before that, she was a reverse marketer for six years with the same for-profit agency as Troy. She and her husband previously ran their own smallgoods business. Like Troy, she sees Pegasus' work culture as 'totally different' to her previous agency in that 'they're not after your blood'. At the for-profit agency, 'it was all about the almighty dollar at the end of the line and it didn't matter who you were, really there was no loyalty'. Hearing that view from both Claire and Troy is fascinating to us. It is at odds with our own survey research, which has

---

19   Senate Education and Employment References Committee 2019, 170.

persistently failed to turn up operational differences between for-profit and not-for-profit agencies. For instance, when we surveyed the Jobactive workforce in mid-2016, we found no statistically significant differences between the responses of frontline staff working in for-profit and not-for-profit agencies on over 90 per cent of survey items.[20] This included their perceptions of clients and the extent to which they were 'work-first' in their approach. But perhaps that is the benefit of ethnographic research. While our survey data tells us that there is no difference, our own intuition, based on many hours speaking to employment services professionals at conferences and elsewhere, tells us something else. It seems that Claire and Troy side with our intuition.

Our impression of the Wilmore office, from the frontline staff we speak to and observe, is of an organisational and office culture that is highly supportive and person-centred. On the first day we visit the site, we repeatedly overhear the staff talking about the Kris Kringle presents they are going to give each other at the upcoming office Christmas party, which seems to be a highlight on their social calendar. Regularly, we see staff offering to buy their colleagues a coffee or a juice as they step out for their coffee break or a quick cigarette. As in most of the sites that we visit during the research for this book, collective smoking breaks appear to be routine at the Wilmore office, generating additional opportunities for informal team bonding. From what we can see, work–life balance seems to take priority over targets and deadlines, and we learn from Sharmaine and the other employment consultants that they are locked out from entering data on their computer systems between 8 pm and 8 am. 'You are encouraged to have a life outside work', Sharmaine tells us. And if you need to take time off for personal reasons, 'they're very supportive of that'. This is something we observe first-hand during the research for this book, when two of the office staff each take multiple weeks of compassionate leave to grieve the deaths of close family members. The general consensus of the management and frontline staff – or at least that is conveyed to us – is that it's an organisation that's 'great to work for' with 'normal targets' and 'lots of supports' for staff.

---

20 Considine, O'Sullivan, McGann and Nguyen 2020.

Claire's official job title is post-placement support specialist. This means she delivers 'in-work support', taking over the management of cases once clients have been successfully found employment. It's a largely phone-based role that involves checking in on clients every two weeks 'to confirm that they are still working' and to identify any issues so that site staff 'can intervene to save that placement' or rescue the outcome by rapidly placing them into alternative employment. Mostly Claire's role seems to entail following up to ensure that clients are declaring their earnings fully to Centrelink and, if not, chasing them for the payslip evidence Pegasus needs to verify the outcome. However, the boundary between where the employment consultants' role ends and where Claire's begins is far more blurred in practice.

The Wilmore office's organisational attempt to formally delineate job placement from in-work support invariably runs up against a system that demands job-seeking conditionality from those in part-time work who remain on benefits. What this means is that these underemployed clients still need to regularly attend appointments with their consultants about what they are doing to increase their working hours. The formal distinction between job placement and in-work support quickly unravels, in practice, as we quickly discover. This becomes evident on our second day at the Wilmore office, when Sharmaine meets with Danush, a mature-age jobseeker from Libya who would remain on her caseload for the duration of the study, despite being in full-time employment for much of this time.

Danush is one of Sharmaine's Stream C clients, but it's not obvious why. He speaks good English and ran his own engineering business before coming to Australia as a humanitarian refugee less than a year before. But his engineering experience counts for little in the world of Jobactive, and Danush is now working 38 hours per week as a steel labourer in what Sharmaine describes to him as 'a survival job'. It's a job that the Wilmore office brokered him into after just his second appointment. 'All work is muscle working', Danush complains, having left work to make the 4 pm appointment. Sharmaine responds: 'We've found you a job, and I know it doesn't pay much, but we're looking at entry-level work. Because you've studied engineering in Libya. But it doesn't translate in Australia ... We need to start somewhere ...'

Danush wants to do an apprenticeship, possibly in carpentry, so that he can work in construction and earn a higher salary to support his family. But Sharmaine wants him to stick at the full-time job he already has, warning that he will be on even lower wages if he does an apprenticeship: 'My suggestion would be that you think long and hard about it… We've got you a job, you're earning more than you were [on Centrelink], you're building a work history.' The rest of the appointment continues in this vein, with Sharmaine trying to convince Danush to lower his expectations. Eventually she becomes exasperated by his insistence that he wants a better job than the one they have got for him. So, she wraps up the appointment with 'I have another client waiting', sarcastically promising to call him 'if anything comes up that pays $300 an hour'.

Danush is one of the success stories that we follow at the Wilmore office. Despite his protestations to Sharmaine, he stays in the steel-labouring job long enough for Pegasus to claim a full 26-week employment outcome. His case is highly unusual in that he's still attached to the office throughout his employment and even beyond his first six months of paid full-time work. This means, as Sharmaine tells us in a later interview, that the Wilmore office is 'eligible to go through that whole process again' and earn a second outcome payment if they re-anchor Danush in another job. During our study, this is exactly what they do after Danush injures his back and can no longer work as a steel labourer. Almost immediately, Troy brokers him into a job working in the dispatch section of a bakery supply company. Again, it's a smaller employer that Troy has known for years. Drawing on this relationship, Troy is able 'to sell' Danush purely on his work ethic, since Danush has no dispatch experience.

The Wilmore office staff never discover why Danush remains on their caseload – whether it's a system error in their favour or whether something else is going on behind the scenes of his Centrelink payments. Even Claire, who manages the Wilmore office's outcomes claims, is at a loss to explain it:

There's still something we just don't know. Normally somebody would declare, declare … [and] would get exited [by Centrelink] because of their income. Sharmaine and I have discussed it, we're

86

not 100 per cent sure whether it's something to do with his racial background, whatever is behind the scenes in his file. He's never exited for any of it.

Danush is just one of thousands of cases in which Jobactive providers have received multiple outcome payments for the same jobseeker. Data provided to a Senate inquiry into Jobactive showed that, during the first three years of the contract, providers repeatedly received outcome payments 'for placing the same 4765 people in seven or more different jobs'.[21] What makes Danush's case rather unique is that the two outcome payments the Wilmore office received were both for full-time jobs lasting over six months.

When we conclude our research, Danush is still with the Wilmore office and, for all we know, he may remain on its caseload today. Following his case gives us insight into the complexity of the administrative systems that jobseekers and frontline employment services staff must navigate daily, and their impact on client outcomes. These impenetrable administrative processes are a stroke of good luck for the Wilmore office in Danush's case. But they do not always work to clients' advantage, as we will see later when we encounter one of the Wilmore office's clients who, due to a bureaucratic error, is still formally required by the system to attend appointments and undertake Work for the Dole despite having a newborn baby. And even from Danush's perspective, it means that he is compelled to remain in frequent contact with his Jobactive provider despite working more than 30 hours per week.

'New Australians'

Like Danush, the jobseekers that the Wilmore office manages are predominantly from overseas. While the Stream C caseload includes a small number of mature-age jobseekers, early school leavers and 'a

---

21   Data provided by the Department of Jobs and Small Business (as it was then called) to the Senate Education and References Committee. See Senate Education and Employment References Committee 2019, 173.

few ex-offenders', a significant proportion are humanitarian migrants from Tibet. These people, Troy tells us, are 'generally hard working' in that 'they'll maintain employment once given it', but have limited English. So the most straightforward path, at least for the Tibetan-born men, is to find them process work in small businesses that manufacture 'building supplies, food and other general products', where language may not be as much of a barrier, because most of their co-workers will also be migrants. However, as some of the staff admit during moments of reflection, this strategy of seeking to place their Tibetan-born clients in process jobs requiring little English can create a 'catch-22', where the short-term goal of achieving payable outcomes hinders their clients' longer-term progression – for example, by stifling their opportunities to learn and improve their English.

It's a tension that is invariably resolved in favour of immediate employment. 'If something comes up, well, surely you put them forward, because that's our job to do it', explains Sandra, a part-time consultant who works with the Wilmore office's stream B and C caseload. She offers this reflection after we observe a ten-minute appointment with her client Vu, a 17-year-old migrant who has lived in Australia for only six months. Vu's uncle acts as the translator for the meeting. Via his uncle, Sandra asks Vu about the type of work he is willing to do and whether he would consider factory process work. The uncle assures Sandra that Vu would, so she asks Troy to join the meeting to gather Vu's details. After the brief appointment, Sandra worries that Vu's uncle may be pushing the idea of factory work. 'I think the uncle, that's what he wants for him, so it's a catch-22': 'I would love to see [Vu] increase his English first. I think if he goes into a factory where it's predominantly Tibetan-born migrants, his English isn't going to increase as fast as it should. He will be continually reliant on other people to speak for him. That's my concern.'

Sandra, like her colleague Sharmaine, is new to the industry. When we first meet her, it's only her fifth month working as an employment consultant. She tells us that she used to work in the 'corporate world', for a facilities and building management company, but became disillusioned working for an organisation that was 'all about the bottom dollar' and which did not 'really give a shit'. 'So I left a very high paying job, I couldn't do it.' She's the third staff member we speak with to sharply contrast their experience of working for the Wilmore office with what they recall was a more cutthroat, commercial organisational culture.

A mother of five, Sandra thinks of herself as 'a people person', but says that she is still developing 'her style' and probably needs 'to get a bit tougher with clients'. It's not a quality that comes naturally to her. In the appointments that we observe, she assumes more of a nurturing and, at times, 'mothering' tone.

Her next appointment is an early school leaver, Roger. He's in his early 20s, appears to be homeless and presents as visibly affected by drugs. It's a re-engagement appointment, meaning that Roger's payments were stopped when he missed a previous appointment. So, he now must reconnect with Sandra to have them restored. Roger's experience of being 'NARed' (the industry term for having a Non-Attendance Report filed against you) has become commonplace for jobseekers since changes to the jobseeker compliance framework in July 2014 gave providers a new power to directly stop clients' payments. Unlike PRs, which must be reviewed by Centrelink before any payment penalties are applied, NARs almost instantaneously stop jobseekers' payments until they 're-engage'. They have become a go-to tool for providers to prod jobseekers to attend and were routinely applied to the jobseekers that we followed in this study. Sandra later tells us that she gives jobseekers a 15-minute window to arrive for their appointment, before calling them to find out why they have not shown up. If they do not respond within half an hour, 'then I'll submit a NAR': 'Sometimes it's the only way you engage with them … Roger's a classic example. The only way you engage with Roger is when you've NARed him and he needs his payments.'

Slouched, and looking vacantly at the wall, Roger says there's nothing Sandra can do to help him. 'Don't you ever say that you are unhelpable', she abruptly responds. 'You may think that I can't help you, but you may say something that twigs something in my brain that I can help you with.' Turned away from her computer, and leaning over towards Roger, Sandra probes further until Roger eventually opens up, telling her he has a court appearance coming up for cannabis possession. He does not see why he should face court for cannabis possession, likening it to drinking. Then he cracks what seems to be a joke, asking, 'What's the alternative to using cannabis – euthanasia?'

But Sandra treats his offhand remark very seriously, telling him that she cannot let him leave until she's reassured herself that he's not *actually* thinking of self-harming. She makes him promise to see a doctor or a psychologist, giving him a list of counselling services in the area. As she does this, she tells him: 'I see a confused, very young man that's crying out for help – maybe it's the mother in me.' Twenty-five minutes later, Roger leaves with his payments restored, a list of counselling services to visit and a promise that he will see a doctor within the next two weeks. Sandra brings Roger's next appointment forward, from three weeks to two, so that she can follow up with him on this.

Unlike this encounter with Roger, many of the appointments that we sit in on are much briefer. Some last for as little as four minutes, as consultants and jobseekers, only fluent in very different languages, struggle to understand each other. We see little use of professional translation services, at any of the four sites we visit. In most cases it is considered simpler – by all involved – to muddle through, often aided by a younger family member or friend joining the appointment to translate what they can. 'Hopefully next year we can find you some factory work; keep practising your English and I will see you just before Christmas', Sharmaine tells Ang, another young Tibetan-born jobseeker, as she concludes the appointment after only five minutes.

The Wilmore office used to organise interpreters as a matter of course but have stopped doing this. Sharmaine starts to tell us that it was too expensive but backtracks and says that 'the money wouldn't matter if it were effective'. In her view, the best way for 'New Australians' – as she euphemistically calls them – to learn English is to be forced to use it. It's a perspective shared by Sandra, who explains 'that's where the Italians and the Greeks learned their English, by being at work … having to speak.'

Interpreters and English language classes are peripheral to the business of finding employment, which becomes evident during an appointment Sharmaine takes with Cetan, a Tibetan-born jobseeker in his mid-40s, who is in Stream C and attending English language classes.

To break the ice, Sharmaine asks Cetan how he is getting on with this English. 'Very hard', he hesitates. 'You pretend, it's better than you think', Sharmaine says encouragingly in a tone that masks the implication that Cetan is not being upfront with her. It's a tactic she repeats in several of her conversations with Tibetan-born clients that we observe. The conversation moves quickly onto whether Cetan is interested in working in a factory or kitchen, possibly even cleaning? Cetan insists he does not want to do cleaning, so she turns to a kitchen job in the aged care sector. 'I can chop vegetables', he volunteers. 'Is it okay if it's an aged care place, not a restaurant?' Sharmaine wants to know. After taking some time to explain to Cetan what aged care is, she begins organising a referral in his Job Plan to an information session about working in aged care, which is being held the following week. It's not clear Cetan fully understands that he's been referred, so she warns him politely that 'If you say "yeah" then you have to go'. The information session is on the other side of Melbourne, and Cetan has no car or driver's licence. He will have to go by train, which means missing his scheduled English classes for that day. 'You may have school but don't go,' Sharmaine tells Cetan as she confirms the referral in his Job Plan.

Whereas it's mostly manufacturing jobs for the 'New Australia' men, the pathway from welfare-to-work for new 'sheilas' is predominantly via a mop and bucket. The Tibetan-born women we meet are overwhelmingly encouraged to take casual cleaning jobs in the area. However, most of the cleaning jobs that the office can broker depend on jobseekers having access to their own car, as they are either too far away from public transport or require workers to carry their own equipment.

'You can't carry mops and buckets on the train, can you', Sharmaine jokes as she concludes a regular appointment with Bennu, a middle-aged Tibetan-born woman. Bennu has little English, but she does have one of the most prized commodities among jobseekers in outer suburban labour markets: a driver's licence. If she can only gain access to a car, she can take one of the cleaning jobs that the Wilmore office has on its books. This is the hook of Sharmaine's appointment with Bennu, as Sharmaine repeatedly relays over the nine minute meeting that she has jobs for Bennu *if she can get a car*. What about after Christmas? Is there any chance that Bennu and her family will get a car in the new year? We later learn that the Wilmore office will support their clients into work by paying for their car registration and motor vehicle insurance. But clients must have a formal offer of employment before the Wilmore office will commit to this financial assistance, and Sharmaine does not make Bennu aware of this during the appointment. When we meet Bennu, she is already in a casual cleaning job, working 10 hours per week. But it's below her required 30 hours of paid work per fortnight, so it does not count as a trackable job placement for the Wilmore office. The next time we follow up with Sharmaine about Bennu, she's been automatically exited from the caseload by Centrelink for missing an income declaration: a fortnightly report of earnings that people on benefits must submit to Centrelink to continue receiving payments. Bennu never returns to the Wilmore office and leaves no trace in the system to tell us whether she became discouraged – and dropped out of the labour market and off payments altogether – or continued working. Sharmaine suspects the latter as she 'wasn't on much of a payment', so potentially 'just decided to not worry about it and just continue on without a payment'. But it's only Sharmaine's guess, as she was unable to contact Bennu again.

Disappearing without a trace

This pattern of jobseekers disappearing from the Wilmore office's caseload without a trace, we soon learn, is not uncommon. Bennu is one of three Stream C jobseekers that we track at the office to whom this happens. The profile of the Wilmore office's clients means that language presents a real barrier to keeping jobseekers engaged or following up with clients who drop off the system. As Sharmaine tells us in relation to Nilar, another older Tibetan who, like Bennu, falls off her caseload just months into the study:

> Well I can't even phone her … There is no one in the house who speaks English and there is no way that she can communicate on the phone. She could have found full-time employment … She could have passed away. Realistically, how do we know?

Cases like Nilar and Bennu raise a broader concern about the effectiveness of behavioural conditionality policies in supporting transitions from welfare-to-work. While econometric analyses and large-scale evaluations of active labour market programs show that policy instruments such as enforced job searching effectively reduce *benefit claiming*, the evidence is more mixed on whether they move people *into work*.[22] For example, in a study comparing post-unemployment outcomes between sanctioned and non-sanctioned jobseekers in Switzerland over the period 1998–2003, Patrick Arni, Rafael Lalive and Jan van Ours found that the exit rate from benefits to *non employment* was more than double among jobseekers who experienced or were threatened with a payment penalty.[23] Similarly, in a UK study, Barbara Petrongolo found that while the introduction of job-search conditionality requirements in the late 1990s had a significant impact on the short-term exit rate from unemployment benefits, it also reduced benefit recipients' probability of working over a longer-term four-year period.[24] She attributed this partly to the impact that job-search conditionality requirements had on the likelihood of benefit recipients subsequently claiming disability payments, which increased by up to three per cent after these requirements were applied. More recently, in a studying examining the rise in sanctioning of people on unemployment benefits in the UK over the period 2011–14, Rachel Loopstra and her colleagues found that the increase in sanctioning did correspond to a 'substantial increase' in people exiting unemployment benefits, but most of them exited 'to destinations unrelated to work.'[25] In other words, while behavioural conditionality policies may speed up the rate at which some people move off welfare, there is also international evidence to suggest that they push others to drop off benefits to non-employment – the hidden unemployed – or to move to payments with less onerous conditions.

From a policy perspective, this constitutes a significant implementation problem because it results in the exact opposite of the desired outcomes. As Tania Raffass points out, when people on benefits 'disappear from welfare rolls but do not reappear as jobholders … they effectively manage to decommodify themselves, which runs

---

22   For reviews see: Kluve 2010; Card et al. 2015; Martin 2015.
23   Arni et al. 2013.
24   Petrongolo 2009.
25   Loopstra et al. 2015, 11.

against the active labour market policy ambition to expand labour market participation.'[26] This issue is yet to receive adequate attention in Australia, although there is some evidence that a significant proportion of people are moving from the employment services system to non-employment rather than work. For example, in the 12 months to 31 December 2018, 17.5 per cent of the Jobactive participants that left the system were not in the labour force three months later – meaning that they were neither in a job nor unemployed and looking for work.[27] Our research for this book suggests that one way in which frontline workers manage the tension between enforcing behavioural conditionality and responding to the personal and social issues affecting jobseekers' lives is by encouraging their clients to seek medical or personal crisis exemptions. But this comes at the cost of temporarily removing clients from services, meaning that they are unable to work with those clients in other ways such as, for example, supporting them through training or rehabilitation counselling.

For a system that is designed to activate people into work, Jobactive has a very high number of jobseekers who are suspended from their mutual obligation requirements on the grounds of ill-health or personal crisis. Information provided in response to data we requested from the department showed that, on 31 December 2017, more than 22 per cent of all Stream C jobseekers registered with a Jobactive provider were suspended due to a personal crisis, medical exemption or incarceration. In the employment region where the Wilmore office is located, this suspension rate was well above 30 per cent.

As in other offices that we visited, the Wilmore staff would often encourage clients 'to get a medical certificate to Centrelink' in order 'to stop the clock' on their mutual obligation requirements, or if clients intimated that they were unable to meet their job search or Work for the Dole requirements. Occasionally, staff would actively intervene to secure such exemptions on jobseekers' behalf. For example, one jobseeker that we tracked at the Wilmore office, Melinda, a single mother in her mid-50s who suffered from drug dependence combined with several mental and physical health issues, received a total of seven

---

26 Raffass 2017, 358.
27 See Department of Employment, Skills, Small and Family Business 2019a, 13.

different medical exemptions. On one occasion, Laura, the Wilmore office manager, personally intervened when the local Centrelink office would no longer accept Melinda's doctor's certificates. To save Melinda from having her payments stopped, Laura decided to validate Melinda's appointments even though she had missed several meetings without a valid medical exemption. She also contacted Centrelink directly to put in place a longer, formalised exemption on Melinda's behalf.

Citizen or state agent?

Alongside offering employment support, frontline employment services staff are often called on to help their clients troubleshoot administrative problems with their activation and benefits status. At times their role becomes absurd, calling for them to effect activation with clients who are in no way positioned to look for work. On the morning of our third day at the Wilmore office, Sharmaine takes an appointment with Chris, one of her younger Stream B clients who has phoned ahead to let her know that he has a broken pelvis. Chris' girlfriend has driven him to the meeting because Chris' car has also just been stolen. Sharmaine takes all this in her stride, as Chris sits in visible pain. With genuine empathy in her voice, she tries to lighten the mood, telling Chris, 'Don't you just want to be a bit boring, get a job, go to work?' The three then chat about how long it will take for Chris' pelvis to heal. Maybe 18 months, although Chris has yet to see a doctor or go to hospital. His girlfriend will drive him there straight afterwards, but Chris' payments have been suspended because he missed his last appointment, and he has no medical certificate to suspend his mutual obligations. So, the appointment must proceed *as if* Chris is still required to fulfil his jobs-search conditionality requirements of 20 applications per month, even though it is obvious that he is in no condition to look for work. Apologetically, Sharmaine tells him that she still needs to give him a 'basic Job Plan', handing him a fresh dole diary to fill out for his next appointment. As she does so, she remarks on the performative nature of this action. If he can get a doctor's certificate to Centrelink in the afternoon, she tells him, 'we both know you don't have to do it'. But until then 'we have to pretend … You know the drill, you have to look for work, yada, yada.' Conscious of Chris' pain and the urgency of his need for medical treatment, Sharmaine quickly wraps up the appointment. 'Alright guys, get to the hospital.'

In another example, Naledi, a Tibetan-born woman whose trajectory we followed, gives birth but continues to attend appointments at the Wilmore office because the system deems her to be on Newstart Allowance. In the previous months, Naledi has been on an 'expectant mother' exemption from mutual obligations due to the high-risk nature of her pregnancy. But when she gives birth that exemption ends. When we follow up with Naledi's consultant, Amelia (who has returned from parental leave), she tells us that Naledi has been in the Wilmore office in the previous week:

> She said that she went to Centrelink and they said she was on the right payments, but we checked her MyGov together, and I've also double-checked the system, it says Newstart Allowance … They've [Centrelink] said she can't have an exemption for having a child that young, she needs to be on parenting payments, otherwise she needs part-time work.

At this point Naledi's baby was 10 weeks old, but she was showing up in the system as overdue for her Work for the Dole referrals, and 'going against' Amelia's 'Work for the Dole stats'. As Amelia, who herself has young children, explains: 'I need to have her referred, as of last week. So, I've said to her she needs to urgently get on to Centrelink … She doesn't have even an exemption in the system, whilst her parenting payments are pending, or anything.'

Naledi's and Chris' cases show how frontline workers must juggle the tension between managing compliance and looking after the best interests of their clients *as people*. Steven Maynard-Moody and Michael Musheno describe this as case managers' professional identities being pulled in two different directions. On one hand they are state agents: publicly contracted workers 'charged with carrying out the plans and policies of government agencies' and whose job consists in following and applying pre-determined rules.[28] On the other, many prefer to view themselves as citizen agents who 'act in response to individual citizen-clients in specific circumstances' and who see their jobs as primarily about looking after their clients. The fundamental tension of street-level work, as Maynard-Moody and Musheno see it, 'is that the needs of citizen-clients exist in tension with the demands and limits of rules'.[29]

It's a tension that our research shows case managers are acutely aware of. They recognise that they are part of a policy apparatus that demands compliance, and that they can ill afford to ignore this aspect of their work. But, at least at the Wilmore office, case managers try to make this as comfortable an experience as possible for clients. When we ask Sandra what skills and qualities are most important in consultants, she tells us it's 'a fine line between empathy and compliance … and a good knowledge of the guidelines too.' She elaborates: 'Don't get me wrong … I will always be compliant. Do I use a bit of discretion? Yes, I do. But that's the latitude we are provided, but we don't have a lot of it.'

Sometimes this latitude stretches to case managers bending the rules if they can get away with it. This is more feasible – though still not without risk – if their clients are in Stream C, where they have wider discretion under the department's formal procedural guidelines to depart from using heavily standardised Job Plans with specified job-search requirements. Notably, four of the Stream C jobseekers that we followed at the Wilmore office had no job-search requirements in their Job Plans for periods of the study. This included one mature-age Tibetan-born woman, Zar, a client of Sharmaine's, who almost never had job-search requirements while we followed her. Sharmaine did not see the point in giving this 'little old lady without a word of English' job-search requirements, although she was careful to claim it was a very rare case and that if she was 'to be questioned by the department' about how she was managing the case, she 'would definitely have a problem'. But it was a risk she was prepared to take, keeping Zar's appointments short and sweet: 'She's a beautiful sweet lady … Comes in with a smile on her face to every appointment. And I ask her how she is, and she says "good". I say how's her English and she laughs. And we make her another appointment and off she goes.'

28   Maynard-Moody and Musheno 2000, 337.
29   Maynard-Moody and Musheno 2000, 349.

Zar's case is not the only example of Sharmaine bending the rules for jobseekers she thinks the system treats unreasonably. On the morning of our third day, we observe a cheery appointment with Ben, who's Australian-born and in his 40s. Ben comes bearing gifts – one of the cartons of juice he is selling for his part-time job as a sales rep with a fruit juice company. It's a job Ben seems passionate about. When we meet him, Ben is full-time activity tested on Centrelink, meaning he should be looking for 35 hours of paid work per week. The job he has is well under this, but Ben has a medical condition that limits him from working full-time. Unfortunately for Ben, Centrelink won't recognise his condition because he refuses to be treated with traditional medicine, preferring alternative therapies. So, he continues to have job-search requirements on top of his sales rep job and, in theory, is obliged to accept any suitable vacancy referrals for full-time employment Sharmaine directs his way.

But Sharmaine has little intention of making life difficult for Ben, telling us that, in her view, Ben should really only be required to look for part-time work. While she cannot change the fact that he must undertake job searches to continue receiving his payments, she can make things as easy as possible for him by not pushing any additional jobs on him. It's a stance she's open with Ben about during the appointment, telling him warmly: 'If you were part-time tested, you would already be out of the system. So, we're not going to give you a hard time here.' No new jobs or vacancy referrals are discussed and much of the meeting involves casual chitchat about organic juice, and what the warmer weather will mean for Ben's juice sales. All up, the conversation goes for six minutes. As Ben leaves, he promises to bring Sharmaine apple juice the next time!

Backstage

When we first observe the Wilmore office, these appointments play out behind closed doors and out of earshot of colleagues or other jobseekers – in the small interview rooms along the corridor behind the reception area. Things are very different when we return 12 months later. Two of the interview rooms have been demolished, and consultants now take client appointments at their own desks – in the large, open-plan area at the rear of the office. In some ways, this closes the professional distance between jobseeker and case manager. Jobseekers can now glimpse their case managers' personal lives through the family photos and other memorabilia pinned to the partitions dividing consultants' desks. But jobseekers' own lives are also now much more on public display.

With two of the interview rooms gone, there's also a line of sight to the reception and waiting area. This affords us occasional glimpses of the warmth with which the receptionist Gill greets clients as they come in, such as when she discovers a young woman, whom she greets by name, is now five months pregnant. Gill stands up and leans over her reception desk to hear all about it, visibly delighted for the client.

When frontline staff are not meeting with clients at their desks, they finish off file notes, scan documentation, browse the Pegasus jobs database, and discuss cases and other work issues with colleagues. They also spend much time chasing jobseekers by phone about their Work for the Dole attendance, Centrelink reporting or payslip evidence. 'Do you have it all sorted with Centrelink? Why? Have you taken a medical certificate to them?' Sharmaine calls down the receiver to Charlie. 'If you took a medical certificate to Centrelink, that would be A-okay … Can you be here between 10.30 and 10.45? Just do your best. 'Cause I need to see you to re-engage you.' Then she's onto the next call to Brad: 'Did you commence work today … Are you still all good to go? Beautiful, that's awesome.' Later in the morning, she calls Karl, who is supposed to have commenced Work for the Dole: 'Are you at Work for the Dole? Why? … Your payments will be cut as soon as Centrelink finds out you haven't gone. I suggest you jump on the bus and get yourself there now. The sooner you commence, the less financial penalty you will have. Okay, thanks Karl, bye!' Meanwhile, the reverse marketer Troy is talking to an employer on his mobile phone as he paces the corridor. He's someone we rarely see sitting still at his desk: 'We've got a few people who are interested in doing an apprenticeship but, because of their age … Would you be interested in that? … So, it would be like a carpentry apprenticeship? … Alright, terrific.'

It's a loud and bustling room, filled with the hum of frequent exchanges between co-workers, repeated phone calls to clients and the ever-present sound of the radio. Whether by accident or design, it's an eclectic playlist that soundtracks our days at the Wilmore office: from the Beastie Boys to U2 to the Cranberries to Jimmy Barnes to INXS via Prince, and even Chumbawamba, whose Tubthumping plays on the radio as Sharmaine refers Trev, the Stream B jobseeker sitting next to her desk, to various labouring and hospitality jobs. 'This could be good for you', Sharmaine says as she searches the jobs database. 'It is in Smithtown, printing company, seeking an all-rounder ... You meet all those requirements.' Trev responds with, 'Yep, no worries', and she quickly sends his CV into the ether. Then she reads out another advertised job. It's for a kitchen hand. 'Skip that', Trev says, so they move on before settling on a front-of-house job that Trev is interested in. He already has a casual job working for a catering company. The shifts that he is getting are not enough to meet his requirements, but his hours have been increasing since Sharmaine arranged and paid for him to do a short course in the Responsible Service of Alcohol. It means 'I can be the bar man or a waiter', Trev tells her, explaining that he's been told to put his name down 'for loads of shifts'. Sharmaine updates Trev's work in his Job Plan, and they agree to reduce his job search requirements to 10 per month. 'We don't hold a knife to your throat that you do that', she reassures him as she confirms this on the computer.

There's an egalitarianism to how the desk spaces are configured in this open-plan office. Site managers brush elbows with employment consultants in adjoining cubicles, ensuring that their perspective remains grounded in the material realities of casework. Perhaps, more importantly, it gives the consultants easy and immediate access to their manager's institutional knowledge and expertise, especially as all have many years of direct case management experience themselves. For example, at various points while we are at the Wilmore office, the consultants momentarily step out of appointments to clarify procedural issues with the site manager, or the details of courses and information sessions that Pegasus is running for jobseekers. 'What days does Squad run?' Sharmaine interrupts her appointment to ask Jessica, her manager, while Sandra interrupts another appointment to ask if there's anything they can do for a client who has lost his licence for drink-driving. Nothing, unfortunately, Jessica says, so they will have to look at getting him into something that does not require a licence.

From a site manager's perspective, sitting in an open-plan configuration gives them a real-time window into the office's caseload and the nature of the issues that clients and staff are dealing with, insights they wouldn't get from 'pull[ing] down a caseload list and study[ing] names'. Laura – Jessica's replacement – tells us that she gets to see and hear a lot in the open-plan office: 'Claire will be talking about due claims … or Troy's got vacancies and we're talking about referrals … and you can hear that dialogue happening'. It's a dialogue that frequently plays out in front of us during the days that we are onsite, along with regular conversations between staff about individual clients and the degree to which they are 'job ready'. What's most notable about these conversations is that all the clients are known to almost all the staff – from the site manager to the reverse marketer to the consultants, including those not directly managing the case – by first name. 'Did Andy get the job?' Sharmaine calls over to Troy, who's sitting at the desk perpendicular to hers. 'They want to trial him again', Troy responds without hesitation before conjecturing about Andy's motivation. 'Something has changed in him. I don't know if he wants to work anymore'. Rarely do the Wilmore office staff have to consult file notes or look up details on their computers to hold court about clients or respond to queries that colleagues may raise aloud.

In another example, Sandra calls out to Troy as he enters the back office that she's just updated the phone number of a jobseeker in the computer. She refers to the jobseeker by his first name, Max, and Jessica, who overhears, chimes in that she's 'just got an email about him'. It turns out that Max is one of several jobseekers from the Wilmore office who've been sent to an information session for food manufacturing jobs with a major labour hire company. Following this, jobseekers are pre-screened by phone by the company, and the successful candidates will be sent to a five-day Food Handling and Preparation course being run out of another Pegasus office. 'Pretty much they're just fast-tracking him into the course', Jessica tells Sandra and Troy. A minute later Sandra is on the phone to Max, telling him: 'You must be there, because we've pulled a few strings for this …'

The (blurred) boundaries between disability and unemployment

Now reconfigured to accommodate places for jobseekers to sit, the back office houses a multitude of staff. This includes not just the Wilmore office's six Jobactive staff – three employment consultants, the site manager, the reverse marketer and post-placement support specialist – but also Pegasus' Disability Employment Services (DES) team, which is co-located in the Wilmore office. It's the only one of the offices that we visit to also deliver the DES program, and Pegasus is one of the largest DES providers in Australia. But, besides sharing Gill, the office's sociable receptionist, the Jobactive and DES programs are treated as entirely separate entities – each with their own manager and separate case management staff. The Jobactive and DES case managers physically sit with their separate teams, at partitioned desks. It's almost as if they are separate wards in a hospital, treating patients with altogether different ailments and injuries. One is an emergency room for fast-tracking the unemployed into work; the other a rehabilitation wing for gradually managing people's recovery from chronic conditions.

At a program design level, this is how the Australian government would like to think of the difference between DES and Jobactive. One is managed by the Department of Social Services and the other by the Department of Employment. If you're a client in the former, you do not have any Work for the Dole requirements whereas Work for the Dole looms large over Jobactive participants. Yet, as we will see in the remaining chapters, the boundary between the two programs – administratively and in terms of the cohorts they target – is far more porous and fluid than policy designers and public managers care to admit. It is not uncommon for newly commenced Jobactive participants to have come directly from a DES provider following a Centrelink reassessment, or for Jobactive clients to present with significant physical or psychological health issues that lead case managers to think they should be candidates for DES.

One among many examples we witness of this is Prue, a woman in her mid-30s who commences on the Wilmore office's caseload just two months after her partner was killed. When Sharmaine first meets with Prue, who she describes as an 'extremely angry' and chronically depressed woman who is 'not ready to work on anyone but herself',

Prue is in Stream B with full-time activity requirements. Sharmaine's first priority is to try to get Prue 'up-streamed'. She intervenes with Centrelink and manages to organise another Employment Services Assessment (ESA), where Prue is reclassified as a part-time activity-tested jobseeker in Stream C. But Sharmaine 'wanted her up-streamed further', to DES:

> I explained she needed medical evidence, I printed off the forms. I found her a local doctor that bulk billed. I said, 'This is what you need. Make sure you get this, make sure you get that' ... I had to write notes to Centrelink and get her to go there. And I said, 'You're going to need medical evidence and please go prepared.'

We learn from the Wilmore office's employment consultants that the office contracts a psychologist to come in one day per week to assist with circumstances such as this. Sandra tells us that she's had a couple of clients 'where I've sent them to her and they've ended up being referred to DES, which is probably more suitable for them'. In another example, when Amelia meets Barry, a homeless jobseeker in his early 30s with psychological and drug issues, her first manoeuvre is to get him an assessment with the psychologist: 'It's just a one-off assessment and then basically what happens, when we get that assessment, is we use that as evidence for a reassessment by Centrelink'. This happens with Barry, whose work capacity requirements are eventually reduced to between eight and 14 hours per week. This means that he is now an 'hours person', as clients with part-time requirements are colloquially referred to in the industry, referring to the fact that providers can earn payable employment outcomes with these clients by placing them into jobs with the requisite number of hours work per fortnight. Those with full-time requirements, by contrast, are known as 'money people', because providers must place them into jobs that earn clients enough money that they no longer receive payments. When Barry becomes an 'hours person' with a very limited part-time work requirement, he is also volunteering with a not-for-profit organisation, writing research reports. When his work capacity requirements are reduced, Sandra who takes over Barry's case when Amelia goes on parental leave – persuades Barry to approach the not-for-profit to hire him as an independent contractor rather than a volunteer. Barry continues in this job for the remainder of our research, declaring eight hours of paid work per week to Centrelink. And because Barry is an 'hours' rather than a 'money' person, the Wilmore office is able to claim a full-employment outcome.

Barry is an example of the increasing number of jobseekers on Newstart Allowance who have been assessed by Centrelink as having only a partial capacity to work due to major illness or disability (see Figure 3.1). Between June 2014 and June 2019, there was a 60 per cent increase in the number of Newstart recipients with an assessed partial capacity to work, up from 180,646 recipients to 289,489 recipients. At the same time, the total number of Newstart recipients has declined, meaning that people with a partial capacity to work accounted for 42 per cent *of all Newstart recipients* in June 2019 compared to just 26 per cent five years previously.[30] Several dynamics are feeding into these demographic changes, but a critical catalyst is the tightening of eligibility conditions for the Disability Support Pension (DSP). There were almost 85,000 fewer people on the DSP in June 2019 than in June 2014. People who would've been on the DSP were instead put on Newstart Allowance, with the result that the average duration on income support among those on Newstart Allowance blew out from 230 weeks in June 2014 to 296 weeks in June 2019. In other words, people receiving Newstart in June 2019 were on income support payments for an extra 16 months, on average, compared with those receiving Newstart in June 2014. This should put paid to any notion that Newstart Allowance is a temporary unemployment benefit.

These changes in the profile of Newstart recipients point to an increasingly challenging caseload for frontline employment services staff. They are in line with the changes in the composition of their caseload reported by frontline workers in our survey research. For example, when asked to estimate the proportion of their caseload that was more difficult versus easier to place into employment, those we

---

30 These data are taken from the Payment Demographic data published quarterly by the Department of Social Services (2019). In June 2014, 830,454 people were receiving the DSP compared with 745,673 DSP recipients in June 2019.

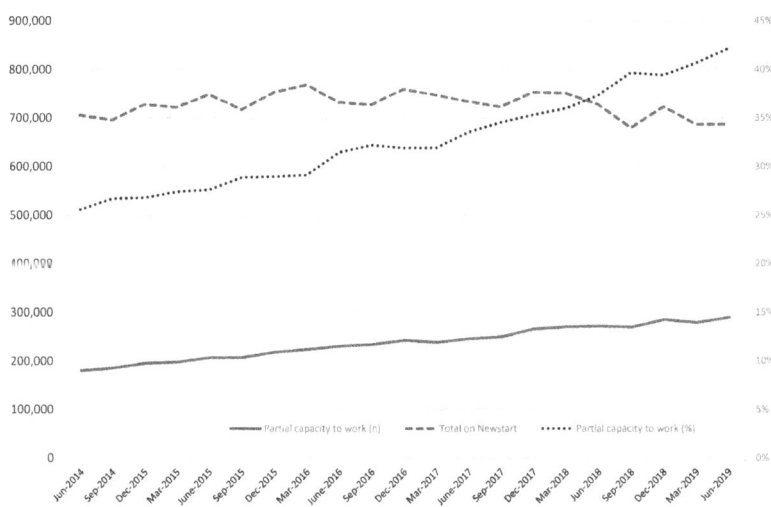

Figure 3.1. Rise in the number of Newstart recipients with an assessed partial capacity to work, June 2014 to June 2019. Data source: Department of Social Services 2014–19.

surveyed in 2016 considered that about 42 per cent of their caseload, on average, was 'more difficult to place'. In the previous survey in 2012, by contrast, this proportion was estimated to be below 36 per cent.

Public displays of performance

Besides the physical divide between Jobactive and DES at the Wilmore office, one of the most striking features of the open-plan area is the array of whiteboards adorning the walls. A board on the back wall notes the dates and locations of upcoming training courses, group interviews and information sessions about jobs the Wilmore office is trying to anchor its clients into. There's a soft skills course coming up in the new year, along with a Squad life-coaching program, both of which are run from another Pegasus office, as the Wilmore office isn't large enough for a training room. There's also a Hospitality Ready course being run over two days, along with information sessions being hosted by an aged care provider recruiting for kitchen hand staff and by a large, international business that has won a contract to operate call centres for the Australian Tax Office. Were it not for their limited English, some of the Wilmore office's Tibetan-born clients may well end up being referred to work for a company that also operates the centres that previously detained them. The board lists another information session being run about the food manufacturing roles that Max, Sandra's client, has just been pre-screened for.

A further board on the adjacent wall, we can see from the capitalised font on the top, belongs to 'Troy the Marketer'. It's a calendar of performance indicators for the month, broken down by each week and each stream: job placements achieved, number of jobseekers to be marketed, wage subsidies to be negotiated, vacancies listed on Pegasus' jobs database, new employers contacted and so on. On the bottom of the board is a list of specific clients (by name) to be marketed week-by-week – what the consultants later tells us is their 'find a job for this girl while she's hot' list. Another board, about a metre away, tracks how each of the Wilmore office's three employment consultants are performing for the month: the number of vacancy referrals they have made, the number of job placements they have and the quantity of employment outcomes they have achieved. Again, these are broken down by stream and by week *for each employment consultant*. It's a very public signalling of their performance, although the boards only list the actual outcomes and placements that Sharmaine, Sandra and Amelia have individually achieved each week and for each stream (A, B and C), not the personal targets they have been individually set. However, four A4 sheets Blu-Tacked to the top of the board do show targets for the Wilmore office as a whole, and how they are collectively tracking towards those targets, so it wouldn't be too difficult to work out whether staff members are pulling their weight to maintain the office's five-star performance rating – which is visibly celebrated in large cut-out letters and a smiley-faced star just above the board tracking the consultants' placement and employment outcomes: :) F I V E S T A R S.

When we commence the research for this book, the personal and collective performance targets for the Wilmore office and its staff are set by Pegasus' senior managers each month. Targets 'come down from above, Jessica, the site manager tells us, based on historical data and projections of 'how many claims or places' the office needs 'to get to be region best'. Jessica, along with the other office staff, also has access to a software tool, internally developed by Pegasus, that enables her to see in real time 'how you are tracking for placements, how you are tracking for outcomes'. Staff can also produce reports, at the touch of a button, about consultants' or the office's Work for the Dole attendance rates, the number of clients with no future appointments or suspensions, and how many placements they have tracking towards an employment outcome. However, in the middle of our fieldwork, the Wilmore office is empowered to set its own monthly targets, perhaps reflecting the change in leadership at the site from Jessica, who had less than two years' management experience, to Laura, who had managed various Pegasus sites for close to a decade. She sets the office's monthly targets using a spreadsheet tool to forecast the office's likely number of job placements and outcomes over coming months and whether this would make it the best-performing Jobactive site – not just the best-performing Pegasus site – in the region.

The performance boards in the Wilmore site's back office are a visible display of the phenomenon that we and our colleagues have elsewhere described as double activation.[31] Much like how welfare-to-work policies, and the case managers implementing them, try to activate jobseekers through financial penalties (e.g. sanctions) and codes of conduct, agency managers try to discipline frontline workers through performance monitoring and performance-related payments. While Pegasus does not pay performance bonuses, the Wilmore office staff have monthly personal placement and outcome targets, and their outputs are publicly documented on the office walls – walls that their clients can now see as they approach consultants' desks for appointments.

---

31   Considine, Lewis, O'Sullivan and Sol 2015.

Overall reflections

We conclude the Wilmore office fieldwork with the strong sense that much of employment services work is about surviving the system and coping with dysfunctional bureaucratic controls that frustrate case managers as much as jobseekers.

There's an impressive team dynamic and work culture at the Wilmore office that clearly goes a long way towards explaining its higher performance. It's also an agency that places a premium on employer engagement and ensuring jobseekers are actively referred to employment opportunities – not just sent to search for themselves. This focus on working with employers, international research suggests, is critical for welfare-to-work programs to be effective,[32] but it's not a systemic strength of the current employment services system, with studies suggesting that as few as one in 20 Australian employers draw on Jobactive agencies to recruit for vacancies.[33] The Wilmore office consultants and other frontline staff all appear to genuinely care about their clients, seeing them first and foremost as people with unique and varied lives rather than commodities in the welfare market. This person-focused orientation is also reflected, from what we can observe, in the Wilmore office's organisational culture and how its management treat and value frontline staff. Indeed, several of the Wilmore staff explicitly remark on the absence of a cutthroat or mercenary work culture in the organisation compared with other providers they have worked for.

Yet, for all of these positives, much of what we observed was transactional and limited. Wilmore is a busy office and the frontline staff – even those managing the 'harder' clients in streams B and C – have heavy caseloads of around 150 clients each. Appointments are often brief, at times lasting less than five minutes. The client meetings we observed were certainly more than the 'tick-and-flick' interactions described in previous studies highlighting the systematic 'carelessness'

---

32   For discussions of the important of employer engagement in active labour market programs in the international context, see van Berkel et al. 2017; Ingold 2018.
33   See Bowman and Randrianarisoa 2018.

encountered by jobseekers at the welfare frontline[34] – what sociologist Richard Sennett describes as a form of 'institutional indifference'.[35] Nonetheless, there was little time during appointments to focus on much beyond the immediate task of job searching and troubleshooting the latest administrative challenge confronting caseworkers and their clients. Whether this be a stream misclassification issue, a problem with the payment a client was on, or the need to produce medical certificates to validate missed appointments, the Wilmore office employment consultants were repeatedly called on to manage jobseekers' relationship with Centrelink.

Despite the emphasis the Wilmore office staff place on building rapport and trust with their clients, much of their job is consumed by administration and the managing of compliance and payments. The computerised case management systems underpinning employment services delivery leave the case managers with limited discretion to avoid insisting that unemployed people fill their time with mutual obligations. This experience is familiar to many frontline Jobactive staff. IT systems exert a large and increasing influence over the type and quality of employment support that jobseekers receive, with almost half the frontline staff we surveyed in 2016 reporting that their computer system told them 'what steps to take with jobseekers and when'.[36] Twenty years ago, when Mark Considine first started surveying the Australian employment services workforce, only 17 per cent of frontline staff reported relying on their computer systems to tell them how to work with jobseekers.[37] While these systems have been introduced partly to guard against the problems of creaming and parking – where agencies focus their resources on the most job ready clients and provide few services to those considered difficult to place – that plagued the early Job Network contracts, they have given rise to a highly standardised approach to working with jobseekers at the frontline, which leaves little room for frontline staff to personalise services to clients.

---

34   See, for example, Bowman et al. 2016; Marston and McDonald 2008.
35   Sennett 2006, 124.
36   Considine, O'Sullivan, McGann and Nguyen 2020.
37   The original study is detailed in Considine 2001.

While the Jobactive reforms were supposed to introduce greater flexibility for providers to tailor their services to the needs of clients and employers, they appear to have had little effect on reversing standardisation at the frontline. Indeed, our survey research shows that frontline staff report a far higher reliance on standardised rules and procedures under Jobactive than previous systems, coupled with much less room to decide for themselves what to do with clients.[38] Whereas in 2008 close to two-thirds of frontline staff reported that they were free to decide for themselves what to do with individual clients, this proportion had fallen to below 50 per cent in 2016. Arguably more striking was the increase in the proportion who reported that 'standard program rules and regulations' determine the decisions they make about jobseekers from 72 per cent in our 2008 survey to 85 per cent in the 2016 survey. These changes suggest that frontline employment services work has become more administrative over the past decade. This transformation gathered pace during the Job Network (1998–2009) era, de-skilling the frontline workforce as decisions became increasingly based on 'entering responses to standardised questions into a computer program'.[39] What distinguishes the case managers at the Wilmore office is not that they have escaped the administrative monotony of frontline activation work, but that they have managed to transform some of this into a broadly humane experience for their clients.

---

38 We discuss these trends at length in Considine, O'Sullivan, McGann and Nguyen 2020. This paper follows up an earlier paper, which examined the impact of the Job Network reforms on levels of flexibility and discretion at the frontline of Australia's employment services system: Considine, Lewis and O'Sullivan 2011.
39 Marston 2006, 92.

4
'Welcome' to Westgate

The Themis office, located in the outer Melbourne fringe suburb of Westgate, is our second site. Buoyed by our first site study at Wilmore, we approach our second fieldwork site with a range of ideas in mind. As researchers we are naturally looking to confirm patterns via similar observations. Spotting a pattern is our bread and butter. At the Wilmore office we witnessed a range of organisational behaviours that we thought may account for its success with the most highly disadvantaged jobseekers. In particular, the Wilmore office was vibrant and collegial, with all staff energetically pulling together to place a jobseeker. Was teamwork the secret to effectively assisting the most highly disadvantaged jobseekers? Would we see this replicated at the Westgate office? What kind of team would they be? How would they work together? What type of dynamism would the team exhibit? This and much more is on our minds as we make the 50-minute train journey out from Melbourne's Flinders Street Station. As the journey continues, the landscape begins to change: the space between houses opens up as more and more land is given over to light industry, vacant lots and waste. Once we arrive at the station, we walk a further 15 minutes, crossing a major highway, until we at last arrive at the Westgate office, which is situated in a run-down shopping centre, dominated by a large supermarket.

The shopping centre includes shops such as a chemist and a fast-food outlet, but no co-located government services such as Centrelink or VicRoads. Access by train is possible for those who are keen walkers. Some bus services travel to the shopping centre, and free parking is plentiful. As is now common with many welfare-to-work offices, the Westgate office is part of the shopping centre structure but has its own entrance from the car park. Passers-by cannot see into the office, and from inside it is also difficult to see out due to the shop-front style windows being blacked out from below shoulder height. Westgate is not a glamorous or sought-after suburb. The area has an unemployment rate of just over seven per cent, with retail, health care, social assistance and manufacturing the biggest employers. The suburb's attractiveness is most likely linked to (more) affordable, housing. The population out here is predominantly white, overwhelmingly Anglo and largely Australian born. Some cultural diversity is evident, but the rate is modest.

Westgate does appear to have a sizable population of white South African–born residents. The South African influence is evident as soon as we approach the Westgate office. The doorway is shielded by an imposing South African woman in her mid-50s, who is standing outside smoking. We later learn that this is Rose, the Westgate office's formidable receptionist. But she does not tell us her name when we introduce ourselves to her and Sharon, the site manager, who is joining her for an early morning smoke. Sporting blue jeans, white runners, and a Themis branded t-shirt, Sharon looks twenty years Rose's junior but the two seem quite close otherwise. Sharon, we later learn, has been working for Themis for seven years, starting out as a Work for the Dole coordinator, then an employment consultant, before taking over as manager of the Westgate office three and a half years ago. Since then, the site has gone from being a two-and-half to a five-star rated provider, which is no small achievement.

Command and control

The Westgate office is staffed by a site manager, two full-time case managers, one part-time case manager and a receptionist. There is no reverse marketer based at the office, but they have access to an agency-wide specialist instead. One of our first impressions on arriving is how much smaller the Westgate office space is than the Wilmore office. We quickly realise that that is one of many, many differences between the two. The office also has a somewhat unusual configuration, with only one small private office set towards the back. It appears to be a purpose-built addition to their rented space, which was probably a shop in the not-too-distant past, and is reserved for Sharon, Westgate's site manager. Unusually for such a small, enclosed room, Sharon's office has two doors: one facing directly onto the reception desk and office entrance, the other facing onto the side of the office where the employment consultants work. During our visits, these two doors are almost always open, affording Sharon a commanding view of the entranceway and any events or appointments that unfold at her colleagues' desks. For like many welfare-to-work offices, the Westgate office is mostly open plan. Jobseekers meet with their case manager at the case manager's desk, and anyone within earshot can listen to the conversation if they can decipher the hushed tones and muted expressions in which the Westgate staff speak – to each other as well as their clients. This is made more difficult again by the drone of the radio from the back of the office, which is permanently tuned to Triple M. The office atmosphere is a far cry from the hive of bustling activity that we encountered at the Wilmore office. It's more reminiscent of the steady monotony of a second-hand goods store such as Cash Converters, with its jaded furnishings and demeanour.

We enter the Westgate office just after 9 am and put our bags down on desks set aside for jobseekers to undertake online job searches. The fact that we are seated at designated jobseeker computers does not matter; nobody comes to use them. They appear old and probably slow, and the staff do not even bother with the pretence of turning them on.

Rose, the receptionist, is the person who 'greets' jobseekers when they arrive. She has a gruff manner and talks to us little over the three days of our initial site visit. Her desk faces the jobseeker waiting area. While three out of the four offices we visit have receptionists, Rose's role – and indeed Rose herself – is special. Her desk is awash with papers. To the right of her desk is a filing cabinet, above which sits oodles of paper, folders, envelopes and more. Rose does do work online. As with all providers, the staff at Westgate are obliged to run their work through the government's online computer portal. But Westgate is the only office we visit that appears to keep a parallel system of paper-based files about clients.

At the other offices we visit, any documentation that jobseekers hand over to case managers, including dole diaries, Work for the Dole attendance records, time sheets or payslips are digitised then shredded. But at the Westgate office, these paper records remain treasured artefacts that are diligently filed away. If a dispute arises between a client and a case manager about the number of outstanding hours of Work for the Dole – as we observe in one appointment – the case manager will pull out the client's paper file to check 'the evidence', despite the same information being available via the computerised case management system. But more than this, the case managers also keep paper trails of the job placements and employment outcomes they achieve each month in large ring binders on their desks. These binders are filled with clients' payslips, which are a prized commodity in the Westgate office.

During our visits, we routinely see clients dropping off their payslips to either Rose or one of the case managers. This is the documentary evidence that the office needs to claim its employment outcome payments from the department. Although the income declarations that jobseekers provide directly to Centrelink can also be used to claim employment outcomes, Sharon tells us that these are often inaccurate. So, the Westgate office captures their clients' payslips to fall back on when this happens: 'Like sometimes you'll get "oh there's no claim available, they've only declared $200 [in income from work] that fortnight." You grab the payslip, its $1,200. So, then we've got to fix that up and get the claim.' As we later learn, one of the reasons why the Westgate office's clients seem so diligent about dropping off their payslips is that they risk having their Centrelink payments stopped if they do not. Many of the jobseekers who are working, such as lone parents and those with reduced activity requirements, are working part-time and also receiving some form of income support. Provided they send through their payslips to prove they are working, they do not have to attend their fortnightly appointment with their case manager. But if they do not, they risk their payments being stopped, and the

Westgate office is particularly quick about triggering Non-Attendance Reports (NARs) when clients do not turn up. The Westgate office harks back to an older bureaucratic era in which executive control was organised through the discipline of form-filling and filing. Compared to our Wilmore office visit two weeks previously, everything at the Westgate office appears to unfold in slow motion. This is symbolised by jobseekers being required by Rose to 'sign in' on a paper clipboard as they arrive. This is treated as an important formality, and one that the jobseekers we observe have clearly become habituated to. It has echoes of people lining up at the welfare office to 'sign on' to the dole. Indeed, Rose's main tasks seem to be mailing letters and filling out forms. After watching papers come and go from Rose's desk for three days, we conclude that much of her work is probably associated with issuing participation reports (PRs) and NARs. She does this work quietly, but in apparent harmony with the site manager, Sharon. They have the air of long-term colleagues and clearly rely on each other. They are smoking buddies, showing each other funny memes that popped up online, but exchange few words. Indeed, Rose speaks in a deep, quiet, mostly inaudible tone. We sit just metres away from her but manage to catch very little of what she says to jobseekers. Hers is not the demeanour of an empathetic listener, positioned at reception to receive jobseekers with matronly love. She is, rather, Westgate's first line of defence.

To Rose's right is a long, narrow part of the office, housing the three case managers: Thomas sits at one end, Monica in the middle and Catherine at the other end. Not so much as a partition divides them. Catherine is new and has an uncertain poise about her. Monica and Thomas are old hands and appear to have worked together for many years, though they clearly have very different styles. Thomas is a large, sedentary man who speaks in a quiet, reserved way. Monica is chatty and engaged. She has just returned from an overseas trip and has much news to share. A door next to Thomas leads to a small kitchen and bathroom. Nothing special or glamorous. Set at the back is Sharon's small office with its two doors: one leading to where we sit, behind Rose, and another to Thomas' desk. Foucault himself would have been alert to the Panoptican quality of the view. As we observe over the next few days, Sharon spends most of her time at her desk but has an omniscient air. From her angled desk, she can see and hear what is happening both at reception and at Thomas, Monica, and Catherine's desks, with Catherine telling us that Sharon 'knows exactly what's going on' and 'runs a pretty tight ship'.

In the public sector, bureaucrats often talk about the importance of the 'authorising environment' that surrounds their role. While this term can describe the chain of command for public-sector workers, it can also refer to the level of risk and innovation that this chain of command permits workers to take. The 'authorising environment' at the Westgate office is slim and carefully watched by Sharon, whose approval, as we observe over the coming days, is regularly sought for all manner of decisions. Case managers in this office are not empowered, or even encouraged, to think for themselves or deviate from the script when managing their clients.

We quickly learn that the Westgate office has an unofficial, yet highly potent, hierarchy. Sharon is at the apex, followed by Rose, while Thomas and Monica jockey for third position and Catherine who is Australian-born and the self-described 'new person in the office', trails behind them.

When we first meet Catherine, she has been working in the employment services sector for only five months. Before that, she lived interstate where she provided office support to a fly-in, fly-out mining company. By contrast, Thomas has been a case manager for 22 years, while Monica has worked in Australian employment services for 12 years and previously worked for South Africa's Centrelink equivalent for 13 years. When she arrived in Australia, Monica could not get a job with Centrelink because she wasn't an Australian citizen. So, she thought 'Oh, well I'll do something else' and that's how she ended up as a case manager. Monica later tells us that she feels she has reached a glass ceiling at Themis. All that keeps her at the Westgate office is the fact that Themis is prepared to offer her part-time hours, which is a rarity in the industry. Despite the frontline employment services workforce being overwhelmingly female, as we discuss in greater detail in chapter six, our survey data suggests that only eight per cent of frontline staff are employed part-time.[1] But, as Monica tells us, her

---

1   Lewis et al. 2016.

part-time hours do not make up for the fact that Themis is 'one of the lowest paying' providers in the industry, and no longer pays any performance bonuses to staff:

> I can do all my KPIs … There is no incentive. I don't get pay rises … I've never got a pay rise since I've been here … And pretty much I'm on the top of where I can go so there's no incentive for me to stay. But I have been approached by other Jobactive agencies and that was something I've been looking at. And I'm just thinking, 'My gosh, you know.' The idea here is that I've got part-time hours. It's school hours, 9 till 3, it's perfect and it's close to my home. That is the only thing that is keeping me, really. I mean I do enjoy my caseload. I enjoy my colleagues … I love the quiet office …. [But] my husband is saying to me 'you know what, you are worth more than that'.

Sharon, Westgate's site manager, later tells us that she rewards performance in other ways. She mentions a job placement challenge on the whiteboard in the back kitchen that she has set for the month. If Thomas, Monica and Catherine make their targets they'll get some little reward 'whether it's time off, extended lunch'. Thomas tells us in an interview that Sharon pays attention to how the case managers are working 'all the time' and is in constant communication 'about our targets and how we are going'. On another occasion we visit, the kitchen whiteboard displays a league table of Themis sites, ranked by the percentage of their monthly job placement targets they are achieving. The Westgate office's target for the month is 27 job placements. The table mimics a footy tipping competition, with each site named after a football team. The site that finishes on top of the ladder wins a team lunch.

Our position in the Westgate office's invisible hierarchy is hard to place. Fifteen minutes after Rose grants us the wifi password on our first day, we lose the connection. Though the wifi password is long and complicated, we dare not ask Rose for it again. But it is not just access to the wifi password that bestows power on Westgate's receptionist. Catherine jokes, 'I passed the test', as Rose permits her access to the petty cash tin. We also witness Rose advising Catherine of a call, in her low, distant tone. When Catherine asks Rose to repeat the name of the caller, Rose says nothing. She has clearly heard the request – we all have – but Rose ignores it. After all, information is power. And as we learn later on our first day, when Rose barks at the office staff that 'no payslips have come through as yet' – the only time her voice lifts beyond the barely audible – she rarely bothers to turn around when addressing her colleagues.

Service rationing and sanctions

Whereas Catherine may be jostling for position on the case manager ladder, jobseekers are at the bottom of the office hierarchy. Their task is to navigate the service without being sanctioned or financially penalised, which is an ever-present danger in the Jobactive system as a whole and the Westgate office is no exception.

In the last quarter of 2016, when we started the research for this book, employment services providers submitted a total of just under 460,000 NARs.[2] As we discussed in chapter three, these are the most ubiquitous form of sanctioning used by Jobactive providers and result in a payment suspension until re-engagement rather than the payment deductions or financial penalties triggered by PRs and PARs. But most importantly, at the time research for this book, they are applied without any prior review by Centrelink or Services Australia. This gives providers an immediate trigger by which to exact compliance, as we witness first-hand at the Westgate office.

When Eddie, an Australian-born jobseeker in his 50s, does not arrive for a 9.30 am appointment, Catherine stops his payments within minutes. This triggers an automatic notification, prompting Eddie to show up to the office at 10.32 am. Catherine makes a big deal about fitting him into her schedule for a re-engagement, even though moments earlier she tells us that her 10.30 am appointment – Emily, a young mother with substance dependency issues – is no longer coming as she's now on a three-month medical suspension. Centrelink granted Emily the medical suspension after Catherine NARed her for missing

---

2   Department of Human Services 2017.

her last appointment. That sanction prompted Emily to go into Centrelink to get herself exempted.

As Eddie sits at Catherine's desk, he tells her that his hands are 'stuffed' and that he cannot work. It turns out that this is the very first time Eddie has ever met Catherine, which makes the speed at which she stopped his payments (less than one hour from missing his appointment) even more astonishing. Did she know what Eddie's circumstances were or the reason why he didn't show for his earlier appointment? Could she be certain that he was not in a vulnerable situation that might be aggravated by stopping his payments?

Eddie explains that he is usually on a medical suspension because of his hands, but when he last asked for a medical certificate his doctor refused because he turned up to the clinic drunk. So, now he needs to find another doctor. Catherine asks if he wants to be reassessed for DES, but Eddie just wants to keep getting his doctor's certificates. He also asks to be transferred to another Themis office, which he says is easier to get to. Catherine rings to see if they'll take Eddie, which they will. 'Okay, your payments are back on', she tells Eddie as he gets up to leave. When Eddie is gone, she tells us that there wasn't 'any point trying to keep him, he clearly just wanted to get out of here'.

As we discussed in chapter two, one of the challenges that we faced undertaking the research for this book was the high rate of churn and attrition among the Stream C jobseekers at the four sites that we studied. More than a quarter of the jobseekers that we tracked at each site fell off that site's caseload without finding employment due to either moving to another Jobactive site, being incarcerated, or, as we saw in the case of some of the Wilmore office's Tibetan-born clients, being exited from the system with no explanation. Eddie's case is just one of several examples that we directly observe at the Westgate office of clients being transferred to another Themis office or even different Jobactive provider. Indeed, seven of the Stream C jobseekers that we follow at the Westgate office transfer to another office during the period of our study. Often, like Eddie, they do so because the other offices are nearer to where they live or because they move address. Monica, for instance, tells us that their Stream C clients can often be in temporary housing and that the Westgate office is just 'like a stepping-stone' until they secure more permanent accommodation with housing agencies on the other side of the city. 'So, it's just in and out' she says. But in other cases, jobseekers are proactively encouraged to transfer by the Westgate office staff, and partly because it makes case manager's lives more convenient.

For instance, when we return to the Westgate office a year later, we see Monica arrange for two newly referred Vietnamese-born jobseekers to be immediately transferred to another Jobactive provider. The couple, who appear to be in their late 50s or early 60s, are recently arrived migrants with almost no English, and are accompanied by their teenage niece. Notably, like many of the appointments that we witness at the Westgate office, the Vietnamese couple are here for a re-engagement appointment even though they've never met Monica, or any other Westgate staff, before. In other words, their payments have been stopped for missing their first scheduled appointment at the office. Using their niece as her translator, Monica explains that they are entitled to several hundred hours of English language classes through the Adult English Migrant Program. This will satisfy their mutual obligations, as they only have part-time activity requirements due to their age. She explains that they will be better off with another provider that has a 'more accessible interpreter' and walks them through the paperwork to arrange the transfer. We later learn from Monica that the Westgate office had booked two interpreters to come that afternoon, but the interpreters cancelled at short notice. This had cost the site money, so the staff collectively decided to refer the couple to another provider that had a Vietnamese interpreter on site.

This approach to dealing with migrants with little English is in marked contrast to how the case managers at the Wilmore office tried to muddle through in such situations. While the transfer will probably benefit the Vietnamese couple, it's also indicative of how case managers and street-level organisations ration their services 'by allocating them differentially among classes of claimants'.[3] Indeed, the triaging of jobseekers by Centrelink into different streams of Jobactive is one example of how employment support services are supposedly differentiated on the basis of need in Australia. The goal of triaging, in this context, is to optimise the use of scarce employment services

_____

3   Lipsky 2010, 105.

by reserving the most intensive support for those jobseekers who need assistance the most. However, as Michael Lipsky argues, street-level workers also routinely ration services in less formal ways and for other reasons. One reason is because differentiation often assists case managers 'in managing their work loads' and in coping with the 'stresses of their jobs'.[4] Confronted with heavy workloads, case managers may decide to ration services on the basis of which clients they think they can succeed with, or which clients they wish to avoid. For instance, case managers may try to organise their caseloads in ways that limit the number of difficult, aggressive, or time-consuming clients they have to deal with.

The full-time case managers at the Westgate office have a caseload of about 150 jobseekers each, and they are supposed to meet with them every two weeks. Monica, who is part-time, still has approximately 100 jobseekers on her caseload. With limited time and resources, the Westgate office staff place a low priority on retaining clients they perceive as time-consuming or as having limited prospects of working. This is not to say that they deny such jobseekers access to any kind of support. However, if they see a chance to move them off their books they take it. Those who present with language barriers are gently encouraged to go elsewhere, along with other clients with whom the case managers lose patience.

One example is Anne, a jobseeker in her late 20s that Catherine encourages to transfer to another provider after working with her for six months. When we start following Anne, she is dealing with several barriers that she discloses to Catherine including drug use and homelessness. When we next follow-up with Catherine about Anne, she tells us that Anne had missed a couple of appointments so she 'had to cut her off'. A little over two months later, we learn that Anne is now with another provider. 'Basically, she wasn't getting anywhere with me', Catherine tells us. 'Every time I tried to push her for anything she just put up barriers and there was always something going on that she couldn't help,' she explains. So 'in the end, I offered for her to be transferred somewhere closer to her home and she just took it.'

---

4   Lipsky 2010, 106.

As we will see in more detail in chapter five, trying to get clients reassessed by Centrelink and referred into Disability Employment Services (DES) was another common strategy that we saw case managers using to ration their services. At the Westgate office, this approach is pursued with five of the Stream C jobseekers that we follow, including Lenore, an early school leaver 'with a lot going on' that commences on Catherine's caseload a few months into the study. When we start following Lenore's case, Catherine unsuccessfully tries to refer her to a hospitality training course. Catherine does not think Lenore is 'job ready' but, being an early school leaver, Lenore needs to either undertake 25 hours per week of employability skills training or some other accredited course if she is to meet her mutual obligations. Hospitality training is seen as the easier of the two options, but Lenore only lasts two days so Catherine tries to arrange for her to be reassessed. When we follow-up about Lenore two months later, we learn that her activity requirements have been reduced to part-time following the reassessment. Although Catherine has also NARed her in the interim because 'she hasn't been turning up'. It's a pattern that repeats over several months as Lenore is again NARed and even PRed for missing training activities before Catherine eventually secures a second reassessment. This time around the outcome is a referral to DES. 'So that worked, doing those ESAts and getting her reassessed', Catherine tells us, 'because she was not serviceable whatsoever.' She also tells us that the benefit for her of getting 'someone off your caseload that you can't work with' is that it 'opens another spot for someone new to come in to see what we can do'.

Cases like Anne's and Catherine's tell us not only about how the Westgate office tries to ration its services but also about the willingness of the Westgate staff to trigger sanctions; something that we see little of at the Wilmore office but which appears to be common practice throughout Jobactive. Altogether, more than 630,000 NARs, PARs and PRs were submitted by employment services providers in Australia in the last quarter of 2016, with a total of 913,511 jobseekers subject to activity-tested requirements during this period. And while some jobseekers were the subject of multiple sanction reports, the Department of Human Services' own jobseeker compliance data shows that 47 per cent of all jobseekers were reported for some form of sanctioning by providers between 1 January and 31 December 2016.[5] This rate of reporting jobseekers for compliance breaches continued over 2017 and 2018, with 45 per cent of the 870,276 activity-tested jobseekers subjected to a NAR, PAR or PR in the June 2018 quarter.[6] A new targeted compliance framework was introduced in Australia in July 2018.

At the Westgate office, almost a third of the jobseekers we tracked (12 out of 39) were NARed, PARed, or PRed for various reasons. As Westgate's site manager tells us, this might include 'if their job search isn't done satisfactorily', or 'if they don't turn up to their job search appointments without reasonable excuse, they'll get PRed for that one as well, and then obviously Work for the Dole non-attendance.' While this proportion is lower than the national rate of 46 per cent, it is important to bear in mind that the jobseekers we follow are the most disadvantaged cohort of all Jobactive clients. As such we expect to see a much lower rate of sanctioning among this Stream C cohort given the complexity of issues many such jobseekers experience, such as severe mental health issues intertwined with family violence and housing insecurity. Nonetheless, from Sharon's point of view, sanctions 'serve their purpose' and can be an effective tool, even for Stream C's:

> They get the jobseekers to actually start complying again. Say if it's the Work for the Dole activity, they'll go 'Oh okay, we're at risk of losing payment, we'll start attending.' Some might start attending for a week and then off they go, they get PRed again. It becomes a cycle until once they've lost a chunk of their payment ...

In the early days of the Australian welfare-to-work market, many of the not-for-profit, community service providers were vocal critics of devolving responsibility for sanctioning or 'breaching' jobseekers to contracted providers. Advocacy groups such as the Australian Catholic Social Welfare Commission maintained that case management of the long-term unemployed 'should not have any policing element in it.'[7] Breaching jobseekers for non-compliance was regarded as antithetical

---

5   Department of Human Services 2017.
6   Department of Human Services 2018.

to the social justice mission of faith-based and community-sector providers. However, the community-sector providers clearly managed to ease their consciences over enforcing the jobseeker compliance regime, for such sanctioning has significantly intensified over the past 20 years, as our survey data confirms.[8]

One of the questions we regularly ask of frontline staff concerns the proportion of clients they have reported for non-compliance in the previous two weeks. In 1998, at the start of Job Network, the mean proportion of clients reported for sanctioning within the previous two weeks was less than two per cent; by 2012, it had reached above 6.5 per cent; and in 2016, it was a staggering 15 per cent. We suspect that this reflects the introduction of NARs since the earlier survey periods. But our survey data also shows that there are now many more circumstances in which frontline staff say they are prepared to report clients for sanctioning compared to 20, or even 10, years ago.

Since the late 1990s, we have consistently asked frontline staff about whether they would be prepared to report clients for sanctioning in 10 different circumstances. Among other things, these circumstances include if a client refuses a suitable job offer, fails to attend an appointment, voluntarily leaves a job, refuses to apply for a suitable job, and so on. As Figure 4.1 shows, the number of circumstances in which frontline staff say they would be prepared to report clients for sanctioning has steadily increased to the point that 40 per cent of those surveyed in 2016 said they would report jobseekers for sanctioning *in all ten circumstances*, with a further 30 per cent recommending sanctions in nine out of the ten circumstances. In 1998, by contrast, fewer than five per cent of frontline staff were prepared to recommend sanctions in nine or more instances.

Given these trends in our survey data, we shouldn't be so surprised to find that the Westgate office is seemingly enthusiastic about policing jobseeker compliance. Still, it was not what we were

---

7   Fr David Cappo, national director, Australian Catholic Social Welfare Commission 1995. Our values and our skills: an ideal combination for case management. National Summit on Employment Opportunities and Case Management, Sydney, 14–15 March. Quoted in Considine 1999, 189.

8   We discuss this trend at length in McGann, Nguyen and Considine 2020.

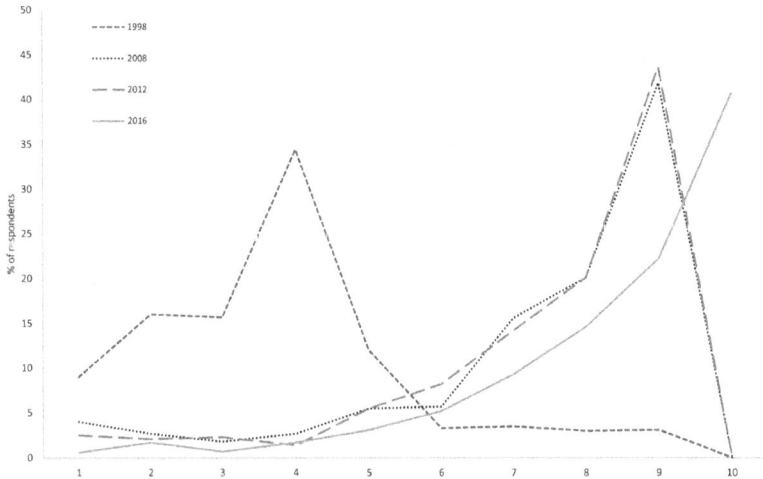

Figure 4.1. Number of circumstances (out of 10) in which frontline staff would report jobseekers for non-compliance.

expecting. This small not-for-profit on Melbourne's outer-suburban fringe is not a welcoming place of refuge for the downtrodden, but it's not a flashy corporate operation either. It is something else: a place of begrudging, meagre aid. How did Themis' Westgate office come to be this kind of environment, and how does it link to their apparent success in working with the highly disadvantaged? All our assumptions have been challenged, and once again, we are reminded that as researchers we must be led by the data.

Mission drift in Australia's welfare-to-work system

When Australia's welfare-to-work system was first privatised, the architects of what would become one of the world's biggest quasi-markets were clear that service delivery needed to be shared equally between private for-profit agencies and not-for profit agencies. They believed each would bring something distinctive and important to the system. As former Australian Prime Minister Tony Abbott famously said of faith-based not-for-profit organisations, 'There is something extra about people with faith in their hearts, and the love of God on their lips, that gives them that extra commitment to jobseekers.'[9]

This roughly equal division between for-profit and not-for-profit agencies was established with Job Network in 1998 and persisted well into the 2010s. But 20 years later, the vision of a system divided between those with corporate skills and those on a mission (often a mission from God), had faltered. In the early 2010s the Australian government, following the UK's lead, began to move towards dealing with a small number of large agencies rather than managing numerous small contracts. And becoming a large agency, with the financial risks that implies, was always going to be easier for a multinational corporation than a small church group from Sydney's inner western suburbs. As we discuss in more detail in chapter six, by the time of Jobactive, for-profits' share of the employment services market had risen to an all-time high of 45 per cent compared with 30 per cent under the previous Job Services Australia contract.[10]

Yet the demise of not-for-profit agencies has not necessarily made much difference to the system overall. Our research has shown that the service provided by most welfare-to-work agencies contracted by the Australian government has become increasingly similar over time. In the late 1990s, there were several important areas of difference between the for-profit and not-for-profit agencies delivering employment services. These included the degree to which line managers supervised and actively monitored frontline staff – it was much higher in not-for-profit agencies than for-profit firms – and the degree to which case managers reported clients for non-compliance, or sanctioning.[11] However, the areas of difference between the responses of staff in for-profit and not-for-profit agencies had markedly declined by the end of the Job Network era – and it has continued to do so. In our 2016 survey, out of the 110 or so different items that we surveyed frontline staff about, the responses of staff in for-profit and not-for-profit agencies differed significantly on only 11 items.[12] In our 2008 survey,

---

9   Quoted in Mendes 2009, 107.
10   Jobs Australia 2015.
11   Considine 1999.

by contrast, their responses differed significantly on 24 items. In short, on almost 90 per cent of the variables that we measure in our survey, there are no discernible differences whatsoever between the responses of frontline staff working in the for-profit and not-for-profit sectors. As Australia's welfare-to-work market has matured, the agencies that have been contracted to deliver employment services have come to increasingly imitate and resemble each other.[13]

The organisational sociologists Paul DiMaggio and Walter Powell coined the term 'institutional isomorphism' to describe this phenomenon of organisations within a shared field of action becoming more alike over time. Importantly, DiMaggio and Powell argue that this trend towards organisational homogenisation is driven by factors other than the competitive drive for efficiency, such as regulatory pressures from government, the dissemination of standardised business practices via industry associations and employee transfer between businesses. Over time, these isomorphic factors lead organisations to change in ways that make them 'more similar without necessarily making them more efficient'.[14] For instance, our own previous research has found that the adoption of more 'business-like' behaviour by not-for-profit employment services providers *did not* result in those organisations becoming more efficient at placing clients into employment.[15]

What DiMaggio and Powell term 'institutional isomorphism', we have tended to describe as 'herding': rather than behaving in entrepreneurial and innovative ways, the agencies contracted to deliver Australian employment services have increasingly offered the same menu of services.[16] Related to this 'herding' is the issue of 'mission drift' among the not-for-profit providers, who have come under increasing pressure 'to become more business-like'. Again, our previous survey research has highlighted that the not-for-profit sector of the Australian welfare-to-work market has become more driven by profit maximisation over time.[17] For example, in 2012, just over 23 per cent

---

12   Considine, O'Sullivan, McGann and Nguyen 2020.
13   See Considine, Lewis, O'Sullivan and Sol 2015, 53.
14   DiMaggio and Powell 1983, 147.
15   See Considine, O'Sullivan and Nguyen 2014a.
16   See Considine, Lewis, O'Sullivan and Sol 2015, 52–3.

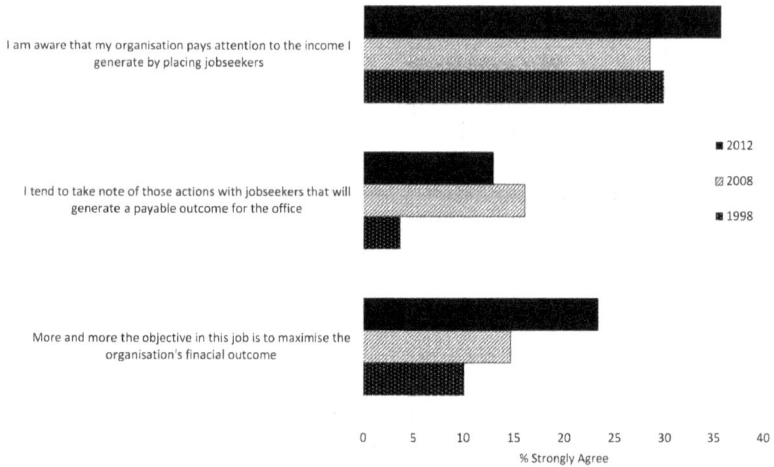

Figure 4.2. 'Mission drift' and the profit maximisation orientation of frontline staff in not-for-profit agencies.

of frontline staff working in not-for-profit agencies 'strongly agreed' that 'more and more the objective in this job is to maximise the organisation's financial outcome', while a further 44 per cent 'agreed' with the statement, a combined total of 67 per cent. In 1998, less than 45 per cent of not-for-profit frontline staff either 'agreed' or 'strongly agreed' with this statement, with only 10 per cent of that cohort strongly agreeing. As Figure 4.2 shows, similar trends towards maximising financial outcomes are also evident in the proportions of not-for-profit frontline staff who 'strongly agree' that (a) they take note of actions which will generate a payable outcome for the office and (b) they are aware their organisation pays attention to the income they generate by placing jobseekers.

All of this suggests that, from a jobseeker's perspective, it matters little whether the office they attend is owned by a church group or a US-based multinational. The Australian government strictly prescribes

---

17   See Considine, O'Sullivan and Nguyen 2014a.

the nature of the services, how much money may be spent on the jobseeker and what constitutes 'success'. (For the record, it means 26 weeks in employment.) With such a rigid system, we are well placed to ask the question: who knows and who cares if an agency is not-for-profit?

While we have been aware of the demise of the distinctiveness of not-for-profit agencies within Australia's welfare-to-work quasi-market, what greets us at the Westgate office is nonetheless a surprise. We are not emotionally or psychologically prepared for what we see. On the wall is a sign that reads 'we do not tolerate aggressive, rude, offensive or threatening behaviour'. While we can absolutely understand why aggressive behaviour is not acceptable, it is untrue that they do not tolerate rude behaviour. The staff *exhibit* rude behaviour, to each other and occasionally to the jobseekers. The feel of the Westgate office left us with many challenging questions, the answers to which were not immediately clear. Why does this agency want to help those without a job? Why do they care about the disadvantaged? If the agency itself is on a mission, what is that mission? And, perhaps most importantly for us as researchers, does it matter why an agency provides a service, so long as they do? Have government contracts fundamentally redefined what it means to be on a mission?

There was something about the drab office environment, with its seemingly downtrodden case managers, that kept begging these and many other questions. Indeed, by the end of the first morning, we are not just asking ourselves about the nature of Themis' mission, we have started openly wondering to each other how this office could possibly be a high performer of any sort, let alone in relation to highly disadvantaged jobseekers.

Do we have a (warehouse) job for you (blokes)!

Of course, Westgate is not all bad – far from it. We see many touching moments of Monica, Thomas and Catherine reaching out to jobseekers, helping them with the little things, which in turn makes the big things possible. On our first morning we see Thomas working with Alex. Alex is in his mid-20s and is well dressed, albeit in activewear. He is

Australian born to white parents and is sporting an expensive mobile phone. He is Stream C, meaning he has been categorised as the most highly disadvantaged type of jobseeker, yet his appearance does not make clear why this should be the case. We later discover that Alex is subject to a court order that requires him to undertake mandatory drug and alcohol counselling. Failure to comply could result in incarceration. While this is serious, and no doubt absolutely qualifies him as a Stream C jobseeker, it's also the kind of thing that will not be immediately evident to a potential employer. Alex has the look of someone who is eminently employable, and we can see that Thomas thinks so too. Alex has also suffered an injury to his head, due to a fall at home. But he has a doctor's certificate and is getting better. He has proactively asked a friend to help him with his CV, and we see him remind Thomas that he is qualified in 'computers and web design'. Thomas does not take a heavy-handed approach with Alex. When Alex cannot remember which jobs he has applied for, Thomas agrees to help him fill out his dole diary.

What Thomas and Alex do, freestyling the dole diary rather than adding real job applications, is technically gaming the system. But Thomas' offer of assistance is not intended to undermine the system. It is intended to stop Alex falling foul of a highly bureaucratic system, in which red tape dominates both the lives of frontline staff and jobseekers. We later learn that this is only the third time Thomas and Alex have met, which is considered a very new relationship when working with a highly disadvantaged jobseeker. What Thomas does to build trust and rapport with Alex will be critically important to whether he succeeds in placing Alex into work. A few dodgy entries on a dole diary that the government is unlikely to ever check is a small price to pay for a quick outcome.

Thomas is sure he can get Alex a job. That will be good for Alex and also good – one more outcome – for Thomas. Sanctioning Alex over paperwork would not be productive, as it would not endear Thomas to Alex and it would not build trust. We can see what Thomas is doing, and it is probably done for the right reasons. It's just unfortunate that it is actually against the rules.

While Thomas' actions are easily justified, and it seems clear that Alex will soon find a job, it is unlikely that the job will be in computers or web design. It is far more likely that Alex, just like most jobseekers who step foot in the Westgate office, will benefit from its location close to a transport logistics hub. Westgate's proximity to Melbourne and cheap land mean the surrounding area is awash with packing factories, warehouses and various forms of light industry. 'We're in a good situation', Monica explains, being close to 'a very high industrial area' and 'on the cusp of being able to access labour hire companies that are close by'. Indeed, labour hire companies are among the largest employers of Jobactive participants. Of the 20 largest recruiters of Jobactive participants from 1 June 2015 to 31 May 2018, 14 were labour hire businesses.[18] Monica tells us that many of the labour hire companies in the Westgate area now 'actually have Jobactive managers' tasked specifically with working with employment services providers to fill their vacancies. And the reason why labour hires want to work with Jobactives? From Monica's perspective, it's 'because we offer wage subsidies, that's a bonus'. Her comments speak to the way in which unemployed labour is doubly commodified under Australia's marketised employment services system. When unemployed jobseekers are placed into work through labour hire supply chains, it is not only the Jobactive provider but also the labour hire agency that earns a commission from the placement. Moreover, the availability of wage subsidies may also enable labour hire agencies to discount the prices they charge employers since any discounts can be offset by the additional revenues from government wage subsidies. In a competitive market for low-wage industrial jobs, these cost savings – paid for by taxpayers – can help labour hire agencies and recruitment firms to win business.

Of course, it's not just the ability to gain access to labour hire companies that matters. Several of the other Jobactive sites that we researched for this book also have connections to labour hire companies that they use to achieve job placements. It's the fact that the Westgate office is located in a part of Melbourne where labour hire companies are looking to fill entry-level warehousing and light industry manufacturing jobs that Jobactive participants can be competitive for. We learn from Sharon that the Westgate office has close relationships with several of the major recruitment agencies in the area 'who hold

---

18   Department of Jobs and Small Business 2018b.

most of the warehousing jobs'. These include Adapt Recruitment, Target Personally and Hume Staffing. 'So we have to keep a good relationship with them if we want to jump the queue or anything'. Importantly, even though Themis, as a provider, employs a reverse marketer to broker jobs with employers for its sites across the region, we learn that the Westgate office holds these relationships with the labour hire companies directly. In other words, it does not have to go through the reverse marketer who works out of another Themis office but can refer its own clients directly to warehousing and labour hire vacancies as they arise. Monica explains that it stems from the fact that they did not have a reverse marketer before so the site 'had to broker our own jobs'. To this day, she says she does not 'give out anything' to any other site unless agencies are looking for 50 people or something, and Westgate cannot fill those vacancies from its own client pool. In blunt terms, 'for us, the advantage is to place our own, not other sites' jobseekers.

Monica sees the proximity to warehousing jobs as a key point of difference between the Westgate office and other Jobactive sites that 'are not close to having that advantage'. It's a perspective shared by Thomas. When we ask him why he thinks the Westgate office is one of the best-performing Jobactive sites for Stream C jobseekers, he speculates that it might have to do more with the local labour market than anything particularly innovative about how they are supporting their clients:

> I've worked in different areas and it could be the area we sit in … has a lot of warehousing jobs. There's a lot of them jobs. It could be the team. I could be gracious and say it's because of the great team that we have here that we work with them, we've got high expectations. But we've had a couple of good workers that have moved to different areas and their site might not be going so well. But it's not because the person has changed the role that they are doing. They're still a good worker. It might be the area or the clientele that they have.

Indeed, one of the very first times we observe Thomas meeting one of his Stream C clients is in relation to a warehousing job. Les is the picture of an Aussie 'battler'. He's in his early 30s and is dressed in blue jeans and a high-vis vest. Les has just been to a pre-employment training session the day before for a container loading and warehousing job, and Thomas is keen to hear how it went. 'Did you get dressed up in your gear?', Thomas wants to know. He's referring to the fact that Les had been into the office yesterday morning to purchase some work clothing to wear to the session. There's a Big W in the shopping centre that the Westgate office uses to kit its clients out with work gear. Thomas then wants to know if it was an 'all day' thing 'or a couple of hours'. Les explains about how it was an induction session to go through 'correct lifting, safety, all those things' and that he had been through it all before with another labour hire that Thomas had sent him to. Les does not know if he got the job or not but is optimistic about his chances.

As we learn over the course of the research for this book, pre-employment inductions and training sessions are part and parcel of life on Jobactive for jobseekers, but they're no guarantee of employment. They're just a series of hoops that jobseekers must jump through for bulk employers, who use them as screening sessions to weed out candidates they think might be problematic or unreliable. It's a 'try before you buy' kind of approach to recruitment that has its efficiencies for employers. Much of the rest of the appointment is taken up with organising a police check for Les should the agency want a background check. As Thomas does this, he also tells Les about another labour hire company that is hiring for warehouse positions. The company specialises in supply chain recruitment, and we later learn from Thomas that some of his other clients have recently been hired by them. Les already has a forklift licence that Thomas helped him to get so Thomas encourages him to just cold call the company to see if they are looking for forklift drivers. As the appointment begins to wind up, Thomas also notices on the computer that Les is due for his annual Work for the Dole activity. He organises a referral to a local charity shop, beginning next week. If Les gets the job, he does not have to go but otherwise he has no choice. 'I'll be working by then', Les assures Thomas.

Les is just one among many, many jobseekers at the Westgate site that we observe being referred for warehousing or labour hire jobs and who are in possession of a forklift licence. Indeed, almost any jobseekers willing to consider warehousing work are put forward by the office for a two-day forklift training course, delivered externally by a private Registered Training Organisation, which is paid for from the office's pool of Employment Funds. If jobseekers land an interview or work trial, they are also routinely kitted out with work clothes, high-vis vests and boots, again, paid for from the Employment Funds.

Another example from Thomas' caseload is Tony, an Australian-born jobseeker in his early 30s who is in Stream C because of an injured back. Thomas helped him to get a forklift licence and then Tony eventually got himself a forklift warehousing job in a place where Tony had worked 'spasmodically' before. There were periods where Tony wasn't attending any training or appointments, so the Westgate office threatened to cut his payments if he did not show up for weekly job-search appointments. As Sharon, the site manager tells us, we 'told him what he had to do and if he didn't do it, what was going to happen - he'd have no payment. So he went off and got his own job.' That forklift warehousing job turned into a full 26-week employment outcome for the Westgate office, as did a warehousing job secured by Mark, one of Monica's Stream C clients. Like Tony, Mark is a young Australian-born jobseeker. He is in his late 20s but has been out of work for the past four years due to some mental health issues and what sounds like a nervous breakdown. For most of that time he was in DES before being reassessed by Centrelink and referred into Jobactive. He arrives on the Westgate caseload with previous warehousing experience and gains employment quickly after Monica starts working with him and refers him for a labour hire position:

> I referred him off to a [labour hire] position. He failed to attend. So I got him in, and I said 'Listen, we need to discuss your capacity to work, if there's any other issues going on'. He said 'No, he wants to go back into the warehousing role.' That's where he was before ... So he just applied for three or four positions and he actually got one in a warehouse. So, he's gone back to the same role that he left say four or five years ago, and he's been there ever since.

A pattern is beginning to emerge about how Westgate is achieving its success. Indeed, in the part of Melbourne where Themis' Westgate office is situated, 10 per cent of the workforce are employed in the industrial sector classified as Transport, Postal or Warehousing.[19] Among men, that proportion is even higher at 13 per cent of the local male labour force. These are essentially logistics and storage jobs, the sort of warehousing and forklift jobs that Tony, Mark, and Les have been looking to get. To put this in perspective, these jobs account for only four per cent of total employment in the part of Melbourne where the Wilmore office is located – and even less in the areas where the other two Jobactive sites that we research are based. Structural transformations in the economy since the 1990s, such as the offshoring of heavy manufacturing and transition to a service-oriented economy, mean that these types of jobs have dried up in many parts of Australia, but not in Westgate. The presence of strong warehousing and supply chain infrastructure also makes the Westgate area a good choice of location for light manufacturing industries, and a further 10 per cent or so of the local labour force is employed in manufacturing for the light industries that have developed alongside Westgate's logistics hubs. Indeed, just two months after we first visit the Westgate office, Alex, the younger jobseeker that Thomas helped with his dole diary, goes on to find full-time employment as a powder-coater – a job that he secures through his cousin who is a supervisor at the firm. Again, it's a placement that the Westgate office turns into a full 26-week employment outcome.

What is notable about the warehousing and manufacturing sectors is the gender segregation of the workforce: women account for only about a quarter of workers. This captures a much broader problem of occupational segregation in Australia, which we return to at length in chapter six. As the sociologists Kate Huppatz and Susan Goodwin observe, 'Australia features a highly segregated workforce where certain occupational spaces appear to privilege particular gendered bodies and dispositions.'[20] This leads to a concentration of many Australian men and women in 'own-sex' industries such as health care and social assistance for women, and construction, manufacturing, transport, postal and warehousing for men. This occupational segregation reflects how gender and class intersect to limit the employment options

---

19 This is based on ABS Labour Force Region Data (3A4) – August 2016, for the area of Melbourne where Themis' Westgate office is located. Australian Bureau of Statistics 2016.
20 Huppatz and Goodwin 2013, 292.

available to workers in Australia, and employment services providers are often complicit in reinforcing this gender patterning of employment pathways. Indeed, almost all the jobseekers that we observe at the Westgate office who are referred for warehousing jobs or forklift licences *are men*. Usually, as with Tony, Les and Mark, they are *young men* in the prime of their working lives. Altogether, seven of the Stream C jobseekers that we follow at the Westgate office continue to a full 26-week employment outcome. Of these, five are men and none are over 50 years of age. Indeed, four of the five men are aged 40 or under.

None of the female jobseekers that we observe or follow at the Westgate office are put forward for warehousing jobs or referred to any of the labour hire companies that the site has 'some rapport with', as Sharon, the site manager puts it. Instead, Westgate's female clients were more likely to be directed towards hospitality or, like the Wilmore office, cleaning jobs. One of Monica's clients that we follow, Alicia – a young woman who is in Stream C due to suffering from depression and anxiety – is referred for a casual cleaning position in a pub. The job comes through about six months into the study after a jobseeker that the Westgate office had working there leaves for full-time work elsewhere. The job is for 15 hours per week, spread over five mornings, and suits Alicia's part-time requirements. So, Monica puts Alicia forward for a work trial, and she gets the job. However, the job falls through several months later when Alicia goes overseas for dental treatment that she has been waiting two years in Australia for. Another one of Monica's clients, Andrea, also temporarily finds casual work in a pub shortly after the Westgate office pays for her to do short courses in Responsible Service of Alcohol and Gaming. Again, however, the job falls through after several months. Andrea becomes pregnant and as her pregnancy continues, her shifts begin to dry up until the employer 'wouldn't offer her any more [shifts]'. 'So, a bit of discrimination there,' in Monica's view.

Clutching for answers

Our case study of the Westgate office is small scale and exploratory, so we must be cautious about generalising too much from what we observed or from the jobseekers that we followed at the site. However, the data we gather do suggest that the Westgate office is having less success with its female clients than male jobseekers. Only a ratio of one in seven female jobseekers that we follow at the Westgate office go on to sustain 26 weeks or more of employment compared with one in five of the male jobseekers that we follow. This is likely connected to the highly gendered labour market that the Westgate office is located in, which in turn provides the clue to the site's overall success – proximity to a supply of warehousing and light manufacturing jobs that suit men in Stream C who are willing to drive forklifts and to take low-skilled, labour hire jobs. This seems to be the ingredient driving the Westgate office's success. There is little else remarkable about the site that is clearly the reason for its achievements. The staff here seem neither motivated by any sense of mission or financial reward. Morale is low, as evidenced by Monica's flirtations with leaving the company and the muted conversation between staff. The case managers are kept on a tight leash by Sharon, Westgate's site manager, along with the clients who must tread carefully and supply all manner of paperwork if they are to avoid having their payments cut by case managers who are all too willing to NAR them if they are late. The gloomy air and strange office hierarchy saps any motivation or effort, and we are also struck by the lack of external stimulus. Catherine does not pick up the phone and call a homeless shelter. Thomas is not working closely with Themis' in-house trainer, and Sharon is not chatting with someone from the regional Chamber of Commerce to get a sense of what the local economy might be doing. As Wilmore has shown us, and the Cove will later confirm, a vibrant office is an externally engaged office. It is the coming and going, the seeking advice, the referring that makes an office buzz. But all that is missing from Westgate. If we are right about the key to the Westgate office's success, it's not an ingredient that lends itself to being replicated in other labour market contexts or employment regions. For, despite Sharon's best efforts to 'command and control', it depends on factors that neither frontline staff nor employment services providers can exercise much control over.

5
'Downtown' Crompton

We approach the first day at our third study site with a little more caution than before. With Wilmore we were nervous but excited, not knowing what to expect. By the time we headed out to Westgate we thought we knew what to expect, but our assumptions were soon challenged. So as we meet outside Fox's Crompton office we are more subdued. Westgate has taught us that it's best to assume that we know little of local conditions and let the office and its staff reveal itself to us. Will Crompton be like our first site: collegial, a team pulling as one? Or will it be like Westgate: dark, intimidating and a little unwelcoming? Or will it be something entirely different from both? The Crompton office is also our first for-profit provider. Will their corporate status make a difference to how they do business, or indeed how they welcome us into the office?

We gather outside a little after 9 am. We meet at the site as it is no more than a good walk, or a short ride, from our own university office. This first meeting is at the height of summer, so the morning is already hot. We soon learn that this is not a normal day at the Crompton office. The heat means that the phones were out the day before and remain out on our first morning. Phone and the internet are critical to providers' work. But neither is completely reliable in Australia, even in the centre of very large cities. 'It's chaos here' is something we are told many times over on that first morning.

Yet despite the heat and technology-induced chaos, the Crompton office is doing steady business on the morning of our arrival. Once settled at our temporary desks, we begin the process of trying to work out what makes the office tick. One of the first things we notice, something that immediately marks the Crompton office out from the rest, is that even though it is hot outside, we are cool as cucumbers in this airy corporate office with windows for walls. On the opposite side of the desk, reclining in his leather swivel chair, is a lightly tanned man in his mid-to-late 40s. The site manager, Trev is wearing black slacks, a tight-fitting t-shirt and a broad smile. If this were a bar, he would be the barkeep with his laidback demeanour and protruding biceps. The large pane of tinted glass behind him frames a view of the tall apartment building across the street. Unlike the Westgate office and our fourth office at the Cove, the Crompton staff do not look out onto a flat tarmac parking lot. The apartments that neighbour this office are so close that we can almost see into the residents' kitchens as Trev begins to tell us about what makes Fox Personnel different from other providers. 'I would say the culture,' he says, comparing Fox to Shelter, the not-for-profit agency that he came from a little over two years ago. 'They're very left, whereas we're sort of middle-to-right.' At Shelter, he says that the emphasis was more on supporting clients into housing and education, whereas Fox's philosophy is 'Without a job you won't have a house'. As a manager, he mainly looks for staff with 'some business acumen' rather than a social work orientation, which he dismisses as being about 'let's not get them a job, let's look after all their other issues'. At the end of the day, he says in a matter-of-fact way, Fox's clients have 'signed a *Social Security Act* that requires them to look for work and that's what we sort of do best'.

The rise of the for-profits

Employment services are Fox's core business. The agency is one of an increasing number of for-profit agencies delivering welfare-to-work contracts in Australia. These Jobactive contracts were estimated to be worth a combined $7.6 billion for the period 2015 to 2020, making welfare-to-work services the largest government procurement activity, in dollar terms, outside of defence.[1] Since the introduction of Jobactive, the proportion of employment services delivered by for-profit businesses has increased to about 45 per cent of all contracts, compared with 30 per cent under the Rudd–Gillard's government's Job Services Australia program.[2] One reason behind this corporatisation of employment services was a change in how the government paid providers. The Abbott government followed the lead of David Cameron's Tory government in the UK, moving to a mostly payment-by-results system: paying providers for the employment outcomes they achieve rather than the services they deliver.

While outcome payments have been a feature of the Australian system since it was first contracted out in the mid-1990s, Jobactive significantly intensified the emphasis on payment-by-results. Under Job Services Australia, almost two-thirds of provider payments were for fixed servicing and administration fees, but under Jobactive, outcome payments increased to more than half of all payments available to providers.[3] This adjusted payment model placed much greater financial risk onto providers.[4] Providers would now largely have to self-fund the delivery of employment services upfront, through borrowing or investing capital against forecast, but uncertain, future outcome payments.

Outcomes-based contracting is attractive to policymakers because it transfers the financial risks of underperformance to providers, supposedly ensuring that governments only pay for 'what works'.[5] However, one major concern about this way of contracting social services is the risk that the financial emphasis on outcomes will encourage creaming by providers, where they focus their resources on clients they think can be placed into employment most easily and at least cost. Conversely, jobseekers who are perceived as more difficult to

---

1 Figures reported in Henriques-Gomes 2019.
2 Jobs Australia 2015.
3 See Australian National Audit Office 2017.
4 For a broader discussion of the impact of outcomes-based contracting on the role of not for profit organisations in delivering social services see Shields and Taylor 2014.
5 For a detailed discussion of the advantages and disadvantages of outcomes-based contracting see Finn 2012.

place risk being 'parked' – kept on the books but given no assistance – if providers think achieving an employment outcome with those clients is too difficult or costly.

Some evidence exists that Jobactive's outcomes-based payment model may have motivated creaming and parking. For example, official data shows that the average cost paid by the government per employment outcome in 2016–17 was just $1,453, more than a thousand dollars below the department's own target of $2,500 per outcome.[6] This saving could mean that providers were placing their clients into jobs more quickly than the government anticipated, meaning they received less fixed payments than forecast. But another possibility is that providers achieved a higher number of outcomes than forecast with clients who had lower value outcome payments attached to them (because they were in 'easier to place' service streams or unemployed for a shorter duration) and fewer outcomes with clients who attracted higher value outcome payments.

The contract's differential payment model, offering higher outcome payments for jobseekers in higher service streams (B or C) and who are unemployed for longer was supposed to guard against this risk. However, a key challenge with differential payment models is ensuring that the outcome payment for placing more difficult clients is large enough to offset the additional resources that providers will need to spend to place those clients into work. Or alternatively, these payments for the occasional, opportunistic success story in the Stream C band need to be high enough to improve the profit average overall, given the smaller rate of return on the two other streams. During the Senate inquiry into Jobactive, providers argued that the outcome payments for Stream C clients were 'not sufficient to meet the investments needed to support training and find jobs' for those participants.[7] Perhaps this

---

6   Department of Jobs and Small Business 2017.
7   Senate Education and Employment References Committee 2019. This point was made by Michael Kolomyjec, Group Executive of atWork Australia, a Jobactive provider. Similar points have also been repeatedly made by providers in the UK, in relation to the Work Programme's differential pricing model. See House of Commons Work and Pensions Committee 2015. For a discussion of the relationship between outcome payments and problems of creaming and parking in the UK context, see Carter and Whitworth 2015.

could also be a self-defence strategy for an industry which spends very little on this group, as we saw in most of our cases.

Another concern about contracting social services via payment-by-results is the danger that it will skew the quasi-market in favour of larger, for-profit providers.[8] This arises because payment-by-results exposes providers to fluctuation in their payments and thus to more financial risk, which many smaller, grassroots organisations are either unprepared or unable to take on.[9] They simply do not have the capital reserves or access to borrowing needed to 'buy in' to the market. This was compounded by the Jobactive contracts substantially increasing the geographical size of the service delivery areas being put out to tender. When the Jobactive tender results were announced, the impact of these changes to the composition of Australia's employment services market were obvious for all to see. While this had already happened in the UK, Australian policymakers had not yet learnt that a minor and seemingly sensible adjustment to the policy settings – linking payment to performance – would advantage for-profit providers and immediately disrupt the range of service providers willing to enter the market.

Australia's Jobactive system became dominated by the for-profit providers MAX Employment, Advanced Personnel Management (APM) and Sarina Russo, alongside the global not-for-profit organisation the Salvation Army, giving the employment services industry its very own 'Big Four'. Between them, these four companies operated three out of every 10 Jobactive offices in Australia in 2015.[10] These included many of the larger Jobactive sites, meaning that the proportion of Jobactive participants serviced by these agencies was higher again. Indeed, according to *The Guardian*, MAX Employment

8   See Bennett 2017.
9   For a broader discussion of the impact of outcomes-based contracting on the role of not-for-profit organisations in delivering social services see Shutes and Taylor 2014.
10   According to data published by Jobs Australia, MAX, APM, Sarina Russo and the Salvation Army (the 'Big 4' Jobactive providers) were cumulatively contracted to operate 511 out of the 1,719 Jobactive sites across Australia in July 2015. See Jobs Australia 2015.

alone was managing about 40 per cent of the Jobactive caseload in May 2019.[11]

Fox Personnel is a smaller for-profit agency delivering Jobactive and the only for-profit provider that formed part of our research for this book. This was not because we deliberately avoided for-profit agencies; we made a concerted effort to include for-profit providers in the research. But as we began the process, we discovered that only a small proportion of 'best-performing' Jobactive sites available for us to study were for-profits. We do not know whether the best-performing offices in Victoria and New South Wales were predominantly run by not-for-profits or whether high-performing for-profit providers simply declined to be involved in the study. Either way, despite our best efforts, we were only able to engage one for-profit in this research.

Finding for-profit agencies to be part of our ongoing research work has been extremely tricky. In 2011, and again in 2020, we published research suggesting that very little differentiates for-profit and not-for-profit service providers.[12] But embedded in both those articles is the spread of survey participants: in 2008 we surveyed 392 for-profit staff and 1056 not-for profit staff, and this pattern has repeated in each survey since. For some reason not-for-profits are more willing to give their time to us: perhaps they feel it is part of their mission, or perhaps they are less worried about giving away trade secrets or commercially sensitive intellectual property that they rely on to compete in the market.

Into the great wide open

Tucked away on the first floor of a corner building on a busy urban street, this Jobactive site is a stone's throw from the local Centrelink office, like the Wilmore office discussed in chapter three. A little further on is the large Crompton Point shopping centre. Compared with Wilmore's shopping centre, its shops are more functional than fashionable, but it's a significant upgrade on the shopping centre that

---

11   Henriques-Gomes 2019.
12   Considine, Lewis and O'Sullivan 2011; Considine, O'Sullivan, McGann and Nguyen 2020.

the Westgate office calls home. There's a cinema, several supermarkets, a collection of international eateries in the food hall and even a travel agent. These consumer complexes are fast becoming the backdrop to the Australian experience of welfare-to-work, the public transport connections into these centres making them strategic locations for Jobactive providers.

Entrance to the Crompton office is via a narrow stairwell door sandwiched between two shopfronts. While a lift runs to the first floor of the building, the entranceway is stepped off the street and we cannot see a wheelchair ramp. The stairway to the first-floor office is steeply inclined. Once these steps have been ascended, the office's expansive reception area lies behind a further door. It's by far the largest of the waiting areas that we visit. The entire Westgate office would almost fit into this waiting area, which is about 15 metres long and 10 metres wide. Both the Australian and Aboriginal flags are displayed on the reception walls, along with the usual array of Jobactive posters and guidelines. A large flat-screen TV, the first one we've seen in a Jobactive reception area, advertises various relevant information to waiting jobseekers. This includes details about the location of résumé and cover letter templates on the office's computers, upcoming training courses at various Fox Personnel sites and notices about Work for the Dole placements.

Cathy, a polite and softly spoken women in her 50s, is on the reception desk when we arrive just after 9 am. She greets us warmly and does her best to make us feel at home. This is a welcome relief after our experience at the Westgate office, when we felt outright hostility to our presence. Cathy directs us to the kitchen, at the back left-hand corner of the office, if we want to make coffee during the day. She also shows us where they keep the keys to the bathroom, which is reserved exclusively for staff. The kitchen itself is quite a large room, with a table that can seat six people quite comfortably. Food has an important place at the Crompton office. It's the only site we visit with a dedicated space for eating meals, and we notice that the consultants generally take their lunch breaks in pairs, eating together in the kitchen.

At the far right-hand side, as we enter, is a doorway to the Crompton office's training room. It's a vast, brightly lit room that can easily accommodate about 30 people in a workshop configuration. A bank of four computer terminals runs the length of one wall; unlike at the Westgate office, these are generously spaced and frequently used. Another room of computers sits on the opposite side of the reception area. The site manager's office and another large glass-walled interview room are located beside that computer room. Both look out on the reception area, but they are well insulated for sound.

The left-hand side of the reception area, as you walk in, opens to an even more expansive open-plan area where the employment consultants sit. It's reminiscent of a call centre in size, but the consultants' workspaces take up only a fraction of the available office real estate. All four consultants share a pod of adjoining desks, separated by thin partitions. We are shown to a large boardroom-style meeting table, which sits opposite the pod of consultants' desks and is concealed from the waiting area by the narrow partition wall behind Cathy's reception desk. A large 'performance whiteboard' hangs on the wall behind us, tracking each consultant's job placements for the month, the stream that placed jobseekers are in, and whether jobs are full-time, part-time or casual. Only placement data is written on the board, not the actual performance targets for staff. But, as we will see, the staff at the Crompton office are subject to more intensive performance monitoring than at the other agencies we observe, which filters through to differences in how they approach working with their more difficult clients.

The Crompton area itself is close to the city, about 20 minutes by tram through hipster streets and bohemian suburbs. It's a housing commission area in the throes of gentrification. Disused warehouses are being upcycled into micro-breweries, studio galleries and loft apartments. But the corner of Crompton where Fox Personnel is located has yet to give way to the artisans and urban professionals. It's a largely migrant area, with a sizable South-East Asian and North African–born population. The office staff reflect the area's ethnic diversity: two of the office's four case managers, Katsy and Shanthi, were born overseas in different parts of Asia. So too was Rachel, a life-skills coordinator who works at the site two days per week. It's the only office that we visit where we witness appointments being conducted in a language other than English. At the Wilmore office, as we noted in chapter three, migrants were encouraged to 'practise' English by avoiding the use of interpreters. However, the Crompton office benefits from the fact that Katsy speaks four languages, one of which is an Asian language spoken by a significant proportion of the office's clients. The Crompton office also books in an interpreter for three hours on Friday mornings to translate for clients who speak languages that Katsy lacks.

Katsy is one of the office's two Stream B and C consultants. The other is Belinda, who is Australian born, of European descent. Both are in their mid-to-late 30s and have a caseload of around 100 clients each. Shanthi and Jen, the two other employment consultants, are slightly younger and work predominantly with the Stream A clients. Overall, the Crompton office's consultants are slightly younger than at the Westgate office, which is reflected in their more sociable and vibrant demeanour. The office dynamic is much more like the Wilmore office's, though we will learn that Crompton has a very different approach to working with jobseekers than Wilmore's person-centred way.

Besides language barriers, the other major issue that the Crompton office case managers must contend with is drug and alcohol addiction. Trev tells us of a deepening 'ice epidemic' that he perceives has broken out across the Jobactive Stream C caseload. Consequently, the government's targets for placing Stream Cs, he says, are 'just ridiculous': 'Centrelink send them here, they're high as a kite, and we're telling them, "Here you go, sign this piece of paper. Now you start looking for work."'

This is brought home to us during our first hour at the Crompton office, when the sister of a jobseeker who has an appointment later that day emails through a medical certificate on his behalf. The jobseeker is in hospital after almost dying. Belinda, his case manager, suspects a drug overdose, but does not suspend his payments because of the medical certificate. 'NARing' jobseekers for missing appointments is, however, routine at the Crompton office, with 10 of the 28 jobseekers we track at the office having their payments suspended in this way. While at the Wilmore office, we observed staff calling jobseekers to ascertain why they had missed appointments before stopping their payments, the Crompton office's consultants prefer to sanction first and ask questions later. It is up to jobseekers to make contact and explain why they were unable to attend their appointment. 'I think they have to take the responsibility,' Katsy tells us when we ask about her NARing clients. Belinda says that her strategy is to schedule jobseekers' appointments for the day after clients are due for their fortnightly reporting to

Centrelink. That way she can see if her clients are in work – by checking the income and hours they are declaring to Centrelink. If they are working, jobseekers know they do not have to come for an appointment. But, as Belinda explains, 'if they aren't reporting their hours, or enough hours, I NAR them if they don't come to their appointment'.

Tight-knit and 'can do'

The Crompton office consultants clearly enjoy each other's company and have not been burnt out by the industry, even though both Katsy and Jen have worked in employment services for almost a decade. Other members of staff refer to them as 'the girls', and the group radiates an infectious energy. We observe them frequently being physically affectionate with each other. When the consultants are not meeting with clients or catching up on administration, they spend much of their time talking about all manner of entertainment: new restaurants, shopping, online dating apps, the latest YouTube videos. We soon learn that they are all friends on Facebook and socialise together, enjoying weekends away as well as regular after-work drinks. Cathy, the Crompton office's measured receptionist, is probably old enough to be their mother, but she involves herself in the group dynamic in her own quiet way.

This strong culture is no accident. It has been carefully cultivated by Trev, the site manager, who has been working in the industry for 15 years. He was previously a hospitality manager, and this background is visibly reflected in the importance that the Crompton office attaches to collective meals and after-work drinks. When he began managing the site at the start of the Jobactive contract, Trev brought Cathy and Katsy across from the not-for-profit provider where they all once worked. Shelter had lost its employment services contract, so Cathy and Katsy were more than happy to come with 'the Boss', as they semi-jokingly call him. Belinda also worked previously with Trev at another site before she was hired as a Stream B/C consultant at the Crompton office. So, there is a strong bond among the Crompton office staff that has been carefully cultivated. It's also watered regularly through weekly office drinks. No appointments are booked for after 3 pm on Fridays. This is quarantined time, when Trev, Cathy and the employment consultants gather around the office's meeting table to unwind over ritual drinks. This management style is a far cry from the command-and-control engine of the Westgate office, partly by necessity, since Trev also manages a second Fox Personnel office. He has to trust them to operate unsupervised. He is only onsite at the Crompton office two days per week. The rest of the time Katsy, his most trusted lieutenant, doubles as the office's team leader – running group meetings and setting the daily strategy for consultants to work with clients. Trev is charismatic in style, anchoring his managerial authority in loyalty rather than fear. He tells us that when his father passed away just a few months ago, 'every one of my staff attended' the funeral. 'Stuff like that,' he says, 'makes you know why you are a five-star organisation.' We almost never observe Trev directing his staff about how to do their jobs, being much less 'hands-on' than the managers at other sites. 'Very rarely would I have to see a jobseeker,' he tells us, leaving it largely to the consultants to manage their caseloads. Unlike Sharon, the Westgate office's 'all seeing eye', we never witness Trev intervening in client appointments or telling the consultants what to do about individual jobseekers. Nor do we observe the consultants looking to Trev for advice when they confront administrative difficulties. Instead, they are far more likely to seek guidance from each other whereas Trev is mostly busy 'with the operations and the finances and everything else that goes on behind the scenes'.

Our immediate impression is of a tight-knit staff with a 'can-do' attitude. Problems are there to be solved, such as when the office's phones and internet go down on the first morning of our visit. With so much of consultants' roles reliant on entering data into IT-based case management systems, an internet disconnection for a Jobactive provider is like a power failure at a hospital: it threatens to shut critical systems down, making work impossible. However, the Crompton office staff are unfazed by the telecommunications blackout. They quickly come up with the solution of tethering their computers and diverting the office phone to Trev's mobile. Since the consultants are equipped with laptops plugged into docking stations, rather than fixed desktop computers, tethering their devices to the mobile internet is fairly convenient. But even with laptops, it is difficult to envisage a public bureaucracy responding to a telecommunications blackout with such speed and minimum fuss. On the occasions when we have presented seminars to the department in Canberra, we have always been required to email our presentations in advance, because uploading slides via an external USB stick, like we do in almost every other context, presents too much risk of contamination for the department's IT security. The thought of a multimillion-dollar contract being run off a mobile network would surely keep Canberra's public administrators awake at night.

Meetings with clients happen in the open-plan setting of the consultants' desks, which is not unusual for a Jobactive provider. However, these exchanges are made a little more public at the Crompton office by the two-by-two configuration of desks and low height of the partitions between them. At other offices, staff would at least have to walk a short distance to colleagues' desks if they wanted to interrupt or join a meeting. At the Crompton office, any one of the four consultants can easily insert themselves into colleagues' meetings with clients by standing up. This is a phenomenon we repeatedly observe. Formally, jobseekers are managed by their individual employment consultant but, in practice, they are often 'worked on' by multiple staff simultaneously.

Early in the afternoon on our second day, we sit in on an appointment with Ray, one of Belinda's Stream C clients. Ray is in his mid-to-late 40s, suffers from anger management issues and is suspected of being a heroin user, although it's not something he admits to. When we meet Ray, he has just jumped bail interstate and is in trouble for violating a community corrections order. The issue relates to some of his seven children, who are living with foster parents that Ray accuses of neglect. Despite these issues, Belinda says she has 'a soft spot' for Ray, telling us afterwards that 'he's genuinely not a bad person ... he just gets himself into bad situations'.

Ray is one of the Stream C clients that Belinda has been working with the longest, and she wants to send him to Centrelink for a reassessment. She does not see Ray as ready to work, given all the issues he's dealing with. When she asks him during the appointment what they are going to do for work this year, he tells her that he cannot 'do nothing for work' because he's got no keys, no wallet and is dealing with the corrections system. 'We need an assessment done,' she tells him in response. She talks to him about the office's life-skills coordinator,

Rachel, who can help with organising this for him and seeing if they can get Ray into DES – or, at the very least, getting his activity requirements reduced. Hearing the word 'disability', Ray, who presents with no obvious impairment or health issue, seems hesitant. At this point of the conversation, Katsy stands up from her desk to join the conversation. She leans over to reinforce Belinda's recommendation, explaining that they can refer Ray directly for an employment services assessment because he is already in Stream C. She comes over with a medical certificate form that Ray needs to take to his GP to organise the assessment. Standing over him and speaking firmly, she tells Ray: 'Look … for us to help you, can you come in for your next appointment and we'll do an assessment.' Ray's next appointment is going to be with Rachel, the life-skills coordinator, in two days' time. In the meantime, he must take the form to his GP, who can fill it out with the required medical evidence. After the appointment with Ray, Belinda explains that Rachel has a good understanding of what sort of evidence, mainly medical, jobseekers need to be successfully reassessed by Centrelink. Rachel sends clients to their reassessment appointment armed with a cover letter outlining the reasons why they should either be up-streamed to DES or have reduced participation requirements applied to them, at the very least.

This is just one of the many examples we observe of the Crompton office consultants jointly working their cases. Earlier that morning we observe Katsy and Belinda casually swapping cases. Belinda approaches Katsy to take over one of her clients, Charlie, who she feels at the end of her tether with. Belinda suspects Charlie is working cash-in-hand and not declaring it, but she has not been able to prove it. Katsy, who is standing in the middle of the office when Belinda makes the request, is more than happy to take on the case. We hear her proclaiming loudly to Belinda and everyone else in earshot that 'if you want a job, come to Katsy'. Belinda protests that the issue is not about finding Charlie a job but about getting him to declare that he is already working. This prompts Katsy to reframe her position: 'He doesn't want to declare, so you know what? Bam!' As we soon learn, 'bam' is a short-hand Katsy uses to signal that she will come down heavy on a jobseeker by enforcing compliance to the letter.

Suspicious minds

The suspicion that clients are probably working cash-in-hand jobs begins to strike us as an accusation that the Crompton office consultants commonly make against their clients. While we certainly encounter such suspicions among staff at the Wilmore and Westgate offices, we do not hear or observe them anywhere near as frequently as we do at the Crompton office. Perhaps the Crompton consultants are simply more open and upfront with us about how they view their clients. Ethnographic fieldwork of this kind always has the danger of causing an 'observer effect', when people change their behaviour in response to being watched, or tell you in interviews what they think you want to hear, instead of what they really believe. We do not think an observer effect was too much of an issue during the research for this book, given the comprehensive nature of what we were permitted to see. If they were going above and beyond how they would normally work while we were observing them, this was not obvious to us in any way.

A lurking distrust of clients seems to us to be almost a default setting among the Crompton office's consultants, who frequently form and express moral judgements about whether clients can be trusted or are participating in employment services in good faith. We also witness multiple conversations in which staff collectively strategise to weed out clients they suspect are already working. The case management decisions they make seemed to be based as much on their judgements about clients' morality as they are on their interpretation of policy guidelines or their understanding of clients' needs.

This observation resonates with previous studies of frontline workers or street-level bureaucrats. Steven Maynard-Moody and Michael Musheno, two American scholars who have done extensive ethnographic research with street-level bureaucrats, argue that frontline decision-making is primarily a form of normative rather than administrative reasoning. This means that case managers firstly size up their clients as people, then base their administrative decisions 'on their judgement of the worth of the individual citizen-client', appealing to official policies and rules only 'to rationalise' and enforce their pre-existing moral judgements.[13] Developing this idea further, Joe Soss, Richard Fording and Sanford Schram emphasise that the frontline delivery of welfare-to-work unfolds 'in social contexts where appraisals of personal identity and behaviour are highly salient'.[14] Reflecting on their experience of observing welfare-to-work case managers in Florida, they conclude that few factors influence case managers' decisions as much as their perceptions of their clients as people: whether they are 'a straight shooter, trying hard, or playing games'. These moral judgements underwrite the decisions they make about whether to sanction clients or to go lightly by using their discretion to give people extra time or 'a good-cause exemption'.[15]

Our observations of the Crompton office's consultants often ring true to this analysis. Katsy and Belinda's view that Charlie is probably gaming the system and working cash-in-hand lead them towards using compliance with him and affording him little benefit of the doubt. We witness repeated conversations between Katsy, Belinda and the other consultants about individual clients they think 'have money' or are 'using the system' to their advantage. For instance, on our second day at the Crompton office, we are invited to join the morning 'Buzz Kill' meeting. This is a daily 15-minute meeting between the four consultants to talk about their caseloads and how the office is tracking towards performance targets, among other things. This morning's meeting starts off with Katsy leading a discussion of the office's 'exit list': clients who have been automatically exited by Centrelink because they are no longer claiming benefits. Belinda recognises two of the names on the list as her former clients. She offers up her explanation that they were probably already working cash-in-hand and decided to get off Centrelink when she started to push them to look for work: 'So, getting them in here [job searching] … So that could have been working cash-in-hand, I'm suspecting both of them.' She says that the strategy now will be to try and make contact to confirm they are working. If they are willing to give Belinda their employment details, she can lodge it on the system and track it as an employment outcome for the office. 'They don't leave on bad terms,' she later tells us. 'They

13   Maynard-Moody and Musheno 2000, 347–49.
14   Soss et al. 2011a, 248.
15   Soss et al. 2011a, 249.

just have had enough of coming in here and juggling working', so they drop off the system.

Observing this meeting affords us insights into the teamwork dynamic at the Crompton office. The consultants are all happy to pitch in with their ideas and explanations of cases, and we see little competitiveness between them. But it also gives us a window into the consultants' understandings of their clientele, and their cynicism towards significant proportions of jobseekers. Later that afternoon, we observe Katsy NARing one of her clients, Lang, when she misses an appointment. Katsy appears to take some delight in stopping Lang's payments, speculating out loud while she does the paperwork: 'I know that she has got a job, but she is not reporting.' As Katsy processes the payment suspension, she quietly starts to sing 'Bang, bang!' The rest of the office is quiet, with no jobseekers around. Katsy's colleagues press her to sing her Work for the Dole song for their, and our, amusement. Cathy walks over from the reception desk to join in the amusement. Katsy, blushing with embarrassment, launches into a parody of the theme song from Disney's *Frozen*:

Bang, bang, Work for the Dole.
Bang, Bang, PAR.
We just want to be a six star!

While Katsy may sing loudly about the sorrows of mutual obligation, it's not obvious from the street that the Crompton office is in the business of activation. Its entrance looks like a private recruitment firm, the sort of place you'd go to find temping work. The Crompton office is not screaming to the public that it's a Jobactive provider. The Australian government's Jobactive logo – which all providers are required to display – is barely noticeable on the door. It's been strategically placed well below eye level and to the left-hand side, where it is dwarfed by the company's own logo. We learn from the Crompton office's employment consultants that the company often gets employers walking in off the street, or randomly calling the office, looking for jobseekers to fill vacancies that have just emerged. For instance, one of the jobseekers we track, Kevin, a recovering alcoholic living in a boarding house, secures a permanent job as a storeroom person with a plumbing supplies store.

Belinda tells us that she has 'put it down to luck'. The store 'was only two doors down', and the employer just 'walked in' off the street saying that he needed two staff members. Belinda 'put Kevin up' and 'they employed him straightaway'.

Despite appearing to the outside world as more like a recruitment firm than an Jobactive provider, Katsy tells us that being a five-star rated provider has its advantages in driving employer traffic towards the Crompton office. When employers 'search the local Jobactive ... we always come up at the top', she explains. In one example of a jobseeker that we follow at the Crompton office, Katsy places one of her Stream C clients, Grace, into a part-time job as a medical receptionist. Like Kevin, Grace is in her mid-40s and living in transitional housing. She lands the job when a local medical practice 'up the road' phones out of the blue wanting a mature-age jobseeker covered by the $10,000 Restart Wage Subsidy, which the government offers employers if they hire mature-age jobseekers who have been on unemployment benefits for six months or more. The employer has seen it advertised on TV, which is why they call the Crompton office. Katsy thinks Grace fits 'the criteria for the role perfectly', even though she is looking for employment in security operations, because the employer is prepared to train someone up, it's a part-time position (Grace is only part-time activity-tested) and her age makes her eligible for the subsidy. It's a virtuous circle whereby government investment in Jobactive advertisements directs foot and phone traffic to the higher performing providers, reinforcing their elevated status in the market.

If you can't handle the heat!

Despite these inbuilt advantages, we learn that only a fraction of the Crompton office's outcomes relate to jobs that the agency has brokered with employers. Most of the employment outcomes we track with clients (six out of eight) involve jobseekers finding employment themselves, sometimes with minimal intervention. This includes one part-time activity tested nurse, Hyejeong, who commences on the caseload just two months before we start our fieldwork. Hyejeong already has a casual job working 'a few hours here and there' for a private plastic surgery clinic when Belinda begins working with her, but this on-call job does not meet her activity requirements. Very soon after, however, Hyejeong finds a second job, at a dermatological clinic. The two jobs combined meet her requirement of 30 hours' paid work per fortnight. Hyejeong, who is in Stream C because of her sleep apnoea and other physical health issues, holds down the two jobs for the next six months, enabling the Crompton office to claim a full outcome with her.

In another example, John, a young Stream C jobseeker who is homeless, finds himself a job as a chef's apprentice barely a month after commencing on Katsy's caseload. Katsy helps John 'fix his résumé' and gives him some transport tickets and clothing 'to go for interviews'. But other than that, 'everything he does himself'. Indeed, Katsy only works with John for a matter of weeks. Once John begins the chef's apprenticeship, he stops his fortnightly reporting to Centrelink and is exited from the Jobactive system. But because he remains off benefits for the next six months, the Crompton office receives a full-employment outcome payment despite Katsy having no further contact with him.

The examples of John and Hyejeong highlight the role that luck can often play in providers' success with Stream C clients. 'I'd say only 10 per cent of them are brokered,' Trev tells us about the type of outcomes that the Crompton office generally achieves with its clients. And of those that count as brokered employment, Grace's and Kevin's examples suggest that this may be by accident as much as design.

Trev's admission speaks to the emphasis that Fox places on job-search conditionality. Katsy prides herself on it. 'My philosophy: I'm tough,' she openly admits. She sees herself primarily as an executor of the *Social Security Act*, policing welfare dependence. Her job, as she sees it, is 'to pass on the message that it is not okay to just be on Centrelink benefits … everyone should be able to get a job and get off the system'. Cases like John's simply reinforce Katsy's perspective that the main issue determining whether people can transition from welfare-to-work is their personal motivation. 'This has once again proven to us that if they want to work, they can get a job themselves,' she says when reflecting on John's case.

This understanding of the causes of unemployment is encouraged by policy discourses of welfare dependence and the political rhetoric of Australia as a nation of 'lifters vs leaners', as former Treasurer Joe Hockey liked to put it. These policy discourses and ministerial proclamations that, Michaelia Cash as then Minister for Employment put it, '[t]here are jobs out there for those who want them', turn the social problem of unemployment into the individualised problem of the unemployed person's lack of effort.[16] This motivational framing tends to shape the type of activation strategies that case managers envisage or turn towards with clients. It offers up a 'precursory belief structure'[17] to support any inclination case managers may have towards using 'controlled motivation'.[18]

Of all the sites that we visit, the Crompton office is by far the most demanding of its clients. 'We bring them in very often,' Katsy tells us, sometimes 'three' or even 'five days a week'. This is in sharp contrast to the Wilmore office, which sees clients every three weeks, and especially, as we will see in chapter six, the Cove office, which sees clients monthly. It also partly explains why Crompton's consultants generally have lower caseloads than those at other offices: they are meeting with their clients far more regularly. Belinda sees this more demanding approach to activation as a way of 'flushing out' people who are working cash-in-hand: 'shaking the tree' as the practice is known in the industry. It gels with the office's general suspicion of jobseekers and perception that many are doing undeclared cash-in-hand work. They get frustrated, Belinda tells us, and 'out of nowhere they'll either say, "I've had enough, get me off the system," or they'll say, "You know what, I've found something."'

Belinda is difficult to read. On many occasions, she speaks with great warmth and empathy about her clients. She describes her clients as 'like my babies' and thinks of herself as the good cop on the beat. Mostly, when asked, she says that she does not 'really use the compliance', preferring instead to 'do it in a different fashion' by building rapport. At moments, she even thinks of herself as a quasi-social worker, telling us that she's 'got more of a social worker approach' and probably 'more patience' than Katsy, the Crompton

---

16   See Marston 2013, 821.
17   Jordan 2018, 61.
18   Raffass 2017, 361.

office's self-described 'PR queen'. But at other moments Belinda speaks of 'riding' jobseekers and 'being on their case': 'That's the mentality here, I think. Just push, push … If they can't handle it, they'll go somewhere else. You cannot fly under the radar here … If you're ready to work, you'll get a job here. And we'll make you get it.'

Two important things are embedded in this comment. First, the accent she places on 'making' jobseekers 'get it'. In one appointment that we observe, Belinda openly tells a new client that 'a lot of it is put on the jobseeker' these days; that the government wants 'the jobseeker to look for the job' and that 'a lot of [her] job is administrative'. The government, she tells her client, 'has made it that way. Jobseekers have to look themselves.' The second important aspect of Belinda's comment is her suggestion that 'If they can't handle it, they'll go somewhere else.' The Crompton office appears to have few reservations about losing clients from its caseload if they are perceived as either unable or unwilling to intensively look for work.

Indeed, as in the example of Ray, the jobseeker who jumped bail interstate, that we discussed earlier in this chapter, the Crompton consultants actively try to move people they perceive as difficult off their caseload – by getting them reassessed to Disability Employment Services. Another approach encourages them to think about transferring to another provider. When we return to the Crompton office for a second wave of fieldwork, we observe Katsy and Belinda discussing a group of the office's Stream C clients who are approaching their annual activity phase. One of these is Ray, who never followed through with the referral to see the life-skills coordinator about being reassessed. Instead, he spent repeated periods exempted from his mutual obligation requirements or on payment suspensions for missing scheduled appointments. Almost 12 months later, he is still on Belinda's caseload. When Katsy asks Belinda how things are going with Ray, Belinda tells her that he's due in the next day. Katsy suggests to Belinda that she should try to move him on to another provider. She knows Belinda has a soft spot for him, she says, but has Belinda 'asked him if he wants to go somewhere else?'

These attempts to off-load the office's harder-to-help clients are the flipside of their demanding approach to activation. They are emblematic of the problems of creaming and parking that have plagued outcomes-based commissioning models. A related feature that we observe at the Crompton office is a high caseload churn and suspension rate, which seems to be at least partly a by-product of the site's philosophy of 'riding' its clients. Rather than propelling jobseekers into work, the Crompton office's demanding model of activation often seems to result in clients requesting to transfer or becoming deactivated by seeking a medical or personal crisis exemption. For instance, another of Belinda's client's that we track is Jeremy, 'a pretty well-known musician back in the '90s', who now battles alcoholism, severe anxiety and depression. He has been volunteering as a teaching support worker at a local primary school, to gain experience in a profession he hopes to move into. The agency has paid for Jeremy to study for a Certificate in Educational Support (Integration Aide). But later in our research, Belinda needs to start pushing him harder to look for work. She in turn is being pushed to do this by Katsy, even though she realises Jeremy's mental health issues will 'be an ongoing thing' and are not 'going to be a quick fix'. She is conflicted about it but feels she has no choice. 'I felt like there was no progress, and maybe I was letting him down.' The next time we catch up with Belinda, Jeremy has requested a transfer to another Jobactive provider, with Belinda telling us 'he didn't want to do it'. 'When the pushing started,' she explains, Jeremy transferred out.

Similarly, the Crompton office's comparatively high suspension rate may have also been linked to the demanding model of activation pursued at the site. Overall, a quarter of the jobseekers that we track at the site (seven of 28) receive multiple or long-term medical exemptions from their mutual obligation requirements. At one point during the study, around 45 per cent of the office's Stream C caseload are on suspension. While this figure includes some part-time activity-tested clients who are meeting their mutual obligations through part-time work, it is an exceptionally high suspension rate, with the national suspension rate among the Stream C caseload being just over 27 per cent at the end of 2017. In the employment region where the Crompton office is located it was a little higher than this – at 35 per cent – but still well short of the Crompton office's suspension rate.[19] When

---

19 These data are based on information given to us by the Department of Employment about the profile of the Stream C caseload on 31 December

asked about the office's high suspension rate, Katsy was unsurprised: 'With this aggressive model that we are working on, pushing them into survival jobs, it's not surprising that a lot of jobseekers would switch to [a] passive model on suspension.' Rachel, Crompton's life-skills coordinator, shares this view: 'Sometimes it's the easy option for clients to get a medical certificate and just get an exemption. Otherwise they know the requirements that they have, whether it's Work for the Dole or job search.'

'Survival jobs' is a euphemism for jobs that people don't want but are prepared to do because they need the money to survive. Whether people are willing to accept 'survival jobs' is treated as a litmus test of their motivation to work. People who turn down such jobs are seen by the case managers as difficult, choosy jobseekers with an air of entitlement. In a follow-up interview, Katsy refers to one of her clients, Shane, as 'a long-term survivor'. But being a 'survivor' and taking 'survival jobs' are two different things. What Katsy means by 'survivor' is that Shane knows how to play the system to survive in it. A former high-security prisoner, Shane is on a long-term medical suspension and on route to being transferred to the DES system. Katsy NARs Shane for missing an appointment, and he responds to the sanction by applying directly to Centrelink for a medical exemption. This also triggers a reassessment by Centrelink, who deems that Shane should be moved to DES. Katsy has few regrets about this outcome: 'For some long-term survivors, I think the best thing for me to do is just continue for compliance to push you to go to get your shit together.'

We later learn from Katsy's manager, Trev, that not only is she the highest performing consultant in the whole of the company, she's also the case manager who jobseekers complain about the most to Centrelink. We witness this for ourselves on our second day at the Crompton office, when Katsy has an altercation with one of her clients, Lee. During the appointment, she refuses to accept the job search evidence that Lee hands her because none of his job applications have résumés attached to them. Lee claims that he is not legally obliged to attach résumés but Katsy says she will submit a PR for unsatisfactory

---

2017. This information was a response to a data request made by our research team.

job searching. This is a far stricter approach to the dole diary than we observe at the Westgate office, where Thomas helps one of his clients to come up with entries for a job search sheet, or at the Cove office, where, as we will see in chapter six, jobseekers are given additional time to complete unfulfilled dole diaries.

The prospect of a faked dole diary is not something that Katsy takes lightly, telling us that she will sometimes call employers to verify job search entries or get clients 'to also collect the business card, bring it back to me'. So, she will not accept Lee's unverifiable effort. Lee storms out of the office, refusing to sign his Job Plan and threatening to 'take this further'. After consulting briefly with Trev, Katsy walks back to her desk to do the necessary paperwork, saying that she is 'going to PR him now, arsehole', and telling her colleagues that Lee 'should go and do a law degree' if he wants to challenge her on the rules. Katsy's colleagues laugh the episode off, unperturbed that Lee will face a significant payment penalty. Indeed, Lee is going to be PRed twice: for unsatisfactory job searching and also for refusing to sign his Job Plan. She jokes that her goal is to issue two PRs per day, which she will now get in one hit.

A couple of hours later, notification comes through on Katsy's computer that Lee has requested a transfer. This is *very* welcome news to the Crompton office consultants. 'You need to give me a big hug for this one,' Katsy tells Jen as she gives her the news. Belinda overhears and dares Katsy to 'ring him and say, "I wish you all the best."' They then act out how the call might go.

In-house counselling: the fuzzy side of activation

Of all the frontline staff that we encounter in the research for this book, Katsy is clearly the most assertive. Yet she is equally capable of moments of great empathy and concern for jobseekers. One of the appointments that we observe Katsy taking is with Gemma, a young woman in her early 20s who is homeless and recently pregnant. It's a confronting and emotional meeting for Katsy to take. Gemma is quite distraught, expressing that her life 'is a shambles' and telling Katsy that she has decided to keep the baby even though she's not happy about it. Katsy tries to focus Gemma's mind on the positive things in her life. 'What keeps you going?' she wants to know, and they start to talk about Gemma's little brother, whom she has great affection for. Katsy arranges an appointment for Gemma to meet with the life-skills coordinator, Rachel, the next day at 2 pm. Rachel will try to help Gemma find stable accommodation, with Katsy assuring Gemma that Rachel is 'really good at her job' and has helped several of Katsy's clients to find housing. As she begins to wrap up the appointment, Katsy lets Gemma know that she can always call the office using reverse charges if she is running late or cannot make the appointment. Rachel can even take the appointment with Gemma over the phone, although face-to-face is much better. Katsy gives Gemma the reverse charges number she can call, telling her, 'You look after yourself and we will see you tomorrow.' Gemma, still a little teary, is visibly moved that the office will try to help her out with housing. 'Thank you so much,' she says as she turns to leave.

Katsy's appointment with Gemma affords us a window into how the Crompton office supports clients beyond job searching. Indeed, several of the Stream C jobseekers we follow are assisted to find stable housing by Crompton office personnel. Others are linked into drug and alcohol rehabilitation programs, while still others are referred to specialist mental health support. One fascinating aspect of the Crompton office's case management model is the juxtaposition between the organisation's demanding approach to activation and the resources it puts into specialist non-vocational staff.

The Crompton office's core staff are joined at different points in the week by a supporting cast of counsellors: Noreen, a psychologist, and Rachel, one of Fox Personnel's life-skills coordinators. Rachel and Noreen both work across four of the organisation's sites, so they are only at the Crompton office one to two days per week. They are also managed separately to the rest of the Crompton office staff, reporting to line managers in their own non-vocational teams rather than Trev.

Both Rachel and Noreen have qualifications in counselling, although Rachel tells us she focuses more on linking clients to external social support services in the area, 'telling them what exactly is available, what kind of support services there are [and] explaining to them what it involves'. Most of these external services are state-funded social services, like crisis housing and drug and alcohol rehabilitation. Sometimes her involvement in cases is limited to a single appointment to signpost clients to relevant supports, although she tells us that mostly 'it does take time' before clients are ready to act on her referrals. Fox allows the consultants to refer jobseekers for up to eight appointments with Rachel without needing management approval. These appointments are paid out of the site's pool of Employment Funds, and the Crompton office regularly uses this option. Most of the jobseekers that we track at the office are referred to appointments with the organisation's non-vocational specialists at some point during our research.

Noreen focuses more specifically on the mental health side of things – working on psychological barriers that clients might have. These, she says, 'could just be lack of motivation'. When either Noreen or Rachel meet with jobseekers, they usually do so for an hour and in one of the two private interview rooms off the reception area. This is substantially longer than the employment consultants' appointments with clients, which are allocated as 30 minutes, but, we observe, often run for barely more than 15 minutes. In the case of re-engagement appointments, the meetings can be as short as five minutes.

From Noreen's perspective, the longer duration of non-vocational appointments affords the counsellors the 'opportunity to work on a deeper level with the clients'. In Noreen's case, jobseekers can be referred for up to 10 appointments with her before needing management approval. Again, these appointments are paid from the site's pool of Employment Funds: at the end of each week, Noreen draws down a list of the clients she has seen, and Fox is 'funded from the government for each client that we see'. Co-locating in-house counselling with employment assistance enables providers to generate additional revenue from their clients than if they refer them to externally provided services. While some of the other offices that we visit also employ their own counsellors to work with jobseekers, these counsellors are always located offsite and tend to be used less frequently than those at the Crompton office. Moreover, Fox Personnel's in-house counselling services can be used more intensively given the high number of appointments that individual clients can have.

This model of incorporating in-house counsellors as part of service delivery teams is becoming increasingly popular among employment services providers, especially the larger for-profit agencies such as MAX Employment and Sarina Russo. However, it can put counsellors in the difficult professional position of balancing tensions between client confidentiality and the interests of their employer and colleagues. Unlike external counsellors or clinical psychologists, in-house non-vocational staff have a direct employment interest in encouraging their clients to look for work. As much as they may think of themselves as allied health professionals or social workers, they are not independent advocates for their clients. If their clients withdraw from the labour market, they will soon be out of a job themselves.

We 'are on the same page', explains Katsy when asked about the benefits of referring jobseekers to Fox's in-house counselling services over external services. External counsellors and psychologists, she says, sometimes 'don't encourage their jobseekers to work'. They push back when consultants try to place clients into survival jobs and do not understand that, as Katsy says, 'if you are on unemployment benefits, occupation or job option is not about a choice'. Noreen reflects on the delicate subject of 'survival jobs' when we interview her:

> I think a lot of the time I find that clients don't really know where to head because they're dissatisfied, which is very understandable. But sometimes it's about going, 'Okay, well the system is not necessarily going to support your bigger career goals' … Sometimes it does, but not necessarily … So, 'Okay, we can look at that, but let's look at the survival stuff because you need money, basically.'

The potential for conflict between their professional priority as counsellors and the organisation's interests can be difficult to manage. As Noreen reflects, whereas her 'priority is the clients' wellbeing', the consultants' 'priority is essentially getting them into work'. These mental health and employment outcomes 'don't always line up exactly', she admits, although mostly they do. But there are occasions when clients might be progressing 'really well mental health-wise', which is a great achievement for her personally, but it's 'not really shown … in the work sense'.

Rachel, the life-skills coordinator, started out working with Fox as an employment consultant before moving across to a counselling role. Besides her main role of triaging clients into external social support services, she also draws on her experience as an employment consultant to work with clients 'on interview skills, talk about, I guess, preparation for work'. While her role is formally focused on helping jobseekers into social support services, she says that she also tries to work with clients on their vocational goals and that she does not want jobseekers seeing her role and the employment consultant's role 'as separate services'.

The other professional tension that must be carefully managed is between the voluntary nature of clients' participation in counselling and mental health services and the compulsory nature of activation. In principle, clients' appointments with Noreen and Rachel sit outside the compliance regime, so they cannot be sanctioned for missing these appointments. However, we learn from Noreen that the employment consultants often coordinate the timing of their own client appointments with those of the non-vocational staff. This co-location and co-timing of non-vocational and job-search appointments streamlines meetings for the Crompton office's clients, but it also blurs the program boundaries between mutual obligation and counselling or social support.

These boundaries are also blurred in other ways. As we have seen earlier in this chapter, the Crompton office may refer jobseekers for appointments with either Rachel or Noreen as part of a broader strategy to have their activity requirements reduced, or to try and have clients moved into a higher service stream or out of the Jobactive system entirely. 'First of all,' Rachel explains in relation to the clients that she works with, 'we just look at the suitability to work in itself, and then whether or not they're suitable to part-time and full-time work.' If jobseekers present with any barriers that might impact the type of work they can do, 'then we'll probably organise an assessment for them with Centrelink so they get reassessed, and whether or not Jobactive is the most suitable service'.

Of the 28 jobseekers that we follow at the Crompton office, the consultants and non-vocational staff work together to try to get eight clients reassessed and reclassified into another program, and to reduce the work capacity requirements of two further clients. Noreen, and especially Rachel, are critical components of these strategies. For example, one of the jobseekers on Belinda's caseload is Vinny, an ex-prisoner and former addict now on the methadone program. When we start tracking Vinny's case, he has a part-time 'pick-packing job' that he has secured himself with a local jewellery company. But because Vinny has full-time activity requirements, his job is unable to be counted as a payable employment outcome. Belinda needs to find Vinny further work, but she is pessimistic about his prospects of securing a different, full-time job given his 'pretty bad criminal record and convictions'. So, rather than trying to find Vinny alternative employment, she tries to get his activity requirements reduced. Vinny is referred to Rachel, and together Belinda and Rachel try 'to reduce his capacity' in order 'to get an outcome'. It's a strategy that Katsy similarly pursues with Michaela, a Stream C Aboriginal jobseeker who she describes to us as 'very employable': 'She's meeting our life-skills coordinator now. We are thinking to bring down her capacity to part-time ... She can get jobs easily if she wants to, but somehow every time when she's just about to start a job there's hiccups.'

These examples of working to reduce clients' activity requirements to make outcomes easier to achieve speak to how the performance incentives in Jobactive's payment model can tacitly encourage providers to try to game the classification system. In cases like Vinny's, where providers try to claim outcomes for jobs clients already have, providers are rewarded for practices that produce little social benefit or added economic value.

Another way in which we observe the Crompton office occasionally using its in-house counsellors in response to Jobactive's performance framework relates to Work for the Dole compliance. The star rating system that the department uses to measure provider performance, and to reallocate business share from low- to high-performing sites, was controversially adjusted under the Jobactive contract. One notable adjustment was including Work for the Dole outcomes as a major component of providers' and offices' overall star ratings. The star rating that a Jobactive site receives depends on its outcomes for jobseekers across streams, with Stream C outcomes weighted more heavily (40 per cent of total star ratings) than Stream A or B outcomes (25 and 35 per cent respectively). However, while employment outcomes are still the most important measurement, providers are now also assessed according to the proportion of their clients participating in Work for the Dole during their annual activity phase, and the speed with which jobseekers start a Work for the Dole activity.[20] Each of these indicators contributes 10 per cent towards providers' performance outcomes, meaning that Work for the Dole outcomes are responsible for a fifth of agencies' overall star rating. This significant change to the performance measurement framework is explicitly designed to strengthen providers' emphasis on enforcing mutual obligation.

This means that offices wishing to remain high-performing sites cannot afford to neglect Work for the Dole attendance, something that we observe the Crompton office staff to be acutely aware of. The consultants reiterate this to us during one of their regular team meetings, explaining that keeping on track of Work for the Dole attendance is critical for star ratings but something that not all providers have paid enough attention to. Trev estimates that the Crompton staff spend about 30 to 40 per cent of their time managing Work for the Dole, telling us that 'the administration involved is a nightmare'.

One way that the consultants try to handle this administrative burden is by holding Work for the Dole meetings every Tuesday from 3 to 5 pm, where they collectively go through case lists to discuss clients who are due for their annual activity phase and what to do about jobseekers that are difficult to get into a Work for the Dole activity. Moreover, to ensure that they place people into Work for the Dole activities as quickly as possible, appointments are scheduled with jobseekers for the day before they are due to commence Work for the Dole. This way they can refer people without delay, protecting their Work for the Dole performance stats.

With Stream C jobseekers, consultants have a little more flexibility about the type of activities their clients can undertake to meet their requirements. While the default Work for the Dole activity across the program is a community work placement activity (such as working in an opportunity shop, waste recycling or landscape gardening),

---

20 For a detailed discussion of how star ratings are calculated under the Jobactive contract, see Australian National Audit Office 2017, 56–9.

participation in training, counselling or a health maintenance program can satisfy Work for the Dole requirements for jobseekers in Stream C. On occasion, the Crompton office's clients were referred to appointments with either Rachel or Noreen as they entered their annual activity phase. This enabled the consultants to count their clients as meeting their Work for the Dole requirements without having to refer them to community work placements that they doubted their clients would attend. Belinda takes this approach with Han, one of her Stream C clients that she is trying to get into a drug and alcohol rehabilitation program. Six months into the study, Belinda starts to refer Han for appointments with Rachel, the life-skills coordinator. In the months previously, Han has been quite non-compliant and Belinda has sanctioned him for persistent non-attendance. When we ask Belinda how she managed to persuade Han to meet with Rachel, she tells us that she outlined a choice for him: 'Work for the Dole popped up. And I said, "It's either that, and if you don't want to do that, I need you to do counselling."' Again, this example illustrates how the boundaries between behavioural conditionality and the voluntariness of participation in counselling can easily become blurred, particularly when job search assistance and counselling services are not just co-located but co-managed.

Steps, a motivational and life-skills program, is another activity that the Crompton office regularly uses over the course of our research as a way for its Stream C clients to meet their annual activity requirements. The soft skills program is well known in the industry, being regularly publicised by speakers at industry conferences. Over the period of our research, the Crompton office contracts Steps to run its program out of the office on at least three separate occasions, and six of the 28 jobseekers that we track at the office are referred to the program. One of these is Adam, whom Katsy refers to Steps when he enters his annual activity (Work for the Dole) phase. She knows 'he wouldn't get up to do' a mainstream activity in a Work for the Dole host organisation 'because of his drug factors'. The only activity she can think of is waste recycling on the other side of the city, but that would involve 'a lot of heavy lifting and machinery, and he's going to be blurred all the time'. So, she feels the only option is Steps: 'I told him he's coming in for Steps. And I had a serious chat with him, "From now on… it will be just compliance."'

'Triple' activation

We learn that one reason why the Crompton office staff appear so cognisant of activities that could contribute to the office's star ratings is because they are financially incentivised to do so. As at the Wilmore and Westgate offices, the Crompton staff have regular targets that they are expected to achieve. Their primary key performance indicators are the number of job placements and four-, 12- and 26-week employment outcomes, although their appointment attendance rate is also a secondary KPI. These targets are handed down to the site from Fox Personnel's quality assurance manager each quarter, and it's then up to the site manager to ensure that the staff deliver.

During our first visit to the office, Belinda shares her personal performance targets with us. For the quarter, she is expected to achieve 27 job placements (including seven in Stream C), 18 × four-week outcomes (five in Stream C), 15 × 12-week outcomes (five in Stream C), and 9 × 26-week outcomes (three in Stream C). What's noteworthy about these targets is the fall off from job placements to full outcomes. Fox Personnel sets performance targets on the assumption that only a third of job placements will convert into a full (i.e. 26-week) outcome. One in three jobs placements, it assumes, will fall over before reaching four weeks. And of the job placements that make it to four weeks, half will fail before reaching six months. While 33 per cent might seem like a low job placement to full-outcome conversion rate, it is substantially higher than Jobactive providers achieved nationally in the first three years of the contract.

Data reported by the department shows that from 1 July 2015 to 31 May 2018, Jobactive providers achieved a total of just over one million job placements but fewer than 290,000 full-employment outcomes. Of these, Stream C jobseekers accounted for just under 13 per cent of all job placements and just over 10 per cent of all full outcomes. As shown in Figure 5.1, this gives a placement to full-outcome conversion rate of just under 30 per cent across all streams, and a conversion rate below 22 per cent among Stream C jobseekers who are placed in employment.

With its five-star rating, the Crompton office is ranked in the top 25 per cent of Jobactive sites nationally, so it's not surprising that its performance targets exceed the national average by some distance.

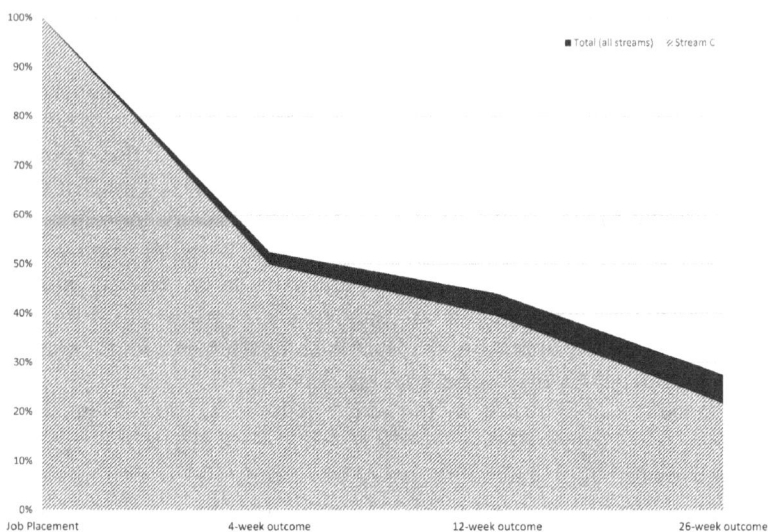

Figure 5.1. Job placement to full-outcome conversion rate, 1 July 2015 to 31 May 2018. Data is drawn from Department of Jobs and Small Business 2018b.

Still, they are considered hard to achieve by some of the staff. Vance, one of Fox Personnel's reverse marketing staff who works across four of the company's sites (including the Crompton office), tells us that his KPIs are unachievable. His performance targets require him to place a minimum of 20 clients into jobs each month, with 12 of those placements progressing to a 12-week outcome and eight progressing to a full 26-week outcome. But he feels, 'There's no way I can achieve my personal KPI.' This is despite being, he claims, the highest performing reverse marketer in the role to date. When we interview Vance, he has been working with Fox Personnel for about six months. But when we try to contact him again, less than a month later, we learn that he has left the organisation. On another occasion that we visit the Crompton office, Cathy, the usual receptionist is on leave. Veronica, a young South-East Asian born woman, is filling in for her. Veronica explains to us that she's one of Fox Personnel's back-fill staff. She used to be in Vance's reverse marketing role, but she was moved out of the role around the time we started the research because she could not meet her targets. So it's not entirely surprising that Vance lasts only months in the job.

It's 'a high-pressure job', Katsy tells us about the pressures to perform. If the site is not doing well, 'the government can take back the contract ... so, to me, I think it's competitive'. 'They're hard,' Belinda says about her personal targets. 'I haven't got my bonus every quarter,' she admits. 'I've had it probably two or three times.' Belinda's admission speaks to a distinguishing feature of how the Crompton office's consultants are managed. Unlike staff in the Wilmore and Westgate offices, who receive no performance-related pay, Fox Personnel incentivises its staff through quarterly performance bonuses. Staff can receive two types of bonuses: $500 per quarter if the site achieves four stars or above for that quarter, and $1000 per quarter for individual staff if they achieve their performance targets. A potential quarterly bonus of $1500 is worth a lot to employees in a very low-paying industry, and during our first visit to the Crompton office we witness Jen and Belinda talking about what their bonus money 'will go towards' if they get it. Jen is hoping to buy a new mobile phone. However, the formula for determining whether staff receive bonuses is convoluted.

To qualify for the $500 bonus for the site's performance rating, individual staff must achieve over 50 per cent of their personal performance targets in each category of placements and outcomes. 'So if someone's not performing, yet the site's a five-star, they won't get it,' explains Trev. In order to receive the $1000 personal performance bonus, staff must achieve over 80 per cent of their targets in each category. This in itself suggests that the company recognises that the performance targets it sets its staff are difficult to achieve. On top of this, staff who make less than 50 per cent of their targets in each category for two quarters in a row enter performance management and the prospect of performance improvement plans. So it is understandable that targets and outcomes are therefore always on the minds of the Crompton office consultants.

During one visit, we witness Belinda, who is below her four-week outcome targets for the month, approaching Jen for advice: 'Jen, I need to pick your brain I need to work out how to know who has an outcome and how to manipulate.' The last part of this sentence is said more quietly, perhaps because Belinda is aware of our presence just metres behind her. Jen, who has been working in the industry for nearly 10 years, knows Excel spreadsheets like the back of her hand. She's a fountain of knowledge for the other case managers and is regularly consulted by Belinda when she runs into an administrative issue that she does not fully understand or know how to handle. In this case, what Jen proceeds to help Belinda with over 45 minutes is how to increase the number of four-week outcomes she has showing in the system. Jen talks Belinda through a spreadsheet tab with tracking data on her job placements and how they are progressing towards a full outcome: 'You see how it started off good, shit, partial then nothing,' she points out to Belinda. They work out that if Belinda lodges some of her clients as job placements, and backdates these by a few weeks, they will automatically convert into four-week outcomes, boosting Belinda's KPIs. This is what Belinda meant when she asked for help to know how to 'manipulate' things.

The job placements they are putting into the system are genuine. 'I'm not lying about my placements,' Belinda explains when we ask her about it later that day. However, Belinda has been holding off lodging them as job placements because she was worried that the jobseekers wouldn't declare their earnings properly to Centrelink, meaning the placements would fall off before reaching four weeks. If that happens, it will jeopardise her and the site's placement-to-outcome conversion rate. This worry comes back to the suspicion Belinda and the other staff have about the trustworthiness of their clientele. 'Because a lot of them are shifty, or they don't report the correct hours or they don't know how to report correctly,' she tells us. Hence why she now waits 'for them to report correctly, and then put it in'.

Jen and Belinda therefore need to work out which of Belinda's clients have been reporting correctly to Centrelink over the past four weeks, so that if Belinda puts in that job placement, it will automatically boost her four-week outcome rate. Jen looks at what one of Belinda's clients has been reporting, double-checking what the jobseeker's activity requirements are with Belinda. It's 30 hours per fortnight, so Jen advises, 'If you place her on the 15 of November that will translate automatically into a four-week claim.' By now, we are already well into December. Belinda wants to make sure Jen is certain before she changes things on the system. 'Your calculations are correct and tie in with the site manager's?' Gen assures her they are. 'I'm not doubting you. I'm just double-checking,' Belinda clarifies for Jen's benefit.

Fox Personnel's use of rewards (bonus payments) and sanctions (performance management) to motivate its staff is emblematic of a broader phenomenon in the employment services field known as 'triple activation'.[21] It is closely related to what we have described earlier in this book (and elsewhere) as 'double activation': the government purchaser's use of financial and contractual incentives to activate providers to place jobseekers into work. *Triple activation* takes this dynamic one step further, embedding this logic of organisational financial and performance incentives into internal employee appraisal systems. If activation is the behavioural management of jobseekers, double activation is the performance management *of* organisations and triple activation is the performance management *within* organisations.

While the use of performance-related pay is not widespread in Australian employment services, other triple activation tactics, such as individualised performance targets for case managers certainly are. In our 2016 survey of Jobactive staff, fewer than 12 per cent of frontline workers agreed with the statement 'In my job, I am *not* influenced by numerical targets'.[22] The vast majority disagreed with this statement, with almost a third of those in strong disagreement. This influence of numerical targets was confirmed by frontline workers' responses to other survey questions. More than 70 per cent of frontline Jobactive staff said that they were aware the organisation they worked for pays attention to the income they generate through placing clients. Nearly two-thirds told us that they took note of those actions with clients that would generate a payable outcome for the office, and 45 per cent said that the need to get an outcome quickly was 'quite' or 'very influential' in determining what activities they recommended to clients.

Should we worry about such a reliance on triple activation tactics to steer the behaviours of frontline workers? One concern arises from how triple activation reshapes what Evelyn Brodkin calls 'the calculus of street level choice'.[23] Performance indicators do more than just

---

21   Van Berkel 2013, 87.
22   The survey data is reported in full in Lewis et al. 2016.
23   Brodkin 2011, i260.

measure what people do. They encourage workers 'to do different things' – directing their attention to those measured activities and outcomes to which rewards are attached.[24] For this reason, scholars who have studied the influence of performance management on frontline service delivery often argue for treating performance management systems as *political* rather than administrative apparatuses.[25] Indeed, influencing how frontline workers make use of and exercise their administrative discretion 'to raise the odds that preferred paths will be taken' is precisely the point of triple activation.[26] The problem, however, is that what has value from a social and public policy perspective is not always adequately measured by performance monitoring systems, and vice versa.

Working with clients to address drug and alcohol addiction, or to secure housing, has enormous public benefits even if it does not lead to an employment outcome. But if providers are rewarded only for activities that produce job outcomes, they may neglect interventions like these that bring people much closer to, *but not all the way* to employment. Janice Dias and Steven Maynard-Moody describe this as the 'performance paradox': when organisational targets redirect workers' behaviours in ways that undermine the achievement of broader policy goals.[27] The most well known example of this paradox is the problem of providers creaming and parking clients in order to maximise financial outcomes. We saw some evidence of this practice at the Crompton office with the re-categorisation strategies, such as trying to reduce clients' assessed activity requirements, described earlier. The triple activation of its staff fed directly into these practices. When we ask Katsy what the benefit to her is of jobseekers being referred into DES, since these jobseekers will not deliver any payable outcome for the office, she explains that they could make it easier for her to achieve her overall personal performance targets (and bonuses):

---

24   van Berkel, R. and Knies, E. 2017, 64.
25   On this point see: van Berkel, 2017.
26   Soss, Fording and Schram 2011, i204.
27   Dias and Maynard-Moody 2006.

Our KPI is based on the number of job seekers in our caseload. So, if we have a bigger case load, that means we have a higher KPI. And we understand that Jobactive is not for every single jobseeker … It works beneficially to both parties. A benefit to us because if you don't have many jobseekers, then our KPI will be lower. On the other hand, for jobseekers, they can get a better service and more appropriate service.

In other words, one way that the Crompton office consultants could respond to performance targets is by making those targets easier to achieve by moving difficult clients onto another Jobactive or DES provider. *And they are very aware of this*, as Katsy's explanation makes clear. The 'paradoxical' element of this strategy is that triple activation works against the first-order activation of jobseekers in these instances: by incentivising case managers to engage in practices targeted at *deactivating* their more challenging clients.

For-profits v. not-for-profits: more that unites than divides

In many ways, the Crompton office is the embodiment of the Australian government's activation agenda as envisaged under a marketised system. Its case managers show a clear disposition towards using the behavioural policy instruments at their disposal – job search conditionality backed by the threat of sanctions for non-compliance – to move their clients from welfare-to-work. More is demanded of jobseekers in the form of job search activities and frequent appointment attendance than at other offices we observe. Stopping jobseekers' payments for missing appointments is also routine, with the consultants adopting a sanction first, ask questions later approach to NARing clients. The proportion of jobseekers we tracked who were NARed for missing appointments, 10 of 28 (or just over 35 per cent), was significantly higher than at either the Wilmore (23 per cent) or Westgate (26 per cent) offices. This may have reflected the greater frequency of appointments at the Crompton office, meaning that clients faced the threat of payment suspensions on a more regular basis. Yet we also observed the Crompton office's consultants at times taking delight in penalising their clients, which we witnessed nowhere else.

The behavioural approach that the Crompton office's consultants adopted with their clients was mirrored by Fox Personnel's performance management of its staff. The consultants were given discretion by Trev to manage their caseloads as they saw fit, but Fox Personnel tried to steer how they directed this discretion (towards payable outcomes) through financial bonuses. In so doing, the organisation took the logic of Jobactive's payment-by-results funding model to its natural conclusion.

The Crompton office was, in some respects, a microcosm of the 'black box' contracting we described in chapter two. While the theory is that this 'hands off' approach to monitoring program delivery frees commercial providers to better tailor services and to 'develop new practices to identify and tackle individual employment barriers',[28] it also increases the opportunities and incentives for providers to engage in creaming and parking.[29] Some of these anticipated problems with 'black box' and 'outcomes-based' contracting were clearly evident at the Crompton office in the repeated attempts that we witnessed to get clients reclassified as eligible for DES or to move difficult jobseekers off the site's caseload.

Yet the Crompton office's success in working with its Stream C clients – in total, we tracked eight full-employment outcomes at the office – did at least show that it is possible to achieve results with highly disadvantaged jobseekers using a demanding approach to activation, albeit at the cost of generating high rates of caseload churn and motivating disaffected jobseekers to seek a medical exemption or transfer out. However, the demanding nature of the Crompton office's approach to working with its clients shouldn't be overstated. Behavioural conditionality seldom worked by itself to deliver results with Stream C clients. In the successful cases that we track, it is

---

28   Finn 2012, 24.
29   We discuss the risk of 'black box' contracting increasing the incentives for providers to cream and park clients, especially when implemented in the context of a Payment-by-Results system, more extensively in Considine, O'Sullivan and Nguyen 2018.

frequently accompanied by referrals to training courses and/or counselling sessions with the agency's life-skills coordinator or in-house psychologist. When clients display an interest in training that could lead to a job in the local area, that training is frequently supported and paid for out of the office's pool of Employment Funds. This includes two female clients, Surini and Grace, who are funded to study certificates in security operations; Jeremy, who is funded to train as an educational support worker; and another migrant jobseeker, Terri, who receives financial support to study beauty therapy.

In Terri's case, the original strategy was actually to try to upstream her into DES, because she keeps telling Katsy that she has 'a back problem'. Katsy refers her to Noreen, the psychologist, in the hope of supporting Terri to be reassessed by Centrelink. As Katsy explains to us, she tells Terri: 'In order for you to go to Disability Employment Services, because you say can't work, you need to see our psychologist'. However, after a few appointments with Terri, Noreen instead recommends that they pay for Terri to pursue beauty therapy, telling Katsy that Terri 'has changed and wants to work' but is 'very particular about what she likes'. It's a course that costs the office more than $2,000, because Terri has unsuccessfully attempted it once before, with another provider, making her ineligible for the Victorian government's Training Guarantee funding (which subsidises jobseekers to upskill their qualifications). Terri eventually goes on to secure a permanent part-time job working for someone that she meets on the course, a job that leads to a full payable outcome for the Crompton office. Terri's case is again an example of how the employment outcomes that the Crompton office is achieving with its Stream Cs appears to be as much by accident as by design. But it also speaks to the broader perspective that we observe at the office: when an opportunity presents itself, the Crompton staff go 'all in', even if this means taking some significant risks along the way.

6
The Casual Cove

We pull our car up outside our final site, an office of the New South Wales (NSW) not-for-profit provider Artemis. Artemis would have once been considered a large provider, with around 80 offices, although many of them are part-time. But within the context of Australia's highly consolidated welfare-to-work sector – once featuring around 300 providers, and now down to around 40[1] – Artemis is now probably considered a small player in the market, especially as not-for-profits have progressively lost market share to for-profit providers and Artemis' footprint is primarily regional. Parking at Artemis' Cove office is plentiful and free, plus public transport servicing the site is also relatively good. We soon learn from the site manager that the office has relocated to this modern, clean, lively shopping centre to be closer to buses. Rural New South Wales has little rail infrastructure, so buses are the better option. The buses in these parts of Australia tend to be privately run, which means that they have a limited timetable and are fairly costly to ride. But, as we are told, 'every single bus in the area comes to the shopping centre', meaning this site is much more accessible than many others throughout regional and remote Australia.

The Cove office is located in regional NSW, a short drive from the ocean. The town the site services has a year-round population of almost

---

1   This is based on data from Jobs Australia 2015.

5,000. But it is around three hours' drive from Sydney and experiences seasonal population surges. The town has a sun- and sand-driven vibe, meaning jobs in the hospitality sector are relatively plentiful. But this small regional town is also situated close to a former industrial centre, so many jobseekers are likely to have a trade or experience working in the mining, construction or allied sectors. A substantial university is within 20 minutes of the site, but the overwhelming vibe is of a town dominated by blue collar workers, retirees and holiday makers.

The population is predominantly Anglo. International cultural diversity is minimal. This is not a site that needs to make extensive use of translation services. But the Cove and its surrounding area are also home to Aboriginal communities. The site manager, Andrew, is a proud Aboriginal man, who also mentors local Aboriginal youth and coaches a local footy team. We quickly work out – although the information is not explicitly advertised – that Kat, the most senior consultant at the site, and occasional manager, is the mother of the office's other consultant Gwen. This is the world we have entered: a small town in which most people know each other and the detail of your life is likely to be less private than in a large city such as Brisbane, Sydney or Melbourne. The jobseekers that the Cove office staff work with are not just their clients but also their neighbours, parents involved in their own children's school or footy team, and people they may have had dealings with in other walks of life. For instance, one Stream C jobseeker that we follow is also known to Gwen as a difficult tenant from her previous career as a real estate agent. We also observe a lone parent asking Andrew during a meeting if she can sign her son up to the footy team that he coaches.

A charismatic office environment

The office is part of the Cove's largest, and most modern, shopping centre. While attached to the shopping centre, it opens onto the car park, meaning jobseekers have the convenience of parking, bus-stops and shops, but they can also visit the office without entering the shopping centre. The shopping centre, however, does not feature other useful government services such as Centrelink or Service NSW. Placing welfare-to-work offices close to such services is common practice in the industry. But government offices are typically in short supply outside large cities, and clearly in this case, co-location is not possible. The exterior of the office features bold and prominent signage, making it unmissable. But the glass is frosted, and from the outside it is impossible to see who is inside. As we walk through the door, we enter a large office space. It is somewhat narrow, but long, and feels as though it may have once been a clothing shop or perhaps a travel agency. Like many welfare-to-work offices throughout Australia, it is open plan. A row of chairs is placed for jobseekers to sit while they wait for their appointment. Computers for job searches also sit near the entrance. A shoulder-high temporary partition is the only barrier between the waiting area and the rest of the office. There is a reception desk but no receptionist, and one never appears. Four desks are set up for case managers to work at and meet with jobseekers. Only three are ever used. The fourth, at the far end of the long office, becomes our workspace and vantage point.

In this office the site manager's desk is no different from the case managers'. Andrew, Kat and Gwen all pick up the phone when it rings – answering the phone is nobody and everybody's job. Egalitarianism seems to be a strong guiding principle. Indeed, Kat quickly tells us how proud she is to see Andrew in the site manager role. Kat is perhaps in her late 50s, and about ten years older than Andrew. Andrew is shy and reserved, whereas Kat is bold and chatty. She shows no ego or jealousy, telling us that she has seen Andrew come up through the organisation and is so pleased to see him now with his own office to manage. Indeed, when we interview Andrew, we learn that, like Jessica, the first manager of the Wilmore office, he too started out in Artemis as a client almost nine years ago:

Before Artemis I was actually a tyre fitter and a farm hand. And then some things happened and I actually was an Artemis client … A traineeship in admin came up so I applied for it, and I got the job. I wasn't suited to the admin role, so they put me in as an employment consultant … Then I done the Indigenous Employment Program … Then after three years, we had Youth Connections, so I decided to throw my hand at Youth

Connections ... and then the manager's role came up at the Cove office at the time, so I applied for that and I've been here since.

Kat is genuinely proud of Andrew's achievement, recalling vividly the first day he walked into the Cove office:

> He had a pair of board shorts and all, stubby shorts and t-shirt and what have you, and he walked through the door and I got up and I said, 'How can I help you?' Because I thought it was one of our jobseekers, it was Andrew ... Because he just was an everyday looking bloke walking through the door. And do you know what? I think that part of his gift is the gift of being the salt of the earth, down-to-earth, approachable, genuine bloke.

She tells us that Andrew has brought 'all the best values to the office' and that, under his leadership, the site has progressed from a two-and-a-half to five-star rating. That is a very big achievement in the world of welfare-to-work, which Andrew himself partly puts down to changing the mentality of the staff – 'opening their eyes up a little bit to ... not be so hard on the jobseeker'. He mentions that some of the staff back then, who no longer work at the office, were 'too quick' to impose penalties on jobseekers 'without finding out what's behind it' first. The Cove office's approach to monitoring jobseeker compliance, as we will see, is a far cry from the 'sanction first, ask questions later' approach that characterised the Crompton office and, to a lesser extent, the Westgate office.

Perhaps implied in Kat's reverence for Andrew is a view that having an Aboriginal man, with strong links to the local community, 'being so successful and being able to represent Artemis in such a positive manner' is good both for the jobseekers and the local community. Indeed, we soon learn that this site has a higher Aboriginal caseload than at any other site we visit. These links to First Nations communities are announced on arrival, with both the Australian and Aboriginal flags on display in the reception area. The other striking focus is on mature-age jobseekers. Posters about Aboriginal Learning Circles and training and subsidies programs for older jobseekers line the wall of the small waiting area.

On our first afternoon in the office, a male jobseeker arrives. His name is Dave, and Kat openly wonders to us whether Dave has suffered some type of head trauma. Clearly, she suspects brain damage but does not know for sure. Kat explains to us that she prefers to leave Dave to meet with Andrew. This is for the dual reasons that Dave is both male and Aboriginal, so Kat feels that Andrew is better placed to work with Dave and 'get to his barriers' (to employment). For young men like Dave, opportunities like this – to work with a male case manager – are few and far between in the Jobactive system. Other than Thomas at the Westgate office, Andrew is the only male frontline staff member at any of the four sites that regularly meets with jobseekers for their appointments. Trev, the Crompton office's site manager, never takes client appointments, while the two other male staff members that we come across, Troy at the Wilmore office and Vance at the Crompton office are reverse marketers with no personal caseloads. This is indicative of the wider gendered division of labour within frontline employment services work, a phenomenon that has deepened over the past 20 years.

Our survey data shows that the frontline of Australia's welfare-to-work system is highly, and increasingly, gendered. In 2016, three-quarters of the frontline workforce were women, employed on a predominantly full-time basis (only eight per cent of frontline workers were employed part-time).[2] By comparison, when we first surveyed the frontline workforce in 1998, only 62 per cent of frontline staff were women. Indeed, Figure 6.1 shows that the number of women employed in social assistance services more broadly has more than doubled over the past two decades, from just under 150,000 in November 1998 to almost 315,000 in November 2016. Over the same period, the number of men working in social assistance services only increased by 32,200. To put this in perspective, the rise in the number of women working in social assistance services accounts for almost 10 per cent of the rise in total female employment over this period. Yet social assistance services is an industry in which just 3 per cent of the Australian workforce is employed.

---

2   Lewis et al. 2016.

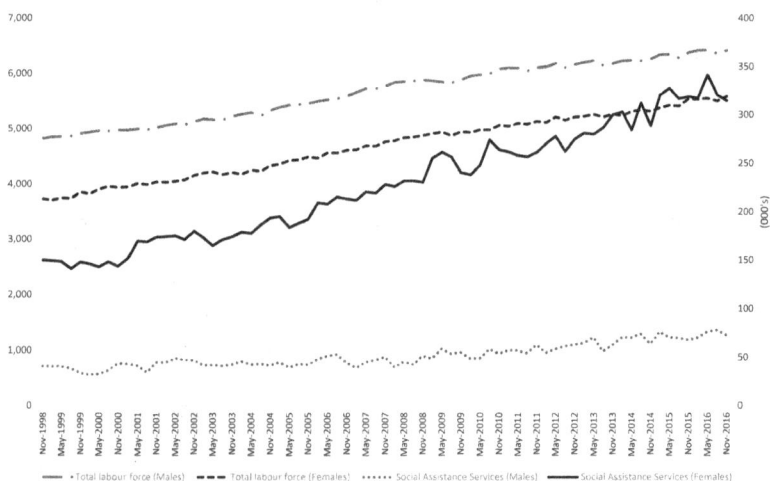

Figure 6.1. Rise in number of women and men working in social assistance services compared to total Australian labour, November 1998 to November 2016. Source: Australian Bureau of Statistics data extracted from Labour Force Australia Survey (Cat. 6291.0.55.003), Detailed, Quarterly, Table 6: Employed persons by industry sub-division of main job.

Besides the increasing proportion of female case managers, the other major shift in the employment services workforce over the past 20 years has been towards the de-skilling and de-collectivisation of frontline staff. We touched upon this issue already in chapter three, but it bears repeating. According to our 2016 survey data, only three per cent of frontline employment services staff are members of a trade union. Only one in four hold a university degree, and over 40 per cent are under 35 years of age.[3] This is a massive demographic shift from the late 1990s, when almost 72 per cent of frontline workers were aged 35 years or older and 39 per cent held a university degree. In the late 1990s, close to half (44.2 per cent) of frontline workers were also members of a trade union.[4] While rates of union membership among Australian

---

3   Lewis et al. 2016.
4   See Considine, Lewis, O'Sullivan and Sol 2015; Lewis et al. 2016.

workers have been declining for many decades, the de-skilling and youthfulness of the frontline employment services workforce is at odds with wider patterns in the Australian labour force towards an older and more educated workforce. Why is it that Australia's employment services workforce has become progressively de-skilled since the 1990s?

One important contributing factor has been the growing use of IT-driven systems and computerised case management tools at the welfare-to-work frontline. Like other forms of public and social services delivery, the provision of welfare-to-work and activation programs has transformed into a form of Mark Bovens and Stavros Zouridis characterise as 'screen-level' bureaucracy. This term captures how contacts and interactions with clients now almost 'always run through or in the presence of a computer screen', not just as a means of recording information into a database but, increasingly, as a device for following standardised protocols and following the guidance of computer-based decision trees.[5] As a result, the nature of case management has become more of an administrative role. This is reflected in our survey data.

In 1998, at the start of Australia's experiment with marketisation, only 17 per cent of frontline staff reported that their computer system told them what steps to take with clients and when. Fewer than 30 per cent reported that they used a standard client classification or assessment tool when deciding how to work with jobseekers. Instead, more than 55 per cent of frontline staff surveyed in 1998 reported that their own judgement was 'very influential' in determining what activities they recommended to clients. By the time of our 2016 survey, that proportion had fallen to below 26 per cent. Almost half of frontline staff instead reported that their computer system now told them 'what steps to take with jobseekers and when', and 62 per cent reported using a standard client classification or assessment tool when working with jobseekers.[6] With structured assessment tools and computerised case management systems replacing 'part of the skill set that a case manager might otherwise need,' professional case managers

---

5   Bovens and Zouridis 2002.
6   The 2016 survey data are reported in Lewis et al. 2016. For the 1998 data on the use of computerised systems and assessment tools see Considine, Lewis, O'Sullivan and Sol 2015, 52–9.

with formal qualifications in fields such as social work, vocational rehabilitation or guidance counselling were no longer required and could be replaced by less-skilled staff with backgrounds in administrative and/or customer service.[7]

Beyond the administrative reconfiguration of frontline work, Ian Greer, Karen Breidahl, Mattias Knuth, and Flemming Larsen argue that there are also inherent tendencies embedded within quasi-markets that drive providers to try to de-professionalise and de-collectivise their frontline staff. In particular, they argue that the competitive pressures associated with open tendering, outcomes-based contracting, and profit maximisation lead employment services providers to try to reduce their costs. And one of the main ways that providers try to do so is through 'lean staffing' measures – replacing professionally qualified staff, who demand higher pay and lower caseloads, with less-skilled staff on lower salaries who are tasked with working with higher caseloads.[8] The need for agencies to be competitive on price during tendering is one factor that motivates providers to 'siphon resources out of services' in this way.[9] Payment-by-results funding models also put downward pressure on providers' staffing costs by shifting more and more of the economic costs and financial risks associated with service provision onto agencies. Providers, in turn, shift these risks onto their staff through their hiring and remuneration practices. The cumulative effect is a 'disorganisation of employment relations' as marketisation leads to the transfer of service delivery away from agencies with highly collectivised and skilled workforces towards lower-cost organisations with leaner workforces.[10]

The Cove office runs somewhat against the grain of these patterns in that two out of the three site staff are well into their 40s and beyond. And although Andrew has no formal university qualifications, Kat is a qualified nurse who 'did six to seven years of nursing' before moving into sales for 20 years and then changing to employment services five and a half years ago.

---

7   Considine, Lewis and O'Sullivan 2011, 821.
8   See, for example, Fuertes and Lindsay 2016, 536.
9   Greer et al. 2017, 141.
10   Greer et al. 2017.

Beyond the charisma and warmth of its staff, one of the things that first strikes us about the Cove office is the generosity of its physical space. The ceilings are high and the four desks in the open-plan portion of the office are wide with space between each. To the left-hand side of the office is a humble-looking enclosed meeting room. The meeting room takes on an air of mystery throughout our initial fieldwork. People come and go from the room throughout the day, but we are never introduced to any of them. Indeed, a semi-constant stream of traffic moves from the car park to the meeting room, often not stopping to acknowledge the case managers along the way. We later discover that the agency owns several other businesses and those businesses provide additional training to jobseekers. The exact nature of the training held in the meeting room is never made clear to us, but we do discover that the agency owns a driver training school. In regional New South Wales, not having a driver's licence and/or a car, or indeed money to buy fuel, is a monumental obstacle to employment. When jobseekers present without a driver's licence, one of the most obvious and simplest things the agency can do to help the jobseeker become 'job ready' is to help them get their licence. Indeed, half of the 12 Stream C jobseekers that we follow at the Cove are assisted to gain their driver's licence and, in one example, the site also pays to register a car that a Stream C client has purchased. On the first day that we visit the office, we also observe an appointment in which Andrew offers to pay six months of comprehensive car insurance for a single mother if she secures a job as a disability support worker that she is interviewing for the following day. He also gives her a fuel voucher to cover the costs of attending the interview.

The Cove uses government money to pay for driving lessons, with Andrew telling us that 'a lot' of the site's Employment Fund 'is spent on driving lessons'. The instructors work for a small business that Artemis owns. When the driving instructor first comes into the office we are amazed at how friendly he is with the case managers. Is this a small town thing? No, the driving school and the employment agency are effectively one and the same. So this is the pattern at the Cove, with numerous people sharing the space, moving through it without the need to greet each other each time. Everyone busy with their own tasks, but all pulling in the same direction – trying to get jobseekers into work.

The office also has a small staffroom out the back, which is overwhelmed by the office computer server and other seemingly discarded IT-items, but which does also feature a small kitchenette and toilet. Kat tells us that the office has started buying its toilet paper from Who Gives a Crap, a company that donates a proportion of its profits to charity. Kat tells us that they support the company because they are building toilets in Kenya. The Cove office's theme of doing what they can to help those in need is dominant throughout our site visit. We are told that they purchase from social enterprises whenever they can. The office is also taking part in a 'bags for dignity' drive, in which members of the local community donate second-hand bags filled with new toiletries such as toothpaste, tampons and deodorant. On occasion, we are told, they give the bags to their highly disadvantaged jobseekers.

The office features the obligatory whiteboard in which placements are celebrated with a red marker. In this office the whiteboard is in the open-plan office, but facing away from the jobseeker waiting area, towards the case managers. It is somewhat understated. We are told that the whiteboard is also used to follow jobseekers in various streams, but that function does not appear active during our visit.

Never set anyone up to fail

Overall, this is the smallest office we visit, with only two staff members there at the time of our first visit – Andrew, the site manager, and Kat, a senior manager within Artemis who looks after staff development and employer engagement but also fills-in as a case manager when staff at various sites are on leave or sick. When we return months later to complete the fieldwork, Gwen is also working with them and has taken over as the site's only full-time case manager. But Andrew is often out of the office, apparently working between two sites. For much of our first visit, Kat is the only person in the office and it immediately becomes apparent that her mode is positive, affirming and familiar.

Soon after we arrive at 9 am, the first client appears. He is an older man, perhaps in his 60s, and Kat gives him a light touch on the shoulder as she refers to him as 'my friend'. As soon as she learns of his volunteer work, by way of friendly chitchat, she immediately encourages him to add the information to his CV. She types away but makes sure the jobseeker can see what she's doing. She ends the appointment with 'keep your phone close. You have the skills they want for the job.' As with almost all the offices we visit, Kat appears to know each and every jobseeker by name, without having to consult her notes. But she tends to refer to them in person as 'love', 'my love', 'darling' or 'mate'. Kat later tells us that she believes in speaking directly to jobseekers, the most important thing being 'to be real across the table'. For Kat, this means being 'down-to-earth' with jobseekers and 'not coming across as judgemental'. She wields colloquialisms like a pro and tells us that she will gladly tell a jobseeker that 'I am not going to kick you up the arse'.

Despite, or perhaps as a result of, the small staff numbers, the office has a positive, airy vibe. Music plays quietly in the background and the staff seem genuinely to enjoy their work and each other's company. That fondness extends to the tone used on the phone when speaking to the agency's head office or one of the other agency sites spread throughout regional NSW.

We later learn from Kat that the agency is proud of its not-for-profit status, but more than that, Artemis' management has explicitly made the decision to be mission driven, not profit or compliance focused. Kat explains to us that this has not always been the case. Under previous management, Kat tells us that they would place jobseekers into 'any job'. Now they work to make sure that the client is 'truly ready' because 'that's what it's all about'. A mantra that we hear repeatedly from the Cove office staff is 'never set no one up to fail'. This applies both to how Artemis, as an organisation, approaches jobseeker compliance but, perhaps more importantly, to how the site prepares its jobseekers for work. 'If we have a jobseeker go to a job,' Andrew tells us,

> We'll get all their work clothes. If they need Eskys, water bottles, we'll get all that. We'll give them fuel for the first week or two weeks, until they get paid from the employer … So just ensuring that they've got everything they need to start that job and fit in straight away.

It seems clear from what we observe during our visits to the Cove that the use of discretionary funds to purchase items needed to help jobseekers into work is commonplace. Andrew later tells us that he's 'a big believer' in spending the office's pool of Employment Funds. 'Because if we're not spending money, we're not moving people forward … [and] if we've only spent $200 for the month, what have we done for a jobseeker?' We see the purchase of fuel cards, car insurance, boots, clothing for interviews, shoes, driving lessons and more. On our second morning, we see an older male jobseeker clearly moved with gratitude when he discovers that the Cove office will buy him clothes for his new job. He asks if he will have to pay them back. Andrew responds 'no', saying that they will do anything to help get him into work: 'so if you need anything, just let us know'. Displays such as this are not common and quite moving, and we also hear of examples of the site's Employment Fund money being used to pay for private rental accommodation to get clients into secure housing and even, in the case of one jobseeker that we follow, for a residential drug rehabilitation program. In Mick's case, Andrew uses the site's Employment Fund to help pay for a residential rehab program that is based in Sydney, thinking that the young Aboriginal jobseeker will have to change providers when he moves to Sydney for his rehab program. In this instance, Andrew is prepared to use the site's money to help pay for the support that Mick needs even though he thinks Mick will soon no longer be a client at the Cove. But, touched by Andrew's gesture, Mick asks Andrew if he can remain as a client on the Cove's caseload:

> What happened there was he needed payment to get into a rehab and detox [program] before he was allowed to go into rehab … I checked it all out and I assisted with that … He rang me up to thank me. Then I advised him that he had been transferred to a company in Sydney. And he said, 'Listen, no one has ever taken the time to help or worried about [me].' But out of the EF [Employment Fund] we actually paid for his entry into rehab. And then when he went to the Sydney provider, he signed the transfer form, I rang the Sydney provider and explained it.

In Mick's case, Andrew arranges to continue working with him over the phone while he's in rehab, speaking to him almost weekly to support his recovery, rather than transferring him to another provider that 'didn't want someone in rehab that they had to keep on not being able to contact and … making their stats not look good'. Mick's case is an example of the Cove office's philosophy of never setting clients up to fail, even if that means going above and beyond what other providers would ordinarily do. Another related pattern that we observe is that if clients are not ready to work, the Cove office does not push them too hard to job search as this might set them up to fail by putting them at risk of a payment penalty. This is a site that is loath to use the stick of job search conditionality, and almost half of the Stream C jobseekers that we follow at the Cove have no job search requirements in their Job Plans for significant periods of our research. This is exceptionally unusual for a Jobactive site. While the program guidelines officially allow case managers and Jobactive sites to exempt Stream C clients from job search requirements, providers rarely use this discretion for fear that they will be audited by the department and asked to explain why their Stream C clients do not have job search requirements in their Job Plans. When we presented early findings from the research for this book at an industry conference, the audience was almost in disbelief that we found such a high proportion of clients without job search obligations for periods of their service.

One example of such a client at the Cove office is Marty. Marty immediately stands out to us due to his 'teardrop tattoo', although Gwen assures us that he's actually 'a really, really nice bloke'. His chequered history, the least of which involves 'a lot of drugs', is well known to the Cove staff. Marty is on parole and suffering severe mental health issues when we start our research at the office. 'We don't force him to supply job search', Andrew tells us, because 'that would put too much pressure on him': 'And then, if we've got it in there, then we'd have to go down the compliance road with him … That's not going to help him. That's going to set him back even more'. It's a philosophy shared by the other Cove staff. While compliance is 'very, very important', Kat says, it's about using 'your flexibility for the right':

> Like, if you've got a jobseeker that has a massive mental health issue and a drug addiction … and you go and put 10 to 20 job searches and they're a Stream C, that's wrong. That's setting them

up to fail. That's making them feel like every time they come in, they've failed at something.

Unlike the Westgate and Crompton offices, we hear no talk in the Cove office about sanctions being applied. Andrew later tells us that they use sanctions 'very rarely'. As he explains, 'Why take something away from them when they haven't got much as it is?' That said, the case managers are far from pushovers. A technique we observe Kat deploy is to mention the government's surveillance to curtail jobseeker behaviour. When Jasmine, a young jobseeker, divulges to Kat that she has applied for only three jobs in the past fortnight, Kat shows Jasmine the online system – which reports back to the government – and tells her 'that's not going to cut it'. She explains that job search activity is monitored by the government and audited. She closes the conversation with, 'At the end of the day I would love to see you applying for 100 to get a job. But the requirement is 20. That's not too much.' Jasmine agrees. This meeting, to which Jasmine was late, starts at 10.19 am. By the close of the meeting, Kat and Jasmine had agreed that Jasmine has until 2.30 pm that day to return to the office with her completed dole diary showing that she has applied for the required 20 jobs. As Jasmine sits there, Kat applies for a 10 hour per week waitressing job on her behalf, found on Seek.com, a commercial online job board. Kat tells Jasmine she can include the waitressing job in the 20 she needs to return to the office later that day. A sanction is mentioned, but not emphasised. While this meeting could be testing in another context, Kat and Jasmine part company on very friendly terms.

By design, all providers within Australia's welfare-to-work system are required to work with jobseekers to help them overcome barriers to employment and ultimately find jobs. Yet providers must also monitor that clients are meeting their mutual obligation requirements and report them to Centrelink for a possible payment suspension or financial penalty if they are not. This means that case managers must balance dual roles: seeking to develop trusting, supportive relationships with vulnerable people; and at the same time, policing them with potentially serious consequences, including loss of benefits payments for up to eight weeks. Staff at the Cove are particularly adept at managing this tricky, multifaceted relationship.

On the morning of our second day, we enter to see Kat on the phone to a jobseeker, whom she has NARed for not attending a scheduled meeting. Yet the call is not terse or confrontational. Rather, Kat chats to the jobseeker about how she plans to stay cool in the hot weather, closing the call with, 'Have a great weekend, Joanne, bye.' Overall, the Cove office does not rely heavily on sanctions to manage jobseekers and drive outcomes. Sanctions are applied as a measure of last resort. The Cove's attitude to sanctioning goes against the grain of a broader industry inclination towards reporting clients for payment penalties and suspensions. In the survey of more than 1,200 Jobactive staff that we undertook just months before beginning the fieldwork for this book, almost two-thirds of frontline staff reported that they were encouraged by their office 'not to be lenient' in the use of sanctions.[11] Moreover, in the years that we have been surveying Australia's frontline employment services workforce, case managers' attitudes towards clients have hardened and their willingness to sanction jobseekers for non-compliance has increased.[12] For instance, when asked, 'Which is more often to blame if a person is on benefits: lack of effort or circumstances beyond their control?' 40 per cent of the frontline workers we surveyed in 2016 blamed 'lack of effort'. By contrast, in the late 1990s, the proportion of frontline staff who blamed lack of effort was much lower, at only 27 per cent.

This tells us that a significant proportion of frontline employment staff now endorse what some scholars refer to as the 'pathological theory of unemployment'. According to this view, long-term unemployment is not primarily due to lack of opportunity caused by economic or structural conditions but 'is rooted in the character or the behavioural problems of the poor': specifically, a lack of motivation and culture of worklessness among those on benefits.[13] Once interpreted in this way, as we discussed in chapter one, the solution to long-term unemployment and welfare dependence becomes what Lawrence Mead – one of the foremost advocates of this theory of unemployment –

---

11 Lewis et al. 2016.
12 We examine this development at length in McGann, Nyugen and Considine 2020.
13 Marston and McDonald 2008, 256.

terms a 'politics of conduct'.[14] Programs must motivate those on benefits to work by attaching 'serious work and other obligations' to the receipt of payments, and imposing sanctions for non-compliance with these new forms of behavioural welfare conditionality.[15] Hence, we see an increasing emphasis on the use of behaviour change instruments such as sanctions, although it is not a value-orientation that we find much evidence of at the Cove or, if Kat is to be believed, at Artemis as an organisation. She attributes this to the leadership of Artemis' CEO, who Kat describes as a woman with the 'right values'.

Kat explains that for an agency to have the values she and Andrew celebrate, of caring for clients and never setting jobseekers 'up to fail', it must 'start at the top and trickle down'. The empathy that Artemis' frontline staff show towards their clients emanates, in part, from how its CEO treats her staff. 'It's a rippling effect,' Kat tells us:

> She cares about her staff but she cares about the jobseekers. That is the magic that makes Artemis work … If you've got care factor up here, then that is a rippling effect throughout your business and that's what we've got. We've got someone at the helm that really, really gives a shit.

While Kat's view of current management may be influenced by her close working relationship with the leadership team, her claims are certainly not baseless. The Cove office is located in a part of Australia that has above average unemployment, six per cent in June 2016 and above eight per cent a year later.[16] The site has around 40 Stream C jobseekers and as noted, a high First Nations clientele, communities that have suffered extreme disadvantage over generations. Yet despite this, it is the highest performing office that we study overall, with a 26-week outcome rate of well over 10 per cent among its Stream C clients.

---

14   Mead 2014, 97.
15   Mead 1986.
16   Data derived from Department of Employment, Small Area (SA2) Labour Market data – June 2016 quarter. Data series available from https://bit.ly/3hFvef5.

Emotional labour at the frontline

Overall, the Cove office tends to be quiet, with only rare instances of a jobseeker waiting to see a case manager. During those quiet times, we quickly discover that Kat's disarming nature is not limited to jobseeker interactions. While we are there she takes the opportunity to share the details of her personal weight loss journey. She shows us 'before' and 'after' photos and offers cosmetic surgery tips. She enquires about our ages and we enter into a frank and fearless discussion about whether we should consider Botox, although this part of the conversation only applies to Siobhan. It is hard to know whether the differential treatment is age or gender related. Kat also strongly encourages us to each take one of her muesli bars, which she tells us are part of her weight loss secret. We politely decline, but she insists on sharing this food.

Kat has a deeper spiritual side, although she's careful to say she's 'not a religious person'. She reveals to us that she has sought the help of a guru called the 'Doctor's Apprentice'. He's an Aboriginal man who specialises in trauma, recovery and resilience counselling, and the person who Kat says has had the deepest impact on her life. Almost proselytising, Kat recounts how she had been trying unsuccessfully to contact him for months by phone and email. Eventually, she persuaded Andrew to take a road trip with her to search out the Doctor's Apprentice just before Christmas. Arriving on his doorstep unannounced, the two of them ended up spending several hours with the Doctor's Apprentice, who told them about how we each wake up every morning and put on different suits. But 'the most important suit is your own skin' and you've got to care for yourself.

It's a message Kat continues to take to heart, especially working in a 'caring industry' like employment services, as she describes it. One of the biggest challenges for frontline staff, she says, is dealing with the trauma they come across every day in the lives of their clients, and how to avoid taking that suffering home with them. The next time we return to the Cove, several months later, we learn that the Doctor's Apprentice is now part of Artemis' staff. The provider has recruited him to help frontline staff deal with the trauma they encounter in their roles and the lives of their clients. Although occasionally he also works with some of the provider's clients and Marty, the jobseeker with the teardrop tattoo, is invited to join one of the sessions with the Doctor's Apprentice organised at the Cove site.

Artemis, and the Cove office especially, seem to be person-centred organisations committed to the wellbeing of their clients and staff in more of a holistic way than we've come across so far. Gwen, Kat's daughter, who later takes over as the Cove office's full-time consultant, tells us that the company is very into 'self-care'. The rationale, she explains, is that you cannot inspire others to get a job if you do not feel well yourself. Gwen, who is around 30 and lives in the Cove area with her young family, has been working in employment services for only 17 months when we meet her. She worked in real estate before that and says that 'the biggest eye opener' for her when becoming a case manager was 'really seeing what you didn't realise was going on here in Australia … that some people just aren't as fortunate as the next'. Clients, she says, open up to her a lot during appointments about sensitive personal issues such as abuse, family violence and drug dependency. While she does not 'have a certified plaque on the wall' to say she's a professional counsellor, 'I can almost guarantee you in every appointment we're treated like that.'

Gwen's point about the importance of self-care touches upon the prominence of *emotional labour* in frontline employment services work.[17] This kind of 'people-work' calls for those working at the frontline to display emotions towards clients such as affirmation, hope and encouragement, even though they may not actually feel those emotions, and to conceal conflicting emotions such as anger, despair and annoyance that, if displayed, could jeopardise their relationships with clients. 'Emotional labour' is the term coined by the American sociologist Airlie Hochschild to describe this 'management of feeling' in frontline service work.[18] She distinguishes between two kinds of emotional labour, surface-acting and deep-acting. Surface-acting is when frontline workers try to feign or simulate professionally desired emotions such as empathy through 'careful presentation' of their gestures, facial expressions and tone of voice.[19] Deep-acting, by

---

17 On the prominence of emotional labour to frontline employment services work specifically, see: Mann 2004; Nguyen and Velayutham 2018.

18 See Hochschild 1983.

contrast, involves frontline workers trying to authentically feel or induce the emotions that they are called on to display in their roles, akin to how method actors prepare for roles by living the personas they are performing.[20] However, frontline employment services work is also often associated with a kind of 'other-focused' emotional labour: trying to change the emotions *of their clients*. It seems reasonable to conclude that this is what frontline workers mean when they tell us that they are trying to instil confidence in jobseekers or give them hope and optimism for the future. The act of managing emotions at work, both those of the client as well as the worker's own, is central to success in frontline employment services as well other kinds of social services work.[21]

Gwen's point about not being able to inspire clients to get jobs if you do not feel well yourself points to this other-focused aspect of emotional labour, although it also speaks to the importance of deep-acting and the sense that feigning emotions is ultimately counter-productive. Tran Nguyen and Selvaraj Velayutham argue that a key form of emotional labour for frontline employment services staff is 'critical empathy'. This involves workers trying to connect with their clients *as other human beings* and 'feeling with them at some emotionally, intellectually and socially significant level'.[22] In one example from the Cove, Gwen recounts during a follow-up interview how she opened up to one of her clients, Penny, about her own experience of an abusive relationship. This expression of vulnerability from Gwen is met with an admission from Penny about the nature of her own experience as not just a victim of but also contributor to a violent family relationship:

> So I said to Andrew, 'Do you mind if I break all protocol and say to her, "Look, I've been involved in this and I know how to help

---

19   For further discussion of this distinction between surface- and deep-acting in the Australian employment services context, see Nguyen and Velayutham 2018.
20   This analogy is drawn by Sandi Mann. See Mann 2004.
21   See Guy and Newman 2004.
22   Nguyen and Velayutham 2018, 168.

you … "' And I think by me saying that, it then opened up to be like, 'Ah well, I'm not just a victim.' And then that opened up for her to admit that she's also the person that's being violent too.

Against this backdrop, the Doctor's Apprentice role at the Cove can be likened to an emotion management support worker – helping frontline staff to sustain, as well as protect themselves from, the emotional labour and critical empathy that they perform through teaching them techniques of 'self-caring'. One important reason why an organisation like Artemis might invest in supporting its staff to manage their emotions in this way is the high rate of burnout in the employment services workforce. As we noted in chapter three, the annual turnover of staff within the industry is estimated by NESA to be well over 30 per cent,[23] and high levels of job stress among frontline staff have previously been cited as a key contributing factor to the high rate of job churn in the industry.[24] The research on performing emotional labour indicates that, particularly when it involves forms of surface-acting, it is strongly associated with increased feelings of work stress and job dissatisfaction as well as employee burnout.[25] This stems from the emotional dissonance and strain that can arise from repeatedly having to portray emotions that are not felt, and the exhaustion of continuous emotion management. The prominence of emotional labour in case management work has also been argued by several scholars to contribute to the status of frontline employment services work as a highly feminised and low-paid occupation. As Mary Guy and Meredith Newman argue, 'the world turns to women for mothering, and this fact silently attaches itself to job descriptions'. As a result, emotional labour of the sort that generates perceptions of rapport, nurturance and empathy becomes conflated with women's work and 'does not register on the wage meter'.[26]

---

23 Maguire 2017.
24 Australian Services Union 2011. More than a third of the 568 frontline employment services staff surveyed by the ASU reported that they 'often' or 'always' felt stressed in their jobs, with a further 44 per cent reporting that they 'sometimes' felt stressed in their jobs.
25 For a more detailed discussion of the relationship between emotional labour, job stress and employee burnout, see Mann 2004.

Relationship building is a core theme for the Cove office staff. Early on our first day at the site, we witness an exchange between Kat and a jobseeker. Kat is out the front of the office having a cigarette. The jobseeker is not there for an appointment but happens to see Kat as he is passing by. He asks her for a cigarette, which she fetches from her desk and takes to him. When she returns, she tells us that he is a Stream C client, and she sees their exchange as part of a relationship-building process: he has told her one of the phone numbers on his paperwork is not correct, which she sees as a big relationship milestone, as now he is 'being honest' with her.

Trust is an important theme for Kat, who sees her job as being about building confidence with jobseekers. From her perspective, the job is about finding out where clients are on their journey into employment, then working with them at that level, always asking, 'What do they need to get into work? Is it about confidence? Is it about training? What can we do to get them job ready?' From what Kat tells us, small milestones are cause for celebration. She relays the story of a client who is a 'drug addict' and would regularly miss appointments. But after they worked together for some time, he started popping in and telling her why an appointment had been missed. She saw this as an important victory, because to her it represented the start of honest communication, which is necessary when working with jobseekers. During our time in the Cove office we witness first-hand many instances of jobseekers willingly disclosing information to Kat, including barriers to employment, small cash-in-hand jobs and other personal information such as having been in a car accident or conflict at home with parents or partners.

Kat, like many case managers we meet while undertaking the research for this book, cares little about a jobseeker's official stream categorisation by Centrelink. She tells us that she works with the individual in front of her and that 'sometimes you will have a very together Stream C and sometimes you will have a very weak Stream A. You need to get to know them and work out how to work with them.' Later in our site visit, after meeting with a young female jobseeker, Kat tells us that the jobseeker is Aboriginal but had been classified as Stream

---

26   Guy and Newman 2004, 293.

A, meaning the least disadvantaged class of jobseeker with limited funds available for support. Kat, like many case managers we meet, appears part distrustful of and part exasperated by the government's streaming process. Establishing that a jobseeker is Aboriginal not only makes them eligible for higher stream classification, it also means that various training programs are offered free of charge. Kat tells us that she has only realised that the jobseeker is Aboriginal via informal conversation outside the official context of the appointment.

As discussed in detail in other parts of this book, the re-categorising of jobseekers appeared to be almost core business in nearly all the offices we visit. It is a practice that reflects concerns about jobseeker streaming that providers have repeatedly expressed since the Job Seeker Classification Instrument was changed and a three-tiered streaming system introduced by the Abbott government under the Jobactive reforms. Almost two-thirds of providers surveyed for the official interim evaluation of Jobactive reported 'that they were dissatisfied with the way jobseekers were allocated to a stream'.[27] Most reported experiencing unexpected streaming results, especially in relation to jobseekers who were ex-offenders or pre-release prisoners, long-term or very long-term unemployed, who had low English proficiency or who were First Nations.

Yet while Kat clearly agrees that the Centrelink streaming process is lacking, and also displays considerable frustration at discovering that jobseekers are not receiving the assistance they are entitled to, due to streaming inaccuracies, the Cove office is less inclined than other sites we observe to actively work to re-categorise jobseekers. Overall, we record only two cases of this office actively working with jobseekers to have them reclassified into a higher stream (although we track fewer jobseekers in total at the Cove office than at other sites). One of these is a young jobseeker, Allen, who has moved from interstate and is referred initially to the Cove office as a Stream A participant. However, Gwen detects at his initial appointment that Allen has 'served time', because he discloses that he's 'missed a lot', including his sister's wedding. The office refers him back to Centrelink, who upstream him to a C, with Kat advising Allen of 'the right things that you need to tell

---

27   Department of Employment, Skills, Small and Family Business 2019, 65.

Centrelink so that you're in the right stream'. The other case is Faye, a long-term client of the site who has not worked in 20 years and has survived gendered violence. Like Allen, Faye was initially referred by Centrelink to the Cove office in Stream A and the site progressively worked to upstream her, first into Stream B before they 'eventually ... got her to a C'. Besides these examples of getting clients up-streamed into a higher service stream, we observe only two instances of case managers working with clients to apply for a temporary exemption from participation requirements, and no cases of jobseekers either being encouraged to apply for another program, such as DES, or a reduction in the jobseeker's work capacity. These four cases of jobseeker re-categorisation stand in contrast to the other three sites, where we witness these practices in relation to 11 jobseekers at one site, 15 clients at another and nine at another.[28] Overall, the prevailing attitude at this office appears to be that you work with the jobseekers you have, but you also make sure they have access to the resources they are entitled to.

Caring professions for the ladies and hard yakka for the blokes

According to labour market data, the Cove office is located in a part of regional Australia in which 10.6 per cent of people work in health and social services; 10.3 per cent work in mining; 10 per cent in accommodation and food services; while retail, construction and manufacturing account for 8.5, 8.2 and 5.2 per cent respectively.[29] As such, the sorts of entry-level jobs in small manufacturing businesses that other offices in the study – and especially the Westgate office – relied on are harder to come by in the Cove. We witness for ourselves that the suite of options presented to jobseekers tends to be rather modest. Women are offered waitressing, housekeeping and café work, although this type of work is often seasonal with fluctuating shifts,

---

28   We discuss these re-categorisation practices at length in an article, see
      O'Sullivan et al. 2019.
29   This is based on ABS Labour Force Region Data (SA4) – August 2016, for the
      area of New South Wales where Artemis' Cove office is located. Australian
      Bureau of Statistics 2016. Data Series available at https://bit.ly/3wFI5SF.

which makes it difficult for the Cove office to achieve sustained employment outcomes for clients placed into these kinds of jobs. One of the Stream C jobseekers we track is Janet, a woman in her late 40s who moved to the Cove to flee domestic violence and is living in her car when she first attends the office. Janet has 'a bit of a cleaning job' at that time, but it is only a couple of hours per day and not enough to meet her full-time activity requirements. Janet eventually finds a house in the area, and Andrew pays her bond and the first two weeks' rent 'to get her into housing'. The next step is to try and find her more stable work, which the staff try to do by brokering her into a housekeeping job with a motel that the office has a relationship with. Janet stays in that job for the rest of the study, working casually, but her weekly shifts are never enough to move off benefits or for the Cove office to claim a full 26-week employment outcome. The most they can claim is a 12-week partial outcome even though Janet works at the motel for almost a year.

The National Disability Insurance Scheme (NDIS) is seen as an opportunity for more viable and sustained work. As Andrew tells one of the clients in an appointment that we observe, 'that would be good to get into because it is so big. That is where all the work will be.' Female jobseekers are encouraged to get their certificate in childcare, disability care or aged care, and police checks permitting jobseekers to work with children are readily arranged and paid for by the Cove office staff. On several occasions, Andrew encourages Faye – the long-term client that Centrelink originally classified as a Stream A jobseeker – to think about working in aged care, mainly because he thinks 'she is nice and soft spoken, and a lovely person'. But she keeps turning down the suggestion until her sister, who is also a jobseeker at the Cove, goes through an aged care course and gets a job from it. This persuades Faye to reconsider the course, and the office then organises her police check and pays the concession fee of $240 for Faye to study a Certificate III in Individual Support. They also pay for her work clothes, because the 12-week course, which includes a 160-hour work placement, is actually run out of an aged care facility, Geris Cove. This means a strong prospect of employment following the course, which is exactly what happens when Faye secures a job almost immediately after finishing her training. Eventually, Faye moves off benefits entirely achieving a full 26-week employment outcome for the office. Andrew later tells us that the Cove has found this particular course, delivered by a training organisation that Geris Cove uses to train all its staff, has 'a very high rate of employment after it'. As he does with any training organisation that tries to sell a course to the office, he first sent a couple of jobseekers on the course 'to test the waters', because 'we don't do training for training's sake'. When those first two jobseekers came out with employment, Andrew began sending 'as many as they would take off us', including Faye and her sister.

One marked difference we observe at the Cove office site from our other fieldwork sites, located in and around large cities, is the limited pool of employers the Cove staff can call on to place their jobseekers. From our first morning at the office we hear repeated references to 'Water View': jobseekers have appointments at Water View, interviews at Water View, need transport to get to Water View or are being bought clothes to start with Water View. In one of the first appointments we observe, Andrew takes Lillian, a lone parent in her late 20s, to Target to buy clothes to wear to an interview at Water View later that day. He does this after learning Lillian is planning to wear the clothes she has on, an outfit from a charity shop, to the interview. He gently suggests that she should wear a black dress instead, which he offers to buy for her. Across the room, Kat interrupts the appointment she is taking to tell Andrew to also buy Lillian a red shirt, 'something bright', and 'a nice pair of shoes', telling Lillian that 'they will love you out there'. Andrew also arranges a police check for Lillian on the spot and offers to buy her petrol to make sure, he tells her, that she 'can get to work in the first few weeks'.

We quickly discover that Water View is a retirement village for veterans and seniors operated by another not-for-profit organisation. Clearly the Cove office staff have developed a good working relationship with Water View's management, which is mutually beneficial as Water View needs workers and the Cove needs jobs for clients. But what is most noteworthy about this arrangement is that the clients being referred to Water View are almost exclusively women. This observation brings the gendered nature of Australia's welfare-to-work system, and the tendency for providers to channel women into stereotypical areas of 'women's employment', more fully into view. Not only is the case manager role gendered, but work referrals are also gendered. We have seen this already at the Westgate office, with the male jobseekers being channelled towards warehousing and forklift jobs and the women towards hospitality and cleaning. It is a pattern that runs even deeper at the Cove, with women being directed towards aged care and cleaning roles and the men towards labouring jobs and light manufacturing. While this may enable women returning to the labour force to gain a foothold in employment in the short-term, the tendency 'to steer women into "women's work"' risks accentuating pre-existing gender divisions and inequalities in the labour market.[30]

As Jo Ingold and David Etherington argue regarding the gendered patterning of welfare-to-work policies, while 'activation ostensibly focuses on maximising women's labour market participation it has been limited by the pathways presented to women'.[31] These pathways are frequently 'at the lower end of the job hierarchy', characterised by low pay and poor employment conditions. Developing this point, Linda Grant argues that the gender bias implicit in the delivery of welfare-to-work is an aspect of active labour market policy that is all too often overlooked.[32] But there is evidence to suggest that it is an important issue across the Australian system. As a Senate inquiry into Jobactive noted, the program 'is not delivering equal outcomes for women and men'.[33] We observed this for ourselves in the case of the Westgate office, where the job placement and employment outcome rates were lower among the female jobseekers that we followed. However, official program data reported in the final report of the Australian government's Expert Advisory Panel on the next generation of employment services reveals that it is a systemic pattern across Jobactive. While women comprise more than half of the Jobactive caseload nationally, the Advisory Panel found that female jobseekers account for only 40 per cent of the job placements that providers achieve.[34] Perhaps more alarmingly, only 44 per cent of jobseekers that providers financially assist through Employment Fund expenditure are women. This suggests that providers are not only placing men into jobs

---

30 Grant 2009.
31 Ingold and Etherington 2013, 635.
32 Grant 2009.
33 Senate Education and Employment References Committee 2019, 69.
34 Department of Jobs and Small Business 2018a, 40.

ahead of women, they are also diverting financial resources away from women to subsidise additional Employment Fund expenditure on men.

On the second day, the flipside of the Water View story comes into focus. We learn that a local company, Rebrand, has won a big contract to refurbish all state-owned emergency service vehicles, and they need staff. Once again, it seems clear that the Cove office staff have a strong working relationship with Rebrand. We later learn from Kat that she brokered Rebrand for Artemis after 'going out and doing some marketing', talking to them 'about what we stand for'; namely, that Artemis 'is not just about putting people into jobs ... We're not going to set people up to fail and we're not going to let employers down.' At this stage, the Cove office has been referring jobseekers to interviews with Rebrand for two to three weeks, and Kat anticipates that Artemis might be able to place 100 jobseekers from across three of its sites over the next 12 months. During our time at the Cove, numerous jobseekers are encouraged to think about Rebrand as their next employer, and some of the Stream C jobseekers that we track are referred for jobs with Rebrand. One is Allen, the ex-prisoner jobseeker who the Cove office had worked to upstream from A to C. The jobseekers being referred to Rebrand all have something in common: they are all blokes. Many are mature aged; many are retrenched miners. Some have trades, but others, including Allen, do not.

Another significant employer that the Cove works with, we learn, is Tower Fencing, a local company manufacturing picket fences, awnings, security screens and balustrades. Andrew personally manages this employer, having built trust with Tower Fencing's manager over several years. Andrew only sends his best jobseekers to Tower Fencing and, in return, Tower Fencing's manager, Genevieve, is completely loyal to Andrew. She refuses 'to speak with anyone else' in Artemis, and Andrew deals with her face-to-face in a no-nonsense way. 'I don't fluff around with asking her anything; she doesn't fluff around with me,' Andrew tells us. 'There's no big spiel about any guidelines or anything like that. She's not into that.' Importantly for Artemis, Genevieve had previously worked as a nurse in corrective services, so has 'an understanding of' and 'doesn't judge' some of the clientele Andrew might send her.

As with Rebrand, we witness numerous examples of jobseekers being put forward for jobs with Tower Fencing, one of whom is Bradley, a Stream C jobseeker that we follow at the Cove office. Bradley, who is in his late 20s, secures a permanent full-time job with Tower Fencing after the Cove office places him into a trades-assistant job. It is a job that, Gwen and Andrew tell us, fits perfectly with what Bradley tells them he's always wanted: 'a blokey, bloke job'. Because, as with Rebrand, the jobseekers being referred to Tower Fencing are all blokes. This includes one young man, Steve, who walks into the Cove office late in the afternoon on our first day to ask about some extra driving lessons, telling Kat that he has his test coming up the following week. No problem at all, Kat tells Steve, even though it appears that she's never met him before. But more than this, she will even hire an external instructor for Steve if Artemis' instructor is booked up. Then she wants to know if he's working, since he looks fit and healthy. Steve isn't, so she begins the sell. 'A really good job that has just come in. Afternoon shift. Award wage.' She explains they will provide him with all the work gear, and that Andrew has a really good relationship with the woman that runs the business. Steve is genuinely taken aback with excitement about the job, so Kat promises him: 'Right, we will get you a bloody interview.'

Ten minutes before Steve walks into the office, Kat is also trying to sell other jobseekers on Tower Fencing over the phone. 'I've got a job that Andrew wants to put you forward for,' she calls down the receiver to a jobseeker she has seen earlier that day. 'It's with Tower Fencing,' pays award wages with the prospect of penalty rates and will involve a bit of welding and using power tools. She gets off the phone very excited and immediately leaves a message on Andrew's mobile. The jobseeker is 'as keen as mustard' and has 'all the quals and skills' that Andrew is looking for. Before she hangs up, she promises to get Andrew 'another two to three people' that he can put forward to Tower Fencing.

What determines that some jobseekers are recommended for Water View and others for Rebrand or Tower Fencing? Why is it that we see woman after woman walking out of the office with a new blouse and shirt, while the blokes all walk away with a brand-new pair of steel-capped boots? Unconscious bias seems to be an important factor. We hear jobseeker Pete tell Kat that he does not have a trade certificate, but Kat still strongly encourages Pete towards a job with Rebrand. Kat tells him, 'Pete, I am going to push real hard for you my friend. You will be able to hit the ground running.' We observe no such pushing to get unskilled jobseekers into jobs with Rebrand on behalf of female jobseekers. Kat's only requirement is that Pete assure her that he has left his previous employer on good terms: 'cards on the table. So long as there was no issues with them.' This exchange speaks to, in part, the gendered nature of the job allocation process, at least in rural centres. But it also demonstrates the importance of a trusted relationship with employers. The only reason why Kat would not be prepared to push for a Rebrand job for Pete would be if he had a poor track record with his previous employer. In this part of the world, few things matter more than good relationships.

Sitting in on Pete's appointment with Kat affords us valuable insights into a range of factors influencing Australia's employment system. In addition to the gender issues already discussed, ageism in recruitment is also highlighted. Pete is 57. Even though Rebrand has a large contract and needs workers, Kat worries out loud to Pete that his age may work again him. She does, however, dismiss that concern with 'but you are a fit 57 and they know you'. The Rebrand job requires that Pete undergo a drug test. This issue is broached quite candidly. Kat opens with, 'Don't wish to be rude, but I need to ask it as I don't wish to set people up to fail ...' The thought is interrupted as Kat stops to answer the phone. When she puts the phone down, she continues. 'I need to ask, drug and alcohol test?' Pete quickly answers 'no problem' and that test is booked and paid for. Another issue relates to training, skills and certificates. Pete is a boilermaker, but he has no qualifications. He began in the trade before a certificate was required. He also discloses that he has failed his truck licence test. Again, this is not because he cannot drive a truck; the testing process made him nervous, so he did not change gears properly and was failed. This points to another significant issue, the extent to which jobseekers are required to confide in their case managers about personal circumstances. Kat and Pete have a long discussion about the most effective way to change gears on a truck, but the conversation also necessarily diverts towards how Pete is going to remain calm when he next takes the truck licence test. And it also involves strategy: should Pete disclose to Rebrand that he failed his truck licence? They decide he should say nothing unless asked.

Due to the timeframe of our fieldwork, we never find out what happens to Pete. But Kat seems optimistic about his chances with

Rebrand. Some of her words to Pete are 'I think you are a perfect match out there … it's a perfect résumé. I am a little bit excited for you, mate … I feel pretty confident, mate' and finally, 'okay, keep your phone close to you'. Indeed, minutes later Kat says, 'you know, Pete, I think I will go that one step further for you. I think I will pick the phone up and talk to Julie [in HR] about you.' Their appointment concludes with Kat saying to Pete, with a wink, 'Okay, my darling. This is your next appointment in two weeks. Hopefully you will call and say that you can't come as you are working with Rebrand.' We choose to believe that Pete got that job and it was a wonderful opportunity for him, although Allen, the Stream C jobseeker we track who is placed with Rebrand, does not last in the position. We learn from Gwen in a follow-up interview that he was sacked after just two weeks as the work 'was too fast paced for him and the employer wasn't happy, so they let him go there.'

A little more mission than most

Two themes that we have touched on throughout the book are the loss of diversity between employment services providers and the associated drift of not-for-profit providers away from their core mission-driven values. We have described these two patterns in terms of 'provider herding' around the delivery of standardised, low-cost, work-first strategies and 'mission drift' among the not-for-profit segment of the market as faith-based and other third sector providers have increasingly sought to emulate the business practices of their corporate peers. Our case study of the Westgate office in chapter four exemplifies these developments, confirming what we had long suspected based on the research team's survey work to date. Yet, as our study draws to a close in regional NSW, the Cove case offers grounds for more optimism and hope. A strong local history moderates these larger trends in some important ways.

We see marked points of difference in Cove's service delivery approach, including its commitment to brokering job placements for its clients directly with local employers rather than relying on labour hire agencies as intermediaries, as we saw with the Westgate office in chapter four. As Andrew tells us about the Cove office's approach to job brokerage, he looks to broker jobs with local employers 'that have an understanding' of their Stream C clients rather than labour hire companies that 'to be frank, they just want to use and abuse people when they can, put them off when they feel like it, put them back on when they feel like it.' We also see the Cove office make good use of the site's Employment Fund to invest in its Stream C clients in ways that we rarely see at the other sites – paying for driving lessons, securing deposits for private rental housing and even, as in the example of Mick, paying for residential rehabilitation programs so that jobseekers can get the help that they need to address substance dependency challenges. What's most notable about these investments in jobseekers is that they are targeted at helping jobseekers to address long-term and complex barriers to employment, such as homelessness, drug dependency, and lack of access to transport. The Cove is not holding its resources for more immediate investments in polishing 'job ready' clients for the labour market through purchasing work or interview clothing, and paying for the entry-level licences and accreditations to work in fields such as labouring, construction, hospitality and warehousing. The latter are the bread and butter of employment services providers, and the Cove is also making these more immediate investments. But it is going above and beyond to work with jobseekers in a more sustained and enabling way.

Above all, however, what is most remarkable about the Cove is the genuine and deep sense of commitment among Kat, Andrew and Gwen to their clients, not as jobseekers or tradeable commodities but *as people* to get to know, trust, and help. When Kat has a quiet moment, she explains to us that what we are observing is not her normal role. When the office was located at another site, she worked as a case manager. She has since taken on a head office leadership role that she describes as 'motivator and other things'. She has been filling in at the Cove for three weeks while another case manager is away. She is happy to do so as she likes to remain 'connected to the jobseekers and not lose sight of the purpose of the whole thing'. Indeed, we detect no sense that Kat wants to be somewhere else or that she feels she is above the role she's performing. Kat appears to relish her conversations with jobseekers and gives no sense that she has something better to do. When Kat's attitude is considered alongside Andrew's deep commitment, particularly to his Aboriginal clients, you quickly get the sense that this is quite a remarkable site with deep local roots. It seems to us that the staff, either because of who they are as people or because of the organisation they work for, or perhaps both, have managed to retain a sense of mission in a sector that is often accused of being overly rule driven, bureaucratic, lacking in innovation or focused on KPIs at the expense of their vulnerable clients.

On our first morning in the office, a jobseeker finds herself seated alone while Andrew goes to get her a fuel card, which will allow the jobseeker to fill her car with petrol so she can drive to job interviews. The jobseeker turns towards us and says, 'This is the most fantastic place.' She explains that at her previous agency in regional Queensland, 'they did nothing to help' her. She describes the Cove as an office in which people go out of their way to help. Indeed, the jobseeker tells us that by the end of her first appointment at the Cove, she had her 'blue card', which allows her to work with children. At no other site we visit does a jobseeker offer up a similar testimonial about the case management staff. And we can see for ourselves that the staff at this office, at least while we are there, do seem to sincerely care. Not because jobseekers represent star ratings, but because helping makes their clients' lives better. Thankfully for all concerned, we see no evidence that caring jeopardises the Cove's star rating. Indeed, as already noted, this is the best-performing office we visit, working against the odds in a region with fewer job opportunities than in the city.

The Cove staff extend themselves in other ways. We witness a case manager explaining to a jobseeker how to sign her kids up to the local football team. We also see case managers sharing tips that could make the lives of local unemployed people that little bit easier. For example, reminding a jobseeker that her driver's licence is about to expire and encouraging her to get a five-year licence – the longest term available – because it's free now but may not be in the future. These are little things, but they matter a great deal. It takes only a little thought and a minute of conversation to help a jobseeker save money on their driver's licence. To many of us that saving would be insignificant, but to a highly disadvantaged jobseeker, it could fundamentally change the way they are able to celebrate their child's birthday or heat their home in winter.

Yet despite the cheerful, empathetic predisposition with which the Cove's case managers approach their jobseeker clients, much of what occurs in the office is also routinised and reminiscent of the other sites we visit. Relations between jobseekers are mediated through online systems, with the case managers always logged into the government–provider interface. While emphasis is placed on relationship building, we witness Kat telling one jobseeker that she cannot come early to her appointment or Kat will fall behind on her admin – not something that any case manager in the Australian welfare-to-work system can afford to do. Indeed, Kat with her obviously cheery disposition and substantive 'motivational' role at Artemis, does explicitly note the paperwork burden associated with her position. She tells us that her normal practice is to not see the next client until she has done the paperwork for the previous client.

Our survey research over more than 20 years has shown quite clearly that the heavy administrative burden associated with the delivery of welfare-to-work services in Australia has progressively eroded the amount of time case managers can spend in conversation with jobseekers. When we surveyed frontline Jobactive staff in 2016, they reported spending almost 35 per cent of their time each week, on average, on tasks related to contract compliance and administration – up from 25 per of their time each week in 2008 – and only 44 per cent of their time in direct contact with jobseekers.[35] However, for much of our site visit Kat holds down the fort alone, and therefore does not have time to keep her paperwork in check. She does not stop for lunch, although she tells us that it is Artemis policy to do so. Kat also remains at the office after we leave for the day. We do not know for sure what she does there after 5 pm, but it seems reasonable to assume that meeting her government-reporting requirements is probably the key task. We must not put too fine a point on the workload associated with Australia's welfare-to-work frontline, since stopping for regular cigarette breaks is common practice at the Cove and all our other fieldwork sites. Moreover, chatting with colleagues, including about non-work related matters, is also commonplace among all the sites we visited. But we certainly do not begrudge the staff that time: it is also

---

35   Lewis et al. 2016.

team building and collegial, with stories shared, anecdotes and tips exchanged, and jobseekers sized up in advance of the next employment opportunity. And, of course, we each step out for regular coffee breaks during our fieldwork, though we always go alone, leaving the other in the office to quietly observe the fascinating daily encounters and systems at the Australian welfare-to-work frontline.

Conclusion: Success and the significance of difference

In early December 2019, we sent out our annual season's greetings message to people we had worked with over the previous year or so. It felt natural to include everyone involved in our fieldwork for this project. After all, we had spent many days observing them in their offices, sharing coffee and lunch breaks with them, and contacting them by phone and email every eight weeks for 18 months. These frontline staff had become our colleagues, of a sort. What we quickly discovered was that few of the people we had worked with were still at their place of employment two years on. Even the Cove staff, who all seemed to cherish each other's company, and believed fully in Artemis' mission, had moved on. Where to? We do not know. In some cases they will have moved to other offices, perhaps within the organisation or to a competitor. Others will be lost to the industry altogether. They were hairdressers, bakers, flight attendants, hospitality workers, carpenters or themselves long-term unemployed before they took on the job of assisting others into work, and perhaps they are now back doing those things once again. Such is the nature of Australia's welfare-to-work frontline workforce. Local knowledge is accumulated quickly and lost just as fast. The contracts are short, the work can be stressful, the KPIs are relentless, the time to connect with vulnerable people as individuals is curtailed, and the low pay may seem to many people to simply not be worth it.

While the individual frontline workers we profile in the book have moved on, the system is about to do so too. The rules and methods we describe here will in all likelihood be radically overhauled in July 2022. Our jobseekers will face a completely different set of conditions. Like some comparable systems around the world, Australia's unemployed will no longer experience face-to-face assistance in finding work. Under Australia's as yet unnamed new digital system, Centrelink's initial assessments of jobseekers are likely to be done online via a new digitised Job Seeker Classification Instrument that is currently being tested. Once the newly unemployed citizen has been categorised, it is proposed that they will be given access to a government-designed mobile phone application – the Job Seeker App. That app will be their case manager initially. If the app fails, confuses, or overwhelms them the jobseeker will have the chance to seek assistance by phoning a contact centre, which will most likely be run by a large multinational corporation, experienced in government contracting. The help the jobseeker receives from the call centre worker will not be personal. The voice on the other end of the phone will not ask the jobseeker about their long-term goals; they will not enquire about the jobseeker's mother's health or whether the jobseeker is feeling more confident now that they have their driver's licence. The assistance will be technical, focused on getting the app working properly and perhaps also advising jobseekers on the types of information they need to input to ensure that their welfare payment continues.

If using the app does not result in a job within 18 months, the jobseeker – then classified as long-term unemployed – will likely be moved into a face-to-face system, a variant of the one we describe in this book. It is also possible that individuals who simply cannot use the app may enter the face-to-face system from the start. But indications are that the government is determined to have as many people as possible using the app. In the trial of this new employment services model, providers even receive an incentive payment of $400 to move their clients out of enhanced services and into the impersonal world of digital services.[1] Digital illiteracy; extreme poverty; a lifestyle

---

1   The Department calls this a 'Progress in Service Bonus'. See: Department of Employment, Skills, Small and Family Business 2019b.

inconsistent with maintaining a device in working order, such as homelessness; or poor internet infrastructure in one's area are each unlikely to be an adequate reason for entering the face-to-face system. The promise is that the sizable savings flowing from a digital-first system will be invested in assisting the hardest-to-help.

As we document in this book, one of the most consistent features of Australia's welfare-to-work system is its ineffectiveness in assisting the hardest-to-help. This project specifically focused on trying to identify the most fruitful ways to assist highly disadvantaged jobseekers. What we quickly discovered is that there is no underlying formula. Some offices are better at teamwork, while others are more skilled at connecting with employers. But, taken as a whole, the picture we paint is one of relatively marginal returns for the jobseeker. The difference between being an average and an outstanding provider of services to highly disadvantaged jobseekers may be as low as placing a single additional person into a 26-week job.

As such, it is quite possible that there will come a time when we look back on the system described in this book with a sense of lost possibilities. Or we may see in the proposed split between regular jobseekers and those with serious challenges an opportunity to shift resources towards the latter. So, what can we conclude about the practice of using a market-based system for buying and selling contracts for helping the poor in Australia?

This book, as we said at the start, has been an attempt to step behind the service delivery curtain and see how things work at the frontline of a sensitive social program. We wanted to figure out why some agencies do better at helping very disadvantaged people find jobs, when the overall system is weak at doing that. If we could crack that code, we thought we could share the formula to the advantage of all. We picked four agencies with track records that put them in the top echelon. We used a rigorous method to compare the best sites and select four representative cases. We then spent a lot of time observing them, talking with their staff, and following the progress of a selection of their most disadvantaged clients. It is probably fair to say that our most important research resource was shoe leather. We travelled to them on multiple occasions and spent extended time with them. And the most important research method was structured observation. This should not imply that we were neutral about what we were looking for. Certainly not. Nor that we had no idea beforehand what might be going on. That would be naïve. Rather, we worked with the idea that peer-reviewed observations provide an insightful form of situational reading. Each element of the service was identified, all the main transactions mapped, and each standard approach was described. Then we overlaid these systemic observations with more granular points of comparison to see where a given case manager might alter the pattern. Or to note where certain types of clients might evoke different responses.

This kind of situational reading can easily descend into wishful thinking or even bias, of course. That's the 'eye of the beholder' trap. So we worked in pairs and brought all observations back to the research team for testing. The observations that made it into the book had to endure that long journey unscathed. They had to make sense to both the researcher observing them and their companion observer, and then they needed to be compelling to the other independent members of the team. We also tested them carefully with our industry partners to check that we had understood the system requirements properly. Then we took them into open consultation with a room full of 60 to 70 current practitioners at an annual industry conference and asked them to tell us what they saw in our results and conclusions. And even so, there is still some room for difference as we will show. A trained eye can read a Renaissance painting with a predictable interpretation of its symbols and style. But there will still be argument, and important argument, about the significance of small differences. So, too, with observational social science: it's important to show how much we agree upon and then to explore the variations and surprises.

Let's start with what we think is clear in these cases, what anyone who did what we did, with the observational frame we used, would agree was true. The first thing to hold in clear view is the underlying patterns of success and failure for these most disadvantaged jobseekers. The system's partial success with jobseekers overall are much poorer still with the longer-term clients. As we saw in chapter five, about one-third of those one million or so unemployed people placed in work achieve full-time work and the rate for the most disadvantaged group is considerably lower again – only about one in five Stream C jobseekers continue to 26 weeks or more of employment after being placed in a job. We saw in chapter two, when discussing the criteria for high performance, that even among the best-performing Jobactive sites, only between four and 16 per cent of Stream C jobseekers go on to achieve a fully sustained job – defined as 26 weeks of continuous work. What happens to the rest of them along the way is equally striking. Up to a quarter get reclassified in some way – either with reduced work requirements, moved to a different service stream, or referred to DES – and about one in three experience suspension from their mutual obligations for some period of time, as we saw at the Westgate and Crompton offices. Caseload churn is another significant challenge, and between a quarter and a third of the Stream C jobseekers that we followed at each of the offices soon moved on to a different office, or disappeared from welfare rolls for reasons unknown, before providers could place them in work.

These results are not achieved by chance. Our four cases show there is method in the apparent madness of operating a billion-dollar program with such low success rates. Agencies make important choices about the local strategy they will use. One of our four was quick to issue sanctions, forcing almost a third of our sample to suffer suspended payments. These are dramatic penalties which typically result in jobseekers having insufficient funds to pay rent and buy food and yet, as we witnessed at the Crompton office, case managers occasionally take delight in applying them. How case managers perceive their clients' trustworthiness and motivation helps to shape how they wield this sanctioning power. The Crompton case managers repeatedly voiced – to us and each other – lurking suspicions that clients 'had money' or were 'using the system'. They leaned on these motivational framings to explian to themselves why they were taking such a hard-line stance on policing compliance. They also actively encouraged transfers to other agencies when they felt they would find it hard to get an individual into work. Called 'tree shaking', they challenged clients off their list and replaced them with new jobseekers. They found a way to change their client base in favour of newer and perhaps better options. The method was described by one of the frontline staff we profile in that chapter as 'just push, push' and let them 'transfer out' if they could not comply.

One of the things that make this kind of local strategy feasible and even easy is that the system is highly complex, subject to multiple systems of rules and penalties, and involves a variety of decision-stages where agencies can employ their own approach to client services. Helping clients get reclassified is a classic case. Many of the barriers to employment experienced by these disadvantaged jobseekers can be successfully presented as a reason to vary their requirements, to move them to an inactive status, or alter their obligations to find full or part-time work. Having an alcohol problem or experiencing depression may offer a chance to obtain a medical exemption, or to place restrictions on the kind of work to be done. While there is no doubt that many of these are legitimate concerns, the fact that they can improve an agency's performance is problematic and even corrupt, in some cases. It is illustrative of the kinds of 'performance paradoxes' that Janice Dias and Steven Maynard-Moody argue are frequently generated by outcomes-based contracting regimes.[2] In other words, the strategy of relying on performance targets and financial incentives to try to steer frontline behaviour and street-level policy implementation invariably produces unintended effects that work against the achievement of policy goals. In the case of the reclassification strategies described in this book, the performance targets that offices and case managers have been set to try to motivate them to move clients from welfare-to-work produce street-level adaptations that involve trying to reduce clients' work obligations, or even move them beyond the reach of activation entirely, so that performance targets become more manageable and easier to reach.

In defence of the agencies it must also be said that the organisational regime they work under has massive transaction costs. For example, to secure their performance rating for placement of jobseekers into Work for the Dole, some frontline staff need to spend up to 40 percent of their time chasing and recording client movements, while in one case their agency also manipulated the time of their formal enrolment to maximise 'speed to placement' scores. Paradoxically it took more time to improve speed to placement outcomes. All this while caseloads of 150 per case worker were the norm and management expectations involved

---

2   Dias and Maynard-Moody 2006.

a meeting with each client every two weeks. And even where it is not, the practice tilts the daily work towards time-consuming efforts to constantly re-examine eligibility and client classifications.

As we saw, not every agency takes the same approach to managing their clients. While Crompton was often distrustful of clients and pressed them to find their own jobs, only 10 percent of their job placements came from them finding a vacancy for the client. The Cove was caring and connected, using its longstanding contacts with local employers to find jobs for their most disadvantaged clients. They had more social capital to work with, being based in a regional centre and employing staff with good community standing and deep local connections. But they also invested in that capital and spent far less time on disciplinary issues.

Beneath this local variation we saw a difference in approach to the client's background and barriers to employment. The government policy settings provide scope for significant divergence in the 'theory of change' for these disadvantaged people. Jessica from Wilmore is a former jobseeker turned site manager. She was absolutely clear on this point: She said, in her matter-of-fact way, 'we're an employment service, we're not here to manage the barriers.' Others regarded investments in the client to address background barriers to be both humane and motivational in getting them into work. This process of engaging clients was seen to cut both ways. It had practical benefits for the client and it also served to create high spirits among the staff, producing a characteristic team ethos. Sitting within this set of choices lay a deeper different too. For some frontline workers the treatment of clients conveyed a more general humanity, expressed as a real interest in their non-work trials and interests. This was strongest in our tighter-knit local community of the Cove where contact with clients out-of-hours was likely to count as an important dimension of the workplace discussion of their needs and aspirations. This was often expressed as interest in their hobbies, their kids and their culture or Aboriginality and what this meant to them.

Another striking feature of the frontline work with more disadvantaged clients was the amount of administration required to manage the caseload. With up to 150 people on their individual caseload, frontline staff had high levels of accountability to record, verify and report in relation to each jobseeker. This was evident from the very first office we visited, in Wilmore, where much of the job was consumed with managing jobseekers' administrative status in the system. Case managers and jobseekers frequently came up against monotonous bureaucratic rules and apathetic administrative systems that were indifferent to the personal crises and major life events in jobseekers' often precarious lives. So, we find Naledi, the mother of a 10-week old baby, due for her annual activity and going against Amelia's 'Work for the Dole stats'. An algorithm has removed her expectant mother's exemption from mutual obligation but without moving Naledi from a jobseeker to a parenting payment. So, Amelia must work with Naledi to fix her status in the system if Naledi is to avoid a payment penalty or suspension.

The administrative burden of case managers' work was significantly increased by the transitory character of the most disadvantaged group. They often had precarious housing, and this resulted in stop-start eligibility to be on a particular agency's list. Or they experienced health, drug and family crises which meant submitting new paperwork and verification of new personal data. And as individuals left the rolls for one of these reasons, even if temporarily, a complex engagement with Centrelink was needed to then determine what could and should happen next. We tend to think that greater levels of judgement about what to do next with a client indicates greater scope for useful local discretion. In many cases this does not serve to empower better discretionary action so much as more compliance work to simply hold them in the system.

Frontline staff do have some resources to help them in this regard, but they tend to be limited in nature. Some of those limits are to do with the overall design of the Australian system, including the stop-start approach to training that we reviewed in relation to the Keating-Howard-Rudd/Gillard-Abbott transitions. But part of it is self-imposed by the agencies as they navigate ways to use their own resources. They redeem large payments from the government when they place a Stream C client into a job and keep them there. So, in theory, they have significant funds to invest to get this result. But for the most part they do not. They make small investments only in things like phones and clothes, and very brief courses to secure the basic tickets needed for entry-level jobs in warehousing, factory and hospitality work. The Cove office, with its willingness to invest in driving lessons and to assist clients in meeting the costs of rental housing and addiction programs, is the exception that proves the rule among the four offices.

We recall Sharmaine from our first site. She warns Karl that if he does not do Work for the Dole, his payments will be cut. 'It's not me, it's the department,' she tells him. And he has to start the next day. We cannot be sure if this is strictly true or if she is worried about her speed-to-placement figures. He protests, 'That's bullshit' but she has a peace offering, she is buying him a phone. No doubt that is a valuable asset for someone in Karl's position but she makes it clear that it will also improve her influence over him, 'I will phone and hassle you. You will wish you didn't have a phone!'

The 'hassle factor' is a common element in many of the transactions we observe and is part of the lexicon of adviser know-how, like 'tree shaking'. It is reassuring for advisers because it provides a rationale for all kinds of requirements asked of clients, even where the link to employment is less than obvious. It also helps populate the many small meetings – often only five minutes long – with a practical checklist. Did you collect that form? Did you call your doctor? Did you get a new phone charger? Each of these small duties provide a text for the agency reports and departmental audits, demonstrating that being on benefits has to be earned and that clients are active and less likely to be in shadow employment. But we did not see these micro-measures as the kind of heartless process described in some other studies. There was often real content to requirements and exchanges, it was rather that there was too little time during appointments to go beyond the immediate task of job searching and troubleshooting the latest administrative challenge confronting caseworkers and their clients. The latter tended to be misclassification issues, a problem with the payment a client was on, or the need to produce medical certificates to validate missed appointments. We saw this not only at the Wilmore office, as discussed above, but in the other sites too. Complex government requirements rebound from Centrelink back down to the agencies whether this is their formal role or not.

We also noted some remarkable things about the character of not-for-profits in these cases. Admittedly we have a small sample, but it is nonetheless worth reflecting upon the very different ways in which this special mission was expressed at the frontline and in the overall culture of the service. Certainly, we can note that things like performance payments and other corporate financial drivers were less obvious at our not-for-profit sites. The staff notice this difference and those who had come from for-profits said they valued the less instrumental regimes of their employers in these cases. But all of them shared a very target-driven work culture. They all work hard to meet these targets and spend time doing what they can to comply, including a degree of manipulation of the outcomes (or the expected outcomes) in order to stay on the right side of their target. It seems likely that the fact that only our regional not-for-profit had a less instrumental approach was linked to deeper social bonds and a confidence that these would carry the day. Without that support structure, the other not-for-profits resorted to similar tactics found in the for-profit model. But we cannot conclude that being a client in a not-for-profit will involve a different service style. As we saw in one of the sites, the not-for-profit style was both rude and somewhat brutal in the treatment of those who presented as problem cases.

An important part of the explanation for these stylistic traits is the nature of employment for frontline staff. They are largely untrained and unqualified which, in turn, is a legacy of over two decades of marketisation and the nature of the Australian government's commissioning model. The Department of Employment strives to keep program costs low by shifting financial risks onto providers and curtailing price inflation. To remain competitive for contracts and to reduce their risk exposure under payment-by-results funding models, agencies search for cost savings. And in a social services context focused on intensive one-to-one, face-to-face delivery, the salaries of frontline staff account for a significant bulk of agencies' overall costs. So they try to reduce this cost base by increasing the size of case managers' individual caseloads – meaning fewer workers are needed per given number of clients – and by redefining job roles so that they can be performed by a de-professionalised, inexperienced, and low-paid workforce. As a result of this 'disorganisation of employment relationships' within social services markets, as Ian Greer and his colleagues put it, case managers come with no reservoir of knowledge with which to shape a practice methodology.[3] They are not members of a practice network or work community beyond the organisation. Rather they are completely dependent. What they know is what they are told and what they see other staff doing at the desk beside them. The open plan system provides a management oversight to assure fidelity to local methods, not to work independently using a recognised understanding of how to act, how to problem solve, and how to predict the likely impact of their judgements about complex clients. So they simplify. They adopt the methods in good standing in their office. Along with the other characteristics of the local office and the official requirements, this works to shorten the timeframe of action. The client's conditions and aspirations are only relevant if they mesh with immediate job outcomes.

The biographies of the staff underline the focus upon the immediacy of practice. Some are former unemployed clients. Others have worked in hairdressing or sales jobs. These are transactional skills which highlight the role of client advising as one necessitating simple, practical, right-now services with short-horizon outcomes. And no doubt the self-motivated, people management skills of someone like a former airline attendant can soon be transferred to this timeframe focus and the need to manage sometimes problematic client behaviours. Being unhappy about the service is not a reason to question a better approach so much as a rationale for curbing unwanted or resistant behaviour in favour of doing what is required, or being disciplined.

This style of transactional exchange between the client and the adviser had a simple logic in many of our observed exchanges. Compliance with what was being required was only loosely connected to a job outcome but was much more tightly tied to staying eligible for welfare payments. We did not interview clients and it was not part of our methodology to seek to enter their individual worlds. But we could see in their exchanges with advisers that what was uppermost in their minds was avoiding being sanctioned.

---

3   Greer, Breidahl, Knuth and Larsen 2017.

The very high rates of sanctioning observed in these cases and in the system overall provides a drumbeat for the service as a whole. All of the staff and all the clients at our sites were regularly and strongly reminded of the whip-hand that the service holds above them. Supervisors tutor frontline staff in managing these penalties and ways to use their discretion in applying them. It helps make undesirable jobs easier to fill with reluctant clients who would have preferred to be referred for training or to wait on better options. It furnishes a means to meet targets faster and push resistant clients off the rolls. It also shapes the service style by bolstering the power of the staff to increase the dependence of the client, as if being unemployed was not enough in itself. That power was never more evident than in the cases we reported where staff could choose whether to apply a sanction, even if it was available and mandated by the program rules. Paradoxically perhaps, this negative discretion increases the vulnerability of the client. If you happen to get a good adviser she may relax the penalty but this is never certain. Get a more severe adviser and small infractions can quickly lead to loss of income and all the personal hardship that involves. Again, the low training regimes and absent practice community surrounding the service creates heightened vulnerability, not reduces it.

Frontline staff working in the Australian system are taught to distinguish this work from social work. They are not the client's advocate. They are not there to help them solve personal problems and crises. They know they are not trained for that and they tell us that. 'We're not counsellors', is a refrain we hear many times from the case managers profiled in this book. They know they are not seeking those more permanent outcomes. Instead they are there to get job outcomes and improved star ratings. They called these unpopular vacancies 'survival jobs' which openly reinforced the precarious position their clients face. This also helps them define their tasks by knowing what they are not doing as much as they should be doing. It also helps them self-define their roles as something different, something that does not require a professional bond or responsibility to the client. What then sustains their self-identity and work ethic? In our observed cases we see in place of professionalism or recognised methodologies an incentive and motivational framework based on success stories. They celebrate getting any challenging clients into work, against the odds. High comparative performance can be achieved with getting just two or three job outcomes. And when the result is a high star rating their own jobs become more secure. No one worries or experiences a sense of failure that most of their Stream C's remain out of work. Instead the program as a whole rewards their marginal success rate with significant corporate benefits in the form of new contracts and even increased business.

We notice in this process that the frontline staff themselves are highly vulnerable. They possess few independent resources with which to define any other work practices than the ones described here. Their knowledge base is entirely what the local agency articulates for them. For the most part they are women in precarious employment, lacking training and recognised skills that could make them more powerful in defining what they do and how they do it. The nature of the program and the short contract system determines this and then the inevitable business models of the contracted agencies reinforce it. They work in the shadow of a contracting regime that could see their site closed and re-opened in another state, or lost altogether. Investing in further education or skills that might help them become better advisers is irrational. Their employers do not value such investments and might even regard them as a threat if they create more assertive forms of frontline practice. And even if, in the case of not-for-profits, they wished to value such human development of their staff, how could they pay a higher wage to reward it if the competitor down the street then does better in meeting their bottom line by employing cheaper staff?

This race-to-the-bottom knowledge economy points us to a systemic weakness in the work with these more disadvantaged clients. Without a recognised way to invest in skills there is an absence of a knowledge community that can capture and improve best practice. Good advisers are known only to local managers. Best practice remains a fragile element of frontline work. We can see from our four sites, all of them are at the top of the class, but that no consistent approach or method is evident. Bad cop and good cop methods still vie for popularity without any independent rationale beyond the agency's variable local culture, constrained only by the drive for star ratings. There are no practice standards to protect against client bullying, manipulation of the rolls or discrimination based on race, gender or age. Instead the service rationale is not far advanced from the commercial idea that 'if it pays, it plays'.

The gendered nature of the work was noted in several of the cases. It appears first of all as a predominance of women at the frontline. They are doing the emotional labour to motivate, cajole and discipline their clients. More than once we saw this expressed as interventions to improve the way clients dress for interview, helping them select and purchase clothing, get their haircut or practice the way to speak to potential employers. We saw an example of this with Thomas at Westgate. In other words the boundary between the personal and the professional is far more porous than in any other type of work carried out by frontline staff in banks, shops or government agencies. It is often argued in the research on social services that this kind of emotional labour plays into a broader idea of the female role as linking both a nurturing, improving, and a boundary-setting skill with children. Or with running a household while managing the sometimes turbulent experiences of a male breadwinner. It may be that we are thus predisposed to accept a female adviser giving us supportive but tough love. But the large number of women at the frontline could be due to a more simple reality. These are relatively low-paid and precarious jobs and they have no career trajectory or independent standing.

Gender also shows up in the work practices of the agencies. Women clients are offered jobs like cleaning and shop work. Men are sent to factories and warehouses. We saw this result in a tilt towards better outcomes for some of the men. Only a ratio of one in seven female jobseekers that we followed closely during our time at the Westgate office went on to sustain 26 weeks or more of employment, compared with one in five of the male jobseekers. This was connected to the labour market that the Westgate office is located in, which in turn provides the clue to the site's overall success – proximity to a supply of warehousing and light manufacturing jobs. Agencies were evidently more likely to send men in Stream C to those jobs to drive forklifts, pack shelves and do assembly work. No doubt this may also reflect the expectations of employers, compounding the gender challenge.

In addition to gender we also noted the impact of cultural background. There was no common approach to dealing with migrants who have limited English skills. We saw the example of the two older

Vietnamese-born jobseekers who were first sanctioned for non-attendance and then transferred to another agency because the one they were first allocated had, at best, a hit-or-miss approach to using interpreters. Monica at the Westgate office had booked two interpreters to come the afternoon of their appointment, but the interpreters cancelled at short notice. This had cost the agency money, so the staff collectively decided to refer the couple to another provider that had a Vietnamese interpreter on site.

We also noted a set of important conditions for this work in relation to the broader work environment. Our frontline staff were not much involved in outreach to employers. Even the roles described as 'post-placement support' turned out to be mostly concerned with getting payslips to verify the agency's performance payments. The cases where we did see strong employer engagement, the office had so-called reverse marketers to do the work, and in one case the office manager did the network building with local firms.

This profile of frontline work from four sites, when combined with what we know about caseloads, produces a picture of a common business model which varies in style but not in content. It raises an important question about the extent to which the purchaser is able to steer the service in the manner proposed. For the most vulnerable clients this comes down to one critical question: if agencies are paid almost ten times the amount to get Stream Cs into work, why do they not spend ten times the effort doing so? We certainly saw cases where smaller outlays were provided for clothing or a forklift licence but in most cases the strategy was to push these jobseekers towards unskilled work with minimum outlay.

The contract's differential payment model, offering higher outcome payments for jobseekers in higher service streams (B or C) and who are unemployed for longer was supposed to guard against this risk. However, a key challenge with differential payment models is ensuring that the outcome payment for placing more difficult clients is large enough to offset the additional resources that providers will need to spend to get clients into work. Or alternatively, these payments for the occasional, opportunistic success story in the Stream C band need to be high enough to improve the profit average overall, given the smaller rate of return on the two other streams. During the Senate inquiry into

Jobactive, providers argued that the outcome payments for Stream C clients were 'not sufficient to meet the investments needed to support training and find jobs' for those participants.[4] Perhaps this could also be a self-defence strategy for an industry which spends very little on this group, as we saw in most of our cases.

Our conclusion overall is that this system does not work for the most disadvantaged clients. Staff training and competency has not improved. Investments in training and problem solving for clients has only occasionally been the practice. Churning of the rolls and resorting to very transactional methods have remained prevalent, including in the best of sites. All this despite the enthusiasm and deep commitment of frontline staff who keep trying to help their clients succeed with this meagre diet. They celebrate the minority of success stories and do all they can to manage and manipulate the system to get a result. But then they leave the industry in large numbers or transfer out to seek other opportunities. And with that we see the limited knowledge base and tool kit remaining as far too limited to help the majority of the clients who have already waited years to find a way to a better life.

---

4   Senate Education and Employment References Committee 2019. This point was made by Michael Kolomyjec, Group Executive of at Work Australia, a Jobactive provider. Similar points have also been repeatedly made by providers in the UK, in relation to the Work Programme's differential pricing model. See House of Commons Work and Pensions Committee 2015.

Glossary

Activity-tested payments: Types of benefits, including Newstart Allowance, Youth Allowance and Parenting Payment, for which recipients must meet mutual obligations to continue receiving their payments. These obligations usually involve looking for and accepting work, in addition to an annual activity phase.

Assessed work capacity: Centrelink gives people on activity-tested payments an assessed work capacity, or minimum number of hours of paid work to look for and undertake each week. A person with a full work capacity must look for and undertake 30 hours (or more); partial work capacities are typically divided into categories of 0–7 hours, 8–14 hours or 15–29 hours. In the industry, jobseekers with a full work capacity are informally referred to as 'money people' whereas those with a partial work capacity are referred to as 'hours people'. 'Money people' must find employment that earns them enough money to no longer be on benefits if Jobactive providers are to earn a fully payable employment outcome with them. 'Hours people', however, can remain on benefits if they secure a job that meets their assessed part-time hours.

Disability Employment Services (DES): A parallel employment services system predominantly for people receiving the Disability Support Pension.

Employment Fund (EF): A pool of funds that Jobactive providers receive to purchase interventions and services to support their clients to find work. Jobactive sites are allocated a certain proportion of employment funding per client, depending on what stream those clients are in. At the time of writing, sites received approximately $300 for clients in Stream A and $1,200 for clients in Stream C. However, the employment fund is pooled across a site's caseload, meaning that providers can cross-subsidise between their clients.

Employment Services Assessment (ESAt): An in-person assessment, carried out by an allied health professional on behalf of Services Australia (the Australian government agency responsible for administering a range of health, welfare and social services, including Centrelink, and which was formerly known as the Department of Human Services), to determine jobseekers' eligibility for Stream B or C of Jobactive, as well as DES. Jobseekers must be assessed using a Job Seeker Classification Instrument before they are eligible for an ESAt.

Job Plan: An agreement, also known as an Employment Pathway Plan, that all jobseekers enter into with their provider, outlining the activities they will undertake to meet their mutual obligation requirements. A Job Plan generally includes a minimum number of job searches jobseekers must complete each month, a requirement to attend provider appointments and any interviews with prospective employers, and an obligation 'to act on any referrals from employment services providers to specific job opportunities'.[1] Jobseekers who refuse to sign their Job Plan face the prospect of the cancellation of their payments by Services Australia.

---

1   Australian Government 2021. Section 3.11.2, Job Plans. https://bit.ly/ 3wJGECy.

Job Search Sheet: a record, also known as a 'dole diary', of the job searches that jobseekers have undertaken over the past month to meet their mutual obligation requirements. The required number of job searches depends on the service stream that jobseekers are in and their assessed work capacity.

Job Seeker Classification Instrument (JSCI): The statistical profiling tool that Centrelink uses to measure jobseekers' distance from employment when they apply for an activity-tested payment. From the profile, Centrelink either refers jobseekers into Stream A of Jobactive or sends them for an ESAt to determine their eligibility for a higher stream of services. The JSCI relies on people to self-disclose any barriers to employment such as health issues, criminal convictions, relationship or family breakdown, housing insecurity or substance dependency.

Mutual obligation: The behavioural requirements that people receiving activity-tested payments must comply with to continue receiving payments, and which were first legislated by the Howard government in 1997. Because of its close connection to Work for the Dole, both in time and in policy, mutual obligation is sometimes used as a synonym for Work for the Dole. However, it has a far broader meaning that loosely corresponds to the principle of behavioural conditionality now enshrined in international welfare and active labour market policy reforms. At the time of the study, jobseekers had three main mutual obligation requirements: to enter a Job Plan with their employment services provider, to search for jobs and to attend regular appointments with their provider.

Newstart Allowance: The main type of payment available to unemployed or underemployed people at the time of the study, although it was replaced by the JobSeeker payment in March 2020 following the Covid pandemic. While it is often described as Australia's 'primary' or 'main unemployment benefit', having replaced the Unemployment Benefit in July 1991, this label is misleading because many people receiving Newstart (or the JobSeeker Payment) have part-time or casual employment. Unlike many other kinds of social security payments, including the Age Pension or Disability Support

Pension, the value of Newstart payments is indexed to inflation, not wages. Because wages in Australia have grown at a faster rate than inflation since Newstart was introduced, its value relative to average earnings has declined over time. As at January 2020, the rate of the payment varied from $504.70 to $780.70 per fortnight depending on a person's family circumstances.

Non-Attendance Report (NAR): a non-compliance report that providers use to notify Services Australia that a client has missed their appointment and was either uncontactable or provided an unsatisfactory reason for their absence. NARs suspend a jobseeker's payments until they attend a re-engagement appointment, when their payments resume and are fully back paid.

Participation Report (PR): The most serious type of non-compliance report. Depending on the severity of the compliance breach, a PR can result in loss of payments for up to eight weeks, or 12 weeks for jobseekers who have received an allowance to relocate to find jobs. Providers can submit PRs for jobseekers who have either not attended or behaved inappropriately at an activity, job interview or appointment with a third party; refused to enter into a Job Plan; refused suitable employment; or become voluntarily unemployed.

Provider Appointment Report (PAR): A type of non-compliance report that providers can submit when jobseekers miss their appointments, the provider believes they do not have a valid reason for missing their appointment, and the provider wants to request that jobseekers' payments are reduced rather than suspended (as under a NAR). If Services Australia agrees, jobseekers' payments will typically be reduced by 10 per cent for each day they have failed to engage with services.

Star ratings: The system used by the government to measure the performance of Jobactive providers at a site level, from a high of five stars to a low of one star. Star ratings are published quarterly by the Australian government department responsible for managing the commissioning of employment services. At the time of writing, this department was known as the Department of Education, Skills and Employment but it has undergone frequent name changes. Throughout this book, we generally use the name the Department of Employment, which was its name when we commenced the fieldwork for this book.

Stream: When jobseekers are referred to a Jobactive provider, they are classified into one of the three streams (A, B, and C) according to how their distance from the labour market is assessed by Centrelink (using the JSCI and ESAt processes). Jobseekers in Stream A (about 40 per cent of all Jobactive participants) are considered the most 'job ready' participants, whereas those in Stream C (about 17 per cent of Jobactive participants) are considered the most distant from employment. However, the bulk of jobseekers are referred into Stream B. How jobseekers are streamed is very important for several reasons. For jobseekers, it determines the level of mutual obligation and annual activity requirements they must comply with to continue receiving their payments. For providers, it partly determines the value of the outcome payments they can receive for placing and sustaining clients in employment. These payments increase in value the longer clients are unemployed and the higher the service stream they are referred into.

Wage subsidy: At the time of the study, employers could claim up to $10,000 over six months for hiring a jobseeker if they were Indigenous, 50 years of age or over, or under 25 years of age. A wage subsidy of $6,500 was available for hiring jobseekers who were parents, who were aged between 25 and 49 years, and registered with an employment services provider for a year or more. In all cases, the employment must average at least 20 hours per week over a six-month period.

Work for the Dole: After participating in Jobactive (Australia's main welfare-to-work program) for 12 months, jobseekers enter an Annual Activity Requirement (ARM) phase of six months, during which they must complete an additional activity on top of their job-search and appointment requirements. At the time of the study, Work for the Dole was the default ARM for jobseekers under 30 years of age, who have an annual activity requirement of 50 hours per fortnight. The type of activity can vary, but it generally involves a community work placement such as working in a charity shop, community gardening and/or maintenance projects, or undertaking recycling activities. Other than Work for the Dole, and depending on their circumstances, jobseekers may be able to fulfil their ARM by undertaking part-time paid work, voluntary work, the National Work Experience Program, language, literacy and numeracy courses, drug or alcohol treatment, a health maintenance program (for those in Stream C) or joining the Australian Defence Force Reserves.

Works cited

Adkins, L. 2017. Disobedient workers, the law and the making of unemployment markets. *Sociology* 51(2): 290–305. https://doi.org/10.1177/0038038515598276.

APM 2019. APM acquires Konekt. *APM website*, 20 December. https://bit.ly/2U4luIB.

Arni, P., Lalive, R. and van Ours, J. C. 2013. How effective are unemployment benefit sanctions? Looking beyond unemployment exit. *Journal of Applied Econometrics* 28: 1153–78. https://doi.org/10.1002/jae.2289.

Ashby, W.R. 1956. *An introduction to cybernetics*. London: Chapman and Hall.

Attas, D. and De-Shalit, A. 2004. Workfare: the subjection of labour. *Journal of Applied Philosophy* 21(3): 309–20. https://doi.org/10.1111/j.0264-3758.2004.00284.x.

Australian Bureau of Statistics 2016. Labour Force Region Data (SA4) – August 2016. http://lmip.gov.au/default.aspx?LMIP/Downloads/ABSLabourForceRegion.

Australian Council of Social Services 2001. *Breaching the safety net: the harsh impact of social security penalties*. Sydney: Australian Council of Social Services.

Australian Government 2021. Social Security Guide (version 1.277) https://guides.dss.gov.au/guide-social-security-law.

Australian National Audit Office 2014. *ANAO audit report no.37 2013–14: Management of services delivered by job services Australia*. Canberra: Commonwealth of Australia.

Australian National Audit Office 2017. *Jobactive: design and monitoring.* Canberra: Commonwealth of Australia.

Australian Services Union 2011. *Employment services: not just a job.* Melbourne: Australian Services Union.

Bennett, H. 2017. Re-examining British welfare-to-work contracting using a transaction cost perspective. *Journal of Social Policy* 46: 129–48. https://doi.org/10.1017/S0047279416000337

Bennett, O., Dawson, E., Lewis, A., O'Halloran, D. and Smith, W. 2018. *Working it out.* Melbourne: Per capita and the Australian Unemployed Workers Union.

Boland, T. and Griffin, R. 2017. Working backstage: an ethnographic account of social welfare offices. *Irish Journal of Anthropology* 20(1): 12–22.

Boland, T. and Griffin, R. 2021. *The reformation of welfare: the new faith of the labour market.* Bristol, UK: Bristol University Press. https://doi.org/10.2307/j.ctv1qp9gkd

Bonoli, G. 2010. The political economy of active labor-market policy. *Politics & Society* 38(4): 435–57. https://doi.org/10.1177/0032329210381235

Borland, J., Considine, M., Kalb, G. and Ribar, D. 2016. *What are best-practice programs for Jobseekers facing high barriers to employment?* Melbourne Institute of Applied Economic and Social Research.

Bovens, M. and Zouridis, S. 2002. From street-level to system-level bureaucracies: how information and communication technology is transforming administrative discretion and constitutional control. *Public Administration Review* 62(2): 174–84. https://doi.org/10.1111/0033-3352.00168

Bowman, D. and Randrianarisoa, A. 2018. *Missing the mark: employer perspectives on employment services and mature age jobseekers in Australia.* Melbourne: Brotherhood of St Laurence.

Bowman, D., McGann, M., Kimberley, H. and Biggs, S. 2016. Activation and active ageing? Mature-age jobseekers' experience of employment services. *Social Policy and Society* 15: 647–58. https://doi.org/10.1017/S1474746416000245

Brady, M. 2011. Researching governmentalities through ethnography: the case of Australian welfare reforms and programs for single parents. *Critical Policy Studies* 5(3): 264–82. https://doi.org/10.1080/19460171.2011.606300

Brady, M. 2018. Targeting single mothers? Dynamics of contracting Australian employment services and activation policies at the street level. *Journal of Social Policy* 47(4): 827–45. https://doi.org/10.1017/S0047279418000223

Bredgaard, T. and Larsen, F. 2007. Implementing public employment policy: what happens when non-public agencies take over? *International Journal of Sociology and Social Policy* 27(7/8): 287–300. https://doi.org/10.1108/01443330710773863

Works cited

Brodkin, E.Z. 1997. Inside the welfare contract: discretion and accountability in state welfare administration. *Social Service Review* 71(1): 1–33. https://doi.org/10.1086/604228

Brodkin, E.Z. 2008. Accountability in street-level organizations. *International Journal of Public Administration* 31(3): 317–36. https://doi.org/10.1080/01900690701590587

Brodkin, E.Z. 2011. Policy work: street-level organisations under new managerialism. *Journal of Administration Research and Theory* 21: 1253–1277. https://doi.org/10.1093/jopart/muq093

Brodkin, E.Z. 2012. Reflections on street-level bureaucracy: past, present, and future. *Public Administration Review* 72(6): 940–49. https://doi.org/10.1111/j.1540-6210.2012.02657.x

Brodkin, E.Z. 2013a. Street-level organisations and the welfare state. In E.Z. Brodkin and G. Marston (eds), *Work and the welfare state: street-level organisations and workfare policies* (pp. 17–34). Washington, DC: Georgetown University Press.

Brodkin, E.Z. 2013b. Work and the welfare state. In E.Z. Brodkin and G. Marston (eds), *Work and the welfare state: Street-level organisations and workfare policies* (pp. 3–16). Washington, DC: Georgetown University Press.

Brodkin, E.Z. 2017a. The ethnographic turn in political science: reflections on the state of the art. *PS: Political Science and Politics* 50: 131–4. https://doi.org/10.1017/S1049096516002298

Brodkin, E.Z. 2017b. Street-level organizations and US Workfare: insights for policy and theory. In R. van Berkel, D. Caswell, P. Kupka and F. Larsen. *Front-line delivery of welfare-to-work policies in Europe: activating the unemployed* (pp. 36–52). London: Routledge. https://doi.org/10.4324/9781315694474-3

Brodkin, E.Z. and Larsen, F. 2013. The policies of workfare: at the boundaries between work and the welfare state. In E.Z. Brodkin and G. Marston (eds), *Work and the welfare state: street-level organisations and workfare policies* (pp. 57–67). Washington, DC: Georgetown University Press.

Brodkin, E.Z. and Marston, G. (eds) 2013. *Work and the welfare state: street-level organisations and workfare policies.* Washington, DC: Georgetown University Press.

Card, D., Kluve, J. and Weber, A. 2015. *What works? A meta-analysis of recent active labour market program evaluations.* Bonn: Institute for the Study of Labor (IZA). https://doi.org/10.3386/w21431

Carney, T. and Ramia, G. 2002. Mutuality, Mead and McClure: More 'big Ms' for the unemployed. *Australian Journal of Social Issues* 37(3): 277–300. https://doi.org/10.1002/j.1839-4655.2002.tb01122.x

Carter, E. and Whitworth, A. 2015. Creaming and parking in quasi-marketised welfare-to-work schemes: designed out of or designed into the UK Work Programme? *Journal of Social Policy* 44: 277–96. https://doi.org/10.1017/S0047279414000841

Casey, S. 2019. A Bourdieusian analysis of employment services workers in an era of Workfirst. *Social Policy & Administration* 53(7): 1018–29. https://doi.org/10.1111/spol.12478

Casey, S. and Lewis, A. 2020. *Redesigning employment services after Covid-19.* Melbourne: Per Capita.

Caswell, D. and Larsen, F. 2020. Co-creation in an era of welfare conditionality: lessons from Denmark. *Journal of Social Policy* 1–19. https://doi.org/10.1017/S0047279420000665.

Caswell, D., Kupka, P., Larsen, F. and van Berkel, R. 2017. The frontline delivery of welfare-to-work in context. In R. van Berkel, D. Caswell, P. Kupka and L. Larsen (eds). *Frontline delivery of welfare-to-work policies in Europe* (pp. 1–11). New York and London: Routledge. https://doi.org/10.4324/9781315694474-1

Cohen, G.A. 1989. On the currency of egalitarian justice. *Ethics* 99(4): 906–44. https://doi.org/10.1086/293126

Considine, M. 1999. Markets, networks and the new welfare state: employment assistance reforms in Australia. *Journal of Social Policy*, 2(1): 183–203. https://doi.org/10.1017/S0047279499005607

Considine, M. 2000. Selling the unemployed: the performance of bureaucracies, firms and non-profits in the new Australian 'market' for unemployment assistance. *Social Policy & Administration* 34(3): 274–95. https://doi.org/10.1111/1467-9515.00191

Considine, M. 2001. *Enterprising states: the public management of welfare-to-work.* Cambridge University Press.

Considine, M. 2005. The reform that never ends: quasi-markets in employment services in Australia. In E. Sol and M. Westerveld (eds), *Contractualism in employment services: a new form of welfare state governance* (pp. 41–71). Netherlands: Kluwer Law International.

Considine, M. and Lewis, J.M. 2010. Frontline work in employment services after ten years of new public management reform: governance and activation in Australia, the Netherlands and the UK. *European Journal of Social Security* 12(4): 357–70. https://doi.org/10.1177/138826271001200407

Considine, M., Lewis, J.M. and O'Sullivan, S. 2009. *Activating states: transforming the delivery of 'welfare-to-work' services in Australia, the UK and the Netherlands – Australian report back to industry partners.* The University of Melbourne.

Works cited

Considine, M., Lewis, J.M. and O'Sullivan, S. 2011. Quasi-markets and service delivery flexibility following a decade of employment assistance reform in Australia. *Journal of Social Policy* 40(4): 811–33. https://doi.org/10.1017/S0047279411000213

Considine, M., Lewis, J.M., O'Sullivan, S. and Sol, E. 2015. *Getting welfare-to-work: street-level governance in Australia, the UK, and the Netherlands.* New York: Oxford University Press. https://doi.org/10.1093/acprof:oso/9780198743705.001.0001

Considine, M. and O'Sullivan, S. 2015. Introduction. In M. Considine and S. O'Sullivan (eds), *Contracting-out welfare services: Comparing national policy designs for unemployment assistance* (pp. 1–9). Oxford: Wiley Blackwell. https://doi.org/10.1002/9781119016458.ch0

Considine, M., O'Sullivan, S. and Nguyen, P. 2014a. Mission drift? The third sector and the pressure to be business-like: evidence from Job Services Australia. *Third Sector Review* 20(1): 87–107.

Considine, M., O'Sullivan, S. and Nguyen, P. 2014b. New public management and welfare-to-work in Australia: comparing the reform agendas of the ALP and Coalition. *Australian Journal of Political Science* 49(3): 469–85. https://doi.org/10.1080/10361146.2014.931343

Considine, M., O'Sullivan, S. and Nguyen, P. 2015. Governance, boards of directors and the impact of contracting on not-for-profits organisations: An Australian study. In M. Considine and S. O'Sullivan (eds), *Contracting-out welfare services: comparing national policy designs for unemployment assistance* (pp. 55–74). Oxford: Wiley Blackwell. https://doi.org/10.1002/9781119016458.ch3

Considine, M., O'Sullivan, S. and Nguyen, P. 2018. The policymaker's dilemma: the risks and benefits of a 'black box' approach to commissioning active labour market programs. *Social Policy & Administration* 52: 229–51. https://doi.org/10.1111/spol.12309

Considine, M., O'Sullivan, S., McGann, M. and Nguyen, P. 2020. Locked-in or locked-out: can a public services market really change? *Journal of Social Policy* 49(4): 850–71. https://doi.org/10.1017/S0047279419000941

Davidson, P. 2011. Did 'Work First' work? The role of employment assistance programs in reducing long-term unemployment in Australia (1990–2008). *Australian Bulletin of Labour* 37(1): 51–96.

Davidson, P. 2014. Long term unemployment: the 'Achilles heel' of the Job Services Australia model. Paper presented at the Australian Long-Term Unemployment Conference, Surfers Paradise, Gold Coast.

Deeming, C. 2016. Rethinking social policy and society. *Social Policy and Society* 15: 159–75. https://doi.org/10.1017/S1474746415000147

Department of Education, Skills and Employment. 2019. *Employment services outcomes report October 2018 to September 2019 – Jobactive.* https://bit.ly/3itCjzI.

Department of Employment 2015. Evaluation strategy for Jobactive. https://docs.employment.gov.au/system/files/doc/other/evaluation_strategy_for_jobactive.pdf.

Department of Employment 2016a. Employment services 2015 regulation impact statement. http://ris.dpmc.gov.au/2016/02/23/employment-services-2015/.

Department of Employment 2016b. Small Area (SA2) Labour Market data – June 2016 quarter. https://data.gov.au/data/dataset/ef75535c-1f06-4175-ae51-9c72c642e561.

Department of Employment, Skills, Small and Family Business 2019a. *Employment services outcomes report (Jobactive) – January to December 2018.* https://www.dese.gov.au/jobactive/resources/jobactive-employment-services-outcomes-report-january-2018-december-2018.

Department of Employment, Skills, Small and Family Business 2019b. *Evaluation of Jobactive: interim report.* Canberra: Commonwealth of Australia.

Department of Employment, Skills, Small and Family Business 2019c. *New employment services trial deed 2019–2022.* https://bit.ly/3yxkTrt.

Department of Families, Housing, Community Services, and Indigenous Affairs 2010. *Income support customers: a statistical overview 2008.* Canberra: Commonwealth of Australia.

Department of Human Services 2017. *Job seeker compliance data – December quarter 2016.* https://bit.ly/3s2eq5c.

Department of Human Services 2018. *Job seeker compliance data – June quarter 2018.* https://bit.ly/2VBhWaI.

Department of Jobs and Small Business 2017. *Annual report 2016–17.* Canberra: Commonwealth of Australia.

Department of Jobs and Small Business 2018a. *I want to work: employment services 2020 report.* Canberra: Commonwealth of Australia.

Department of Jobs and Small Business 2018b. *The next generation of employment services: discussion paper.* Canberra: Commonwealth of Australia.

Department of Social Services 2019. DSS payment demographic data: June 2019. See duration on payment data. https://data.gov.au/data/dataset/dss-payment-demographic-data/resource/3d7891bc-6861-47c8-b967-f8807059fa83.

Department of Social Services 2014–19. Payment Demographic Data June 2014–2019. https://bit.ly/3xGOD4T.

Works cited

Dias, J.J. and Maynard-Moody, S. 2006. For-profit welfare: contracts, conflicts, and the performance paradox. *Journal of Public Administration Research and Theory* 17: 189–211. https://doi.org/10.1093/jopart/mul002

Dimaggio, P.J. and Powell, W.W. 1983. The iron cage revisited: institutional isomorphism and collective rationality in organizational fields. *American Sociological Review* 48(2): 147–60. https://doi.org/10.2307/2095101

Dingeldey, I. 2007. Between workfare and enablement? The different paths to transformation of the welfare state. *European Journal of Political Research* 46(6): 823–851. https://doi.org/10.1111/j.1475-6765.2007.00712.x

Dubois, V. 2009. Towards a critical policy ethnography: lessons from fieldwork on welfare control in France. *Critical Policy Studies* 3(2): 221–39. https://doi.org/10.1080/19460170903385684

Dubois, V. 2016. *The bureaucrat and the poor: encounters in French welfare offices.* Abingdon, UK: Routledge.

Eardley, T. 2002. Mutual obligation and the Job Network: the effect of competition on the role of non-profit employment services. *Australian Journal of Social Issues* 37(3): 301–14. https://doi.org/10.1002/j.1839-4655.2002.tb01123.x

Esping-Anderson, G. 1990. *The three worlds of welfare capitalism.* Princeton, NJ: Princeton University Press. https://doi.org/10.1177/095892879100100108

Finn, D. 2011. *Job Services Australia: design and implementation lessons for the British context.* London: Department for Work and Pensions.

Finn, D. 2012. *Subcontracting in public employment services: the design and delivery of 'outcome based' and 'black box' contracts.* Brussels: European Commission.

Fowkes, L. 2011. *Rethinking Australia's employment services.* Parramatta: The Whitlam Institute.

Fuertes, V. and Lindsay, C. 2016. Personalisation and street-level practice in activation: the case of the UK's Work Programme. *Public Administration* 94(2): 526–41. https://doi.org/10.1111/padm.12234

Gillard, J. 2008. More flexible, better targeted employment services [Press release]. https://ministers.jobs.gov.au/gillard/more-flexible-better-targeted-employment-services.

GlobeNewswire 2017. Providence Service Corporation completes sale of joint venture Mission Providence to Konekt. *Intrado Global News Wire,* 29 September. https://bit.ly/3ie06lS.

Gofen, A. 2014. Mind the gap: dimensions and influence of street-level divergence. *Journal of Public Administration Research and Theory* 24: 473–79. https://doi.org/10.1093/jopart/mut037

Grant, L. 2009. Women's disconnection from local labour markets: real lives and policy failure. *Critical Social Policy* 29(3): 330–50. https://doi.org/10.1177/0261018309105174.

241

Greer, I., Breidahl, K.N., Knuth, M. and Larsen, F. 2017. *The marketization of employment services: the dilemmas of Europe's work-first welfare states.* Oxford University Press. https://doi.org/10.1093/oso/9780198785446.001.0001

Greer, I., Schulte, L. and Symon, G. 2018. Creaming and parking in marketized employment services: an Anglo–German comparison. *Human Relations* 71(11): 1427–53. https://doi.org/10.1177/0018726717745958

Grover, C. 2009. Privatizing employment services in Britain. *Critical Social Policy* 29(3): 487–509. https://doi.org/10.1177/0261018309105181

Guy, M.E. and Newman, M.A. 2004. Women's jobs, men's jobs: sex segregation and emotional labour. *Public Administration Review* 64: 289–98. https://doi.org/10.1111/j.1540-6210.2004.00373.x

Henriques-Gomes, L. 2019, Punished by the lucrative welfare-to-work industry: 'I was contemplating suicide'. *Guardian* (Australian edition), 4 May. https://www.theguardian.com/australia-news/2019/may/04/punished-by-the-lucrative-welfare-to-work-industry-i-was-contemplating-suicide.

Herzog, L. and Zacka, B. 2017. Fieldwork in political theory: five arguments for an ethnographic sensibility. *British Journal of Political Science* 49: 763–84. https://doi.org/10.1017/S0007123416000703

Hochschild, A. 1983. *The managed heart.* Berkeley, CA: University of California Press.

House of Commons Work and Pensions Committee 2015. *Welfare-to-work: second report of session 2015–16.* London: House of Commons.

Hughes, O.E. 2003. *Public management and administration: an introduction* (3rd edition). Basingstoke, UK: Palgrave Macmillan.

Huppatz, K. and Goodwin, S. 2013. Masculinised jobs, feminised jobs and men's 'gender capital' experiences: understanding occupational segregation in Australia. *Journal of Sociology* 49(2–3): 291–308. https://doi.org/10.1177/1440783313481743

Ingold, J. 2018. Employer engagement in active labour market programmes: the role of boundary spanners. *Public Administration* 96: 707–20. https://doi.org/10.1111/padm.12545

Ingold, J. and Etherington, D. 2013. Work, welfare and gender inequalities: an analysis of activation strategies for partnered women in the UK, Australia and Denmark. *Work, Employment and Society* 27: 621–38. https://doi.org/10.1177/0950017012460306

Jarvie, W. and Mercer, T. 2018. Australia's employment services 1998–2012: using performance monitoring and evaluation to improve value for money. In A. Podger, T.-T. Su, J. Wanna, H.S. Chan and M. Niu (eds), *Value for money: budget and financial management reform in the people's republic of China,*

Taiwan and Australia (pp. 277–97). Canberra: Australian National University Press. https://doi.org/10.22459/VM.01.2018.13

Jerolmack, C. and Khan, S. 2014. Talk is cheap: ethnography and the attitudinal fallacy. *Sociological Methods & Research* 43(2): 178–209. https://doi.org/10.1177/0049124114523396

Jobs Australia 2015. *State of play: Jobactive employment services 2015–2020 tender results.* Carlton South, Vic: Jobs Australia.

Jordan, J.D. 2018. Evidence from the 'frontline'? An ethnographic problematisation of welfare-to-work administrator opinions. *Work, Employment and Society* 32: 57–74. https://doi.org/10.1177/0950017017741238

Keating, P. 1994. *Working nation: white paper on employment and growth.* Canberra: Australian Government Publishing Service.

Kluve, J. 2010. The effectiveness of European active labor market programs. *Labour Economics* 17: 904–18. https://doi.org/10.1016/j.labeco.2010.02.004

Kunze, N.L. 1971. The origins of modern social legislation: the Henrician Poor Law of 1536. *Albion: A Quarterly Journal Concerned with British Studies* 3(1): 9–20. https://doi.org/10.2307/4048468

Le Grand, J. 1997. Knights, knaves or pawns? Human behaviour and social policy. *Journal of Social Policy* 26(2): 149–69. https://doi.org/10.1017/S0047279497004984

Le Grand, J. 2010. Knights and knaves return: public service motivation and the delivery of public services. *International Public Management Journal* 13(1): 56–71. https://doi.org/10.1080/10967490903547290

Le Grand, J. and Bartlett, W. 1993. Introduction. In J. Le Grand and W. Bartlett (eds), *Quasi-markets and social policy* (pp. 1–12). London: Macmillan. https://doi.org/10.1007/978-1-349-22873-7_1

Lewis, J.M., Considine, M., O'Sullivan, S., Nguyen, P. and Michael McGann, M. 2016. *From entitlement to experiment: the new governance of welfare-to-work – Australian report back to industry partners.* The University of Melbourne.

Lipsky, M. 2010 [1980]. *Street-level bureaucracy: dilemmas of the individual in public services* (30th anniversary edition). New York: Russell Sage Foundation.

Longo, M. and Zacka, B. 2019. Political theory in an ethnographic key. *American Political Science Review* 113(4): 1066–70. https://doi.org/10.1017/S0003055419000431

Loopstra, R., Reeves, A., McKee, M. and Stuckler, D. 2015. *Do punitive approaches to unemployment benefit recipients increase welfare exit and employment? A cross-sectional analysis of UK sanction reforms.* Sociology Working Paper number 2015-1. Department of Sociology, University of Oxford.

Maguire, P. 2017. *Employment services workforce survey of remuneration and HRM performance 2016*. Melbourne: National Employment Services Association.

Mann, S. 2004. 'People-work': emotion management, stress and coping. *British Journal of Guidance and Counselling* 32: 205–21. https://doi.org/10.1080/0369880410001692247

Marshall, T.H. 1950. *Citizenship and social class*. Cambridge: Cambridge University Press.

Marston, G. 2006. Employment services in an age of e-government. *Information, Communication and Society* 9: 83–101. https://doi.org/10.1080/13691180500519555

Marston, G. 2008. The war on the poor: constructing welfare and work in the twenty-first century. *Critical Discourse Studies* 5: 359–70. https://doi.org/10.1080/17405900802405312

Marston, G. 2013. On 'activation workers' perceptions: a reply to Dunn (1). *Journal of Social Policy* 42: 819–27. https://doi.org/10.1017/S0047279413000482

Marston, G. and McDonald, C. 2008. Feeling motivated yet? Long-term unemployed people's perspectives on the implementation of workfare in Australia. *Australian Journal of Social Issues* 43: 255–69. https://doi.org/10.1002/j.1839-4655.2008.tb00101.x

Martin, J.P. 2015. Activation and active labour market policies in OECD countries: stylised facts and evidence on their effectiveness, *IZA Journal of Labor Policy* (2015) 4:4. https://doi.org/10.1186/s40173-015-0032-y.

Maynard-Moody, S. and Musheno, M. 2000. State agent or citizen agent: two narratives of discretion. *Journal of Public Administration Research and Theory* 10: 329–58. https://doi.org/10.1093/oxfordjournals.jpart.a024272

McDonald, C. and Chenoweth, L. 2006. Workfare Oz-style: welfare reform and social work in Australia. *Journal of Policy Practice* 5(2/3): 109–28. https://doi.org/10.1300/J508v05n02_08

McDonald, C. and Marston, G. 2005. Workfare as welfare: governing unemployment in the advanced liberal state. *Critical social policy* 25(3): 374–401. https://doi.org/10.1177/0261018305054077

McDonald, C. and Marston, G. 2008. Motivating the unemployed? Attitudes at the front line. *Australian Social Work* 61(4): 315–26. https://doi.org/10.1080/03124070802428167

McGann, M., Nguyen, P. and Considine, M. 2020. Welfare conditionality and blaming the unemployed. *Administration & Society* 52(3): 466–94. https://doi.org/10.1177/0095399719839362

Mead, L. 1986. *Beyond entitlement: the social obligations of citizenship*. New York: The Free Press.

Works cited

Mead, L. 1997. *The new paternalism: supervisory approaches to poverty.* Washington: Brookings Institute.

Mead, L. 2014 [1991]. The new politics of the new poverty. In C. Pierson, F.G. Castles and I.K. Naumann (eds), *The welfare state reader* (3rd edition) (pp. 89–99). Cambridge: Polity Press.

Mendes, P. 2009. Retrenching or renovating the Australian welfare state: the paradox of the Howard government's neo-liberalism. *International Journal of Social Welfare* 18(1): 102–10. https://doi.org/10.1111/j.1468-2397.2008.00569.x

MergerLinks 2018. APM to buy Ingeus from Providence Service Corp. *MergerLinks*, 8 November. https://bit.ly/3r8K2pA.

Murphy, J., Murray, S., Chalmers, J., Martin, S. and Marston, G. 2011. *Half a citizen: life on welfare in Australia.* Crow's Nest, NSW: Allen & Unwin.

National Employment Services Association 2019. *Work for the Dole.* https://bit.ly/3r8XtFO.

Nguyen, T. and Velayutham, S. 2018. Street-level discretion, emotional labour and welfare frontline staff at the Australian employment service providers. *Australian Journal of Social Issues* 58(1): 158–72. https://doi.org/10.1002/ajs4.35

O'Flynn, J. 2007a. *Measuring performance in Australia's Job Network: part A.* Melbourne: The Australia and New Zealand School of Government.

O'Flynn, J. 2007b. *Measuring performance in Australia's job network: part B.* Melbourne: The Australia and New Zealand School of Government.

O'Halloran, D., Farnworth, L. and Thomacos, N. 2019. Australian employment services: help or hindrance in the achievement of mutual obligation. *Australian Journal of Social Issues* 55(4): 492–508. https://doi.org/10.1002/ajs4.82.

Organisation for Economic Cooperation and Development 2006. *Live longer, work longer: Ageing and employment policies.* Paris: Organisation for Economic Cooperation and Development.

O'Sullivan, S., McGann, M. and Considine, M. 2019. The category game and its impact on street-level bureaucrats and jobseekers: an Australian case study. *Social Policy & Society* 18: 631–45. https://doi.org/10.1017/S1474746419000162

O'Sullivan, S. and Walker, C. 2018. From the interpersonal to the internet: social service digitisation and the implications for vulnerable individuals and communities. *Australian Journal of Political Science* 53(4): 490–507. https://doi.org/10.1080/10361146.2018.1519064

Peterie, M., Ramia, G., Marston, G. and Patulny, R. 2019a. Emotional compliance and emotion as resistance: shame and anger among the long-term unemployed. *Work, Employment and Society* 33(5): 794–811. https://doi.org/10.1177/0950017019845775

Peterie, M., Ramia, G., Marston, G. and Patulny, R. 2019b. Social isolation as stigma-management: explaining long-term unemployed people's 'failure' to network. *Sociology* 53(6): 1043–60. https://doi.org/10.1177/0038038519856813

Petrongolo, B. 2009. The long-term effects of job search requirements: evidence from the UK JSA reform. *Journal of Public Economics* 93: 1234–53. https://doi.org/10.1016/j.jpubeco.2009.09.001

Raaphorst, N. and Van de Walle, S. 2018. A signaling perspective on bureaucratic encounters: how public officials interpret signals and cues. *Social Policy & Administration* 52(7): 1367–78. https://doi.org/10.1111/spol.12369

Raffass, T. 2017. Demanding activation. *Journal of Social Policy* 46(2): 349–65. https://doi.org/10.1017/S004727941600057X

Ramia, G. and Carney, T. 2001. Contractualism, managerialism and welfare: the Australian experiment with a marketised employment services network. *Policy & Politics* 29(1): 59–80. https://doi.org/10.1332/0305573012501206

Ramia, G. and Carney, T. 2003. New public management, the Job Network and non-profit strategy. *Australian Journal of Labour Economics* 6(2): 253–75.

Ramia, G. and Carney, T. 2010. The Rudd government's employment services agenda: is it post-NPM and why is that important?' *Australian Journal of Public Administration* 69(3): 263–73. https://doi.org/10.1111/j.1467-8500.2010.00686.x

Ramia, G., Peterie, M., Patulny, R. and Marston, G. 2020. Networks, case managers, and the job-search experiences of unemployed people. *Social Policy & Administration* 54(5): 765–76. https://doi.org/10.1111/spol.12575

Reagan, R. 1986. Radio address to the nation on welfare reform, 15 February. https://www.reaganlibrary.gov/archives/speech/radio-address-nation-welfare-reform.

Rice, D. 2013. Street-level bureaucrats and the welfare state: toward a micro-institutionalist theory of policy implementation. *Administration & Society* 45(9): 1038–62. https://doi.org/10.1177/0095399712451895

Rogers, C. 2009. The impact of the Australian government Job Network contracting on not-for-profit service providers. *Australian Journal of Public Administration*, 66(4): 395–405. https://doi.org/10.1111/j.1467-8500.2007.00552.x

Schram, S.F., Soss, J., Fording, R.C. and Houser, L. 2009. Deciding to discipline: race, choice, and punishment at the frontlines of welfare reform. *American Sociological Review* 74(3): 398–422. https://doi.org/10.1177/000312240907400304

Schwartz, H.M. 1994. Public choice theory and public choice: bureaucrats and state reorganisation in Australia, Denmark, New Zealand and Sweden in the late 1980s. *Administration & Society* 26(1): 48–77. https://doi.org/10.1177/009539979402600104

Senate Education and Employment References Committee 2019. *Jobactive: failing those it is intended to service*. Canberra: Commonwealth of Australia. https://www.aph.gov.au/Parliamentary_Business/Committees/Senate/ Education_and_Employment/JobActive2018/Report.

Sennett, R. 2006. *The culture of the new capitalism*. New Haven, CT: Yale University Press.

Shutes, I. and Taylor, R. 2014. Conditionality and the financing of employment services: implications for the social divisions of work and welfare. *Social Policy and Administration* 48(2): 204–20. https://doi.org/10.1111/spol.12057

Soss, J., Fording, R.C. and Schram, S.F. 2011a. *Disciplining the poor: neoliberal paternalism and the persistent power of race*. The University of Chicago Press. https://doi.org/10.7208/chicago/9780226768786.001.0001

Soss, J., Fording, R.C. and Schram, S.F. 2011b. The organization of discipline: from performance management to perversity and punishment. *Journal of Public Administration Research and Theory* 21(Suppl. 2): i203–i232. https://doi.org/10.1093/jopart/muq095

Soss, J., Fording, R.C. and Schram, S.F. 2013. Performance management as a disciplinary regime: street-level organisations in a neoliberal era of poverty governance. In E.Z. Brodkin and G. Marston (eds), *Work and the welfare state: street-level organisations and workfare politics* (pp. 125–42). Washington, DC: Georgetown University Press.

Standing, G. 2017. *Basic income: a guide for the open-minded*. New Haven, CT: Yale University Press. https://doi.org/10.2307/j.ctv1bvnf53

Struyven, L. 2014. Varieties of market competition in public employment services-a comparison of the emergence and evolution of the new system in Australia, the Netherlands and Belgium. *Social Policy & Administration* 48(2): 149–68. https://doi.org/10.1002/9781119016458.ch2

Thomas, M. 2007. A review of developments in the Job Network. https://www.aph.gov.au/About_Parliament/Parliamentary_Departments/ Parliamentary_Library/pubs/rp/RP0708/08rp15

Thomas, M. and Daniels, D. 2010. *Welfare-to-work: a reform agenda in progress*. Canberra: Parliamentary Library of Australia: Social Policy Section.

van Berkel, R. 2013. Triple activation: introducing welfare-to-work into Dutch social assistance, in E.Z. Brodkin and G. Marston (eds), *Work and the welfare state: street-level organisations and workfare policies* (pp. 87–102). Washington, DC: Georgetown University Press.

van Berkel, R. 2014. Quasi-markets and the delivery of activation: a frontline perspective. *Social Policy and Administration* 48(2): 188–203. https://doi.org/10.1111/spol.12056

van Berkel, R. 2017. State of the art in frontline studies of welfare-to-work: a literature review. In R. van Berkel, D. Caswell, P. Kupka and F. Larsen (eds), *Frontline delivery of welfare-to-work policies in Europe: activating the unemployed* (pp. 12–35). New York: Routledge. https://doi.org/10.4324/9781315694474-2

van Berkel, R. 2020. Making welfare conditional: a street-level perspective. *Social Policy & Administration* 54(2): 191–204. https://doi.org/10.1111/spol.12564

van Berkel, R. and Knies, E. 2016. Performance management, caseloads and the frontline provision of social services. *Social Policy & Administration* 50: 59–78. https://doi.org/10.1111/spol.12150

van Berkel, R., Ingold, J., McGurk, P., Boselie, P. and Bredgaard, T. 2017. Editorial introduction: an introduction to employer engagement in the field of HRM. Blending social policy and HRM research in promoting vulnerable groups' labour market participation. *Human Resource Management Journal* 27: 503–13. https://doi.org/10.1111/1748-8583.12169

Webb, S. and Webb, B. 1963. *English Poor Law history*. With a new introduction by W.A. Robson. Hamden, CT: Archon Books.

Weeden, L. 2010. Reflections on ethnographic work in political science. *Annual Review of Political Science* 13: 255–72. https://doi.org/10.1146/annurev.polisci.11.052706.123951

Welfare Conditionality Project 2018. *Welfare conditionality project: final findings report.* http://www.welfareconditionality.ac.uk/wp-content/uploads/2018/06/40475_Welfare-Conditionality_Report_complete-v3.pdf.

White, S. 2004. What's wrong with workfare? *Journal of Applied Philosophy* 21(3): 271–84.https://doi.org/10.1111/j.0264-3758.2004.00281.x

Whitworth, A. and Carter, E. 2020. Programme form and service user well-being: linking theory and evidence. *Social Policy & Administration* 54(5): 844–858. https://doi.org/10.1111/spol.12582

Wright, S.E. 2003. Confronting unemployment in a street-level bureaucracy: Jobcentre staff and client perspectives. PhD thesis. University of Stirling.

Wright, S. and Patrick, S. 2019. Welfare conditionality in lived experience: aggregating qualitative longitudinal research. *Social Policy & Society* 18(3): 597–613. https://doi.org/10.1017/S1474746419000204

Zacka, B. 2017. *When the state meets the street: public service and moral agency.* Cambridge, MA: Belknap Press. https://doi.org/10.4159/9780674981423

Ziguras, S., Dufty, G. and Considine, M. 2003. *Much obliged: disadvantaged jobseekers' experiences of the mutual obligation regime.* Melbourne: Brotherhood of St Laurence.

Index

www.ingramcontent.com/pod-product-compliance
Lightning Source LLC
Chambersburg PA
CBHW071734270326
41928CB00013B/2678